IMAGES OF POSTMODERN SOCIETY

Theory, Culture & Society

Theory, Culture & Society caters for the resurgence of interest in culture within contemporary social science and the humanities. Building on the heritage of classical social theory, the book series examines ways in which this tradition has been reshaped by a new generation of theorists. It will also publish theoretically informed analyses of everyday life, popular culture, and new intellectual movements.

EDITOR: Mike Featherstone, *Teesside Polytechnic*

EDITORIAL BOARD
Roy Boyne, *Newcastle upon Tyne Polytechnic*
Mike Hepworth, *University of Aberdeen*
Scott Lash, *University of Lancaster*
Roland Robertson, *University of Pittsburgh*
Bryan S. Turner, *University of Essex*

Also in this series

The Body
Social Process and Cultural Theory
*edited by Mike Featherstone, Mike Hepworth
and Bryan S. Turner*

Consumer Culture and Postmodernism
Mike Featherstone

Talcott Parsons
Theorist of Modernity
edited by Roland Robertson and Bryan S. Turner

The Symbol Theory
Norbert Elias

Religion and Social Theory
Bryan S. Turner

Images of Postmodern Society
Social Theory and Contemporary Cinema
Norman K. Denzin

Promotional Culture
Advertising, Ideology and Symbolic Expression
Andrew Wernick

IMAGES OF POSTMODERN SOCIETY

SOCIAL THEORY AND CONTEMPORARY CINEMA

SAGE Publications Ltd
6 Bonhill Street
London EC2A 4PU

SAGE Publications Inc
2455 Teller Road
Newbury Park, California 91320

SAGE Publications India Pvt Ltd
32, M-Block Market
Greater Kailash – I
New Delhi 110 048

British Library Cataloguing in Publication Data

Denzin, Norman K.
   Images of postmodern society: Social theory and
   contemporary cinema.
   I. Title
   791.4301

   ISBN 0-8039-8515-0
   ISBN 0-8039-8516-9 pbk

Library of Congress catalog card number 91-053213

Typeset by Mayhew Typesetting, Bristol, Great Britain
Printed in Great Britain by Dotesios Ltd, Trowbridge,
Wiltshire

Table of Contents

Acknowledgements

I would like to thank Mike Featherstone and Stephen Barr for suggesting this project and encouraging its development. Interactions in the Unit for Criticism and Interpretive Theory at the University of Illinois, Urbana-Champaign and conversations with Carl Couch, Norbert Wiley, Andy Fontana, Joe Kotarba, Patricia Clough, John Johnson, David Altheide, Laurel Richardson, David Maines, James W. Carey, Lawrence Grossberg, Rob Lynch, Peter K. Manning, Gil Rodman, and Katherine Ryan-Denzin helped to clarify my arguments. I also thank Paul Benson for his careful reading of the page proofs and Susan Worsey for her patience and assistance throughout the production process.

The cover illustrations are from *sex, lies and videotape* (A Miramax Films Release © 1989), *Wall Street* (© 1987 Twentieth Century Fox Film Corp; photo credit: Andy Schwartz), *Blue Velvet* (© 1986 De Laurentiis Entertainment Group), *Wild at Heart* (© 1990 PolyGram Filmproduktion GmbH), *Do the Right Thing* (© 1989 Universal City Studios Inc), and *Crimes and Misdemeanors* (© 1989 Orion Pictures Corporation; photo by Brian Hamill).

Preface

'You believe you can think for all times and all men,' the sociologist says to the philosopher, 'and by that very belief you only express the preconceptions or pretensions of your culture.' That is true . . . but where does he [she] speak from, the sociologist who speaks this way? The sociologist can only form this idea . . . by placing him [her]self outside history . . . and claiming the privileged positions of absolute spectator.

(Merleau-Ponty, 1964: 109)

Definitions

Postmodern   *That which follows the modern; after World War II; A phase of capitalism; a movement in the arts; a form of social theory; that which cannot be avoided; undefinable.*

Postmodernism   *Living the postmodern into experience; a set of emotional experiences defined by ressentiment, anger, alienation, anxiety, poverty, racism, and sexism; the cultural logics of late capitalism.*

Postmodern Self   *The self who embodies the multiple contradictions of postmodernism, while experiencing itself through the everyday performances of gender, class, and racially-linked social identities.*

This work is a study of the postmodern self and its representations in two sites: postmodern social theory, and a select number of contemporary, mainstream Hollywood movies. What follows is, in part, a dialogue with Jean Baudrillard and C. Wright Mills. It attempts to fit Mills's call for a postmodern sociological imagination to Baudrillard's reading of contemporary America, perhaps the most postmodern of contemporary social structures. Postmodernism is defined by the following terms: *a nostalgic, conservative longing for the past, coupled with an erasure of the boundaries between the past and the present; an intense preoccupation with the real and its representations; a pornography of the visible; the commodification of sexuality and desire; a consumer culture which objectifies a set of masculine cultural ideals; intense emotional experiences shaped by anxiety, alienation, ressentiment, and a detachment from others.*
This society, Baudrillard argues, only knows itself through the reflections that flow from the camera's eye. But this knowledge, Baudrillard, contends, is unreflexive. 'The cinema and TV are America's reality!' (Baudrillard, 1987b, 1988b: 104). I examine the basic thesis (taken from Baudrillard) that members of the contemporary world are voyeurs adrift in a sea of symbols. They know and see themselves through cinema and television. If this is so, then an essential part of the contemporary

postmodern American scene can be found in the images and meanings that flow from cinema and TV.

The ingredients of the postmodern self are given in three key cultural identities, those derived from the performances that define gender, social class, race and ethnicity. The patriarchal, and all too often racist contemporary cultures of the world ideologically code the self and its meanings in terms of the meanings brought to these three cultural identities.[1] The postmodern self has become a sign of itself, a double dramaturgical reflection anchored in media representations on the one side, and everyday life on the other. Too often this self is reduced to its essential markers which carry the traces of these three terms.

These cultural identities are filtered through the personal troubles and the emotional experiences that flow from the individual's interactions with everyday life. These existential troubles loop back to the dominant cultural themes of the postmodern era, including the cult of Eros, and its idealized conceptions of love and intimacy. The raw economic, racial, and sexual edges of contemporary life produce anxiety, alienation, a radical isolation from others, madness, violence, and insanity. Large cultural groupings (young women, the elderly, racial and ethnic minorities, gays and lesbians), are unable either to live out their ideological versions of the American dream or to experience personal happiness. They are victims of anhedonia, they are unable to experience pleasure (Lyman, 1990: 3). They bear witness to an economy, a political ideology, and a popular culture which can never deliver the promised goods to their households.

A ressentiment (Scheler, 1961) based on the repeated inability to experience the pleasant emotions promoted by the popular culture takes hold. Self-hatred, anger, envy, false self-pride, and a desire for revenge against the other are experienced. Sexism, racism, and homophobia are the undersides of ressentiment. From this spring the violence, prejudice, and hatred that women, blacks, gays, and lesbians confront on a daily basis.

Two problems, then, both of which turn on the terms postmodern and postmodernism organize this book. I offer a reading of postmodern American society and the cinematic selves that inhabit this structure, while outlining the main contours of a postmodern sociology and postmodern sociological imagination that is alive to the current historical moment which goes by a variety of names, including post-industrial, late capitalist, and the society of the spectacle.

The postmodern terrain is defined almost exclusively in visual terms, including the display, the icon, the representations of the real seen through the camera's eye, captured on videotape, and given in the moving picture (see Ulmer, 1989: ix–x). In these traces of the visible and the invisible the figures of postmodern man, woman, and child emerge, as if out of a misty fog. The search for the meaning of the postmodern moment is a study in looking. It can be no other way. This is a visual, cinematic age. The collage and the mixed-media-tele/audio text are the iconic markers of this moment (Hebdige, 1988b: 13–14; Ulmer, 1983, 1989).

This thesis suggests that classical sociological ways of representing and writing about society require radical transformation. If sociology and the other human disciplines are to remain in touch with the worlds of lived experience in the late twentieth century then new ways of inscribing and reading the social must be found. Throughout, my analysis works back and forth between two kinds of texts: social theory (Mills, Baudrillard, Barthes, Habermas, Jameson, Bourdieu, Derrida, M. Morris, poststructuralism, postmodernism, feminist cultural studies, Marxism) and cinematic representations of life in contemporary America. I take six late 1980s award-winning films, *Blue Velvet, Wall Street, Crimes and Misdemeanors, When Harry Met Sally, sex, lies and videotape, Do the Right Thing*, as readings of life in contemporary America, finding postmodern contradictions in these texts which mirror the everyday in this society and its popular culture.[2]

Defining and Writing the Postmodern

The postmodern as postmodernism is four things at the same time. First, it describes a sequence of historical moments from World War II to the present. These moments include: the Vietnam War; the worldwide economic recessions of the 1970s and 1980s; the rise to power of conservative political regimes in Europe and America; the failure of the Left to mount an effective attack against these regimes; the collapse in the international labor movement; the emergence of a new, conservative politics of health and morality centering on sexuality and the family; totalitarian regimes in Europe, Asia, Latin America, and South Africa; the breakdown of the cold war and the emergence of *glasnost*; increased worldwide racism. Secondly, the postmodern references the multinational forms of late capitalism which have introduced new cultural logics, and new forms of communication and representation into the world economic and cultural systems. Thirdly, it describes a movement in the visual arts, architecture, cinema, popular music, and social theory which goes against the grain of classic realist and modernist formations. Fourthly, it references a form of theorizing and writing about the social which is postpositivist, interpretive, and critical. Postmodern theorizing is preoccupied with the visual society, its representations, cultural logics and the new types of personal troubles (AIDS, homelessness, drug addiction, family and public violence) and public problems that define the current age. *At the most abstract level, the cultural logics of late capitalism define the postmodern moment* (Jameson, 1991).

But postmodernism is more than a series of economic formations. The postmodern society, as suggested above, is a cinematic, dramaturgical production. Film and television have transformed American, and perhaps all other, societies touched by the camera, into video, visual cultures.

Representations of the real have become stand-ins for actual, lived experience. Three implications follow from the cinematization of contemporary life.

First, reality is a staged, social production. Secondly, the real is now judged against its staged, cinematic-video counterpart (Baudrillard, 1983a: 152). Third, the metaphor of the dramaturgical society (Lyman, 1990: 221), or 'life as theater' (Brissett and Edgley, 1990: 2; Goffman, 1959: 254–5) has now become interactional reality. The theatrical aspects of the dramaturgical metaphor have not 'only creeped into everyday life' (Goffman, 1959: 254), they have taken it over. Art not only mirrors life, it structures and reproduces it. The postmodern society is a dramaturgical society.

Accordingly, the postmodern scene is a series of cultural formations which impinge upon, shape, and define contemporary human group life. These formations are anchored in a series of institutional sites, including the mass media, the economy, and the polity, the academy and popular culture itself. In these sites interacting individuals come in contact with postmodernism, which, like the air we breathe, is everywhere around us: in the omnipresent camera whenever lives and money exchange hands; in the sprawling urban shopping malls; in films like *Blue Velvet*; in the evening televised news; in soap operas and situation comedies; in the doctor's office and the police station; at the computer terminal.

The cultural formations of postmodernism do not have a direct, unmediated effect on the worlds of lived experience. The meanings of postmodernism are mediated and filtered through existing systems of interpretation. These meanings may be incorporated into a group's ongoing flow of experience and become part of their collective vocabulary and memory (for example the New York postmodern art scene during the 1970s and 1980s). Here the postmodern supports and strengthens a group's scheme of life. On the other hand, the multiple, conflicting cultural meanings of postmodernism may be judged to have no relevance to what the members of a group do, and hence be rejected (for example the rejection of postmodernism by mainstream American sociologists). Still other groups may incorporate portions of the postmodern and reject its other features (for example the cultural conservatives who value nostalgia). In this case the postmodern will have a disjunctive effect, settling into one part of a group's way of life, without incorporation into its overall interpretive scheme. For still other groups postmodernism may disrupt a way of life and even undermine it, as when postmodernists in the academy challenge the traditional literary canons of western civilization and propose radical new reading lists which express the positions of racial, ethnic, and gender minorities (See Blumer, 1990: 88–101 on these several responses to a new cultural system of interpretation).

In writing about this historical moment the sociologist confronts Merleau-Ponty's (1964: 109) observation that there is no privileged position of absolute spectator, for how can the postmodern self write about itself when the very postmodern stuff it is made of conditions what it says, sees, feels and hears? Of course any hint of objectivity predicated on the privileged position of the absolute spectator must be relinquished. As an observer of the postmodern scene I must recognize that I am grafted into every action and situation I write about. My point of contact with the contemporary postmodern world is the origin of my insights into this world (see Denzin, 1987b, 1987c, 1991). I offer, then, a critical ethnographic reading of this world and its meanings, as given in the texts listed earlier.

This means that I am neither a custodian of nor a defender of post-modern culture, and the theories generated about it. I seek, instead to write a postmodernist theory of cultural resistance, which acknowledges and explores my place in the creation of this culture and its meanings.[3] I seek not a theory of cultural indifference (Connor 1989: 181), but a theory of resistance (Fields, 1988). Such a theory examines how the basic existential experiences with self, other, gender, race, nationality, family, love, intimacy, violence, death, and freedom are produced and given mythical meaning in everyday life (Connor, 1989: 228). This must be a feminist, post-colonial cultural studies theory of micro-politics (Foucault, 1982) which sees 'networks of power-relations subsisting at every point in a society' (Connor, 1989: 225). It must be a theory which does not take itself seriously in terms of abstract terms divorced from the worlds of lived experiences. Such a minimalist formation will write the theories of representation and resistance that are lived by ordinary people. This form of theorizing will valorize the freedoms that the present moment, in all its eclecticism and diversity of voices, brings. It will attempt to expose the oppressive limitations to freedom that flow from the current contradictions that characterize the cultural logics of late capitalism (Hall, 1988: 15).

Eleven chapters contain my analysis. In Chapter One I define my key terms (postmodernism, modernism, cultural studies). In Chapter Two I examine the postmodern moment and social theory. Chapter Three discusses in detail the theories of Lyotard, Baudrillard, and Jameson. Chapter Four takes up C. Wright Mills's challenge to sociology and shows where he went wrong. Chapter Five examines the problems of sex, violence, love, marriage, family, and small-town life through a reading of *Blue Velvet*. Chapter Six studies America's nouveau capitalists, and contradictions in late postmodern capitalism on America's premier marketplace, Wall Street, through a reading of the film by the same name. Chapters Seven and Eight read *Crimes and Misdemeanors*, *When Harry Met Sally*, and *sex, lies and videotape*, seeing in these texts neo-conservative statements which react to current postmodern contradictions in American life. I interpret Woody Allen as the paramount postmodern film-maker. Chapter Nine, '*Do the Right Thing*: Race in the USA', contrasts Spike Lee's 1989 radical treatment of race in America with the self-involved, yuppie films of Reiner and Soderbergh, studied in the

previous chapter. Chapter Ten, '*Paris, Texas*: Mills and Baudrillard in
America', presents a playful interpretation of Baudrillard's book on
America, and contrasts his project with Mills's. Chapter Eleven offers an
agenda for a postmodern sociology which attempts to read the cinematic
society through the eyes of Mills and Baudrillard.

Norman K. Denzin
Champaign, Illinois
14 January 1991

Notes

1. Religion and national identity can also mold the self and its multiple meanings. The
postmodern self is a form of subjectivity hailed, or created, by specific sites of ideological
discourse, including film, the media, television, biography, social science, and everyday life
(see Althusser, 1971; Denzin, 1989b).

2. Any number of other contemporary films could have been examined, including films
from earlier moments in the postmodern period (Chapters 1,5,8,10,11). I seek, as much as
possible, a reading of the current moment. Those films selected for analysis come at the end
of the 1980s, are the most popular of the popular, and are highly controversial in their
meanings.

3. As such it should be read alongside Denzin (forthcoming a, b).

PART I

THE POSTMODERN

1

Defining the Postmodern Terrain

> Our private sphere has ceased to be the stage where the drama of the subject at odds with his [her] objects and with his [her] image is played out: we no longer exist as playwrights or actors but as terminals of multiple networks. (Baudrillard, 1988a: 16)

> In addressing the myth of a postmodernism still waiting for its women we can find an example of a genre, as well as a discourse, which in its untransformed state leaves a woman no place from which to speak. (Morris, 1988a: 15)

My topics are the self, lived experiences, and social theory in the postmodern moment. Three crucial identities, grounded in class, gender, and race define the postmodern self. *A single question guides my discussion: 'How are these three identities enacted, and dramaturgically staged in the postmodern culture?'* Phrased differently, my project attempts to interpret how words, texts and their meanings play a pivotal part in 'those decisive performances of race, class and gender relations [that] shape the emergent political conditions [referred] to as the postmodern world' (Downing, 1987: 80).

This guiding question produces three problems which organize my argument. First, how does social theory, in the wake of the theoretical revolutions which have occurred in poststructural, Marxist, feminist, and interpretive thought (Morris, 1988a) orient itself to the terrible and magnificent world of the late twentieth century? (Mills, 1959: 225). Secondly, how can social theory make sense of this mass-mediated, cinematic postmodern world where the boundaries between images and reality have blurred, and the legacies of classical theory (Marx, Weber, Durkheim) appear exhausted? (Becker, 1986a: 220; Giddens, 1987: 28–9). How, that is, can social texts about this world be written, so that the lived experiences of interacting individuals can be captured, represented, and made sense of in a way that allows individuals and groups to begin making their own history, rather than just repeating the ones which have been handed down to them by previous generations? (Marx, 1983; Sartre, 1976; Finkelstein, 1991, Ch. 7; Featherstone, 1990).

Thirdly, how has the postmodern self and its class, race, and gender-linked identities been described in mainstream, Hollywood cinema? I take my lead from Sklar (1975: 3), who argues that 'for the first half of the twentieth century – from 1896 to 1946, to be exact – movies were the most popular and influential medium of culture in the United States.'[1] Jameson (1991: 68) echoes Sklar, 'culture today is a matter of media . . . . For some seventy years the cleverest prophets have warned us that the dominant art form of the twentieth century was not literature at all . . . but rather the one new and historically unique art invented in the contemporary period, namely film.' Paraphrasing Dewey (also quoted by Rorty, 1989: 69), it can be claimed that 'the moral prophets of humanity in the twentieth century have always been the filmmakers.' Barthes (1972) phrases the argument thus, 'ideology follows the route of the popular' (quoted in Ray, 1985: 20).

Accordingly, the six films examined in the second half of this book take up the topics of class, race, and gender in contemporary postmodernist American culture. These texts, directed by David Lynch, Oliver Stone, Woody Allen, Rob Reiner, Steven Soderbergh, and Spike Lee were among the most popular of the popular during the late 1980s. They aroused considerable controversy in the popular press, and continue to be top video rentals in the 1990s. An examination of these texts, and the readings brought to them by film and cultural critics, should reveal the multiple meanings that now surround the cinematically constructed postmodern self as it enacts the central identities grounded in race, gender, and class.[2]

In this chapter I will outline the main contours of my argument, define key terms, and create the opening for a full-scale discussion of social theory in the postmodern period in Chapters Two, Three, and Four. I begin by attempting to define the contemporary moment.

The Term Postmodern

The term *postmodern* is an oxymoron with a short history.[3] How can something be post, or after the modern, when the modern represents the present, or recent moment? (Hassan, 1985: 121). What comes after the present, but another present, or period in history, which is a continuation of the present? (Updike, 1984). It is an oxymoron because it comes at the end of a series of other 'post-isms', most importantly poststructuralism, that amorphous theoretical formation which has theorized language, meaning, and textuality after the semiotic-structural revolution inspired by Saussure (1959) and Lévi-Strauss (1963; see Macksey and Donato, 1972; Derrida, 1972, 1978, 1986). In a sense postmodernism should have come first, for it describes the very conditions of experience these earlier 'isms' responded to. Predictably as postmodernism emerges as a distinct theoretical formation, it comes under attack from the very perspectives it seeks to surround and make sense of (see Morris, 1988a: 1–23; Hall, 1986a; Grossberg, 1988a).

Users of the word are attempting to describe fields of political, cultural, aesthetic, scientific, and moral experiences which are distinctly different from those which were taken for granted in an earlier historical, commonly called modern or Enlightenment, phase of world history. It is not possible to give a precise date to the beginning of the postmodern period, as Virginia Woolf did for modernism, which she said began 'in or about December, 1910' (Hassan, 1985: 122), although we may, with Hassan (1985: 122) 'woefully imagine that postmodernism began in or about September, 1939.'

The terms postmodern and postmodernism simultaneously refer (as indicated in the Preface) to four interrelated phenomena: (1) a movement called postmodernism in the arts;[4] (2) a new form of theorizing the contemporary historical moment (see Chapter 2); (3) historical transformations that have followed World War II; and (4) social, cultural, and economic life under late capitalism. The dramaturgical, postmodern social order weaves the above phenomena into complex, contradictory fields of experience. These fields are connected to a series of cultural formations which revolve around the definitions brought to human subjectivity, the family, sexuality, social class, race and ethnicity, work, wealth, prestige, love and intimacy. These phenomena are woven through the processes which I called in the Preface postmodernism.

Periodizing the Present

The present historical moment, the dawn of the 1990s, is itself the result of several specific transformations in American military, economic, and cultural life. These changes can be marked by specific time periods, mindful that such attempts at periodization give the impression that any historical moment is a massive homogeneity, bounded on each side by distinct historical markers (Jameson, 1984b: 56). This is never the case.

Nonetheless, if the beginning of the postmodern period is marked by the end of World War II, it can be argued that each decade thereafter introduced and signaled significant changes which were then elaborated and articulated in the next decade. The period 1940–65 saw the emergence of a wartime and then post-wartime economy, bracketed by the Korean War, and the onset of the Vietnam War. By the mid-1960s American multinational corporations had established their fixed presences in Asia, Europe, Latin and South America, and South Africa. America's concept of the 'new frontier' was in place, waiting to be implemented by John Kennedy. The decade of the 1960s saw American culture defined and polarized by the Bay of Pigs crisis, the Vietnam War, the Birmingham race riots, the assassinations of John and Robert Kennedy and Martin Luther King, student and counterculture dissent peaking in 1968, the Altamont rock festival death of 1969, the Cambodian invasion of 1970, and the right-wing reaction to protest (Ray, 1985: 250). As the sixties came to an end, marginalized voices (racial minorities, gays, elderly, women), began to be heard. As the counterculture pronounced the death of

America, they proclaimed the dawn of a new metaphorical frontier, 'an image of new possibilities derived from drugs, sexual freedom and a vague spirituality' (Ray, 1985: 255). The new rock-'n-roll (Buffalo Springfield, The Band) inspired images of a 'new west' to be explored through the use of drugs (*Easy Rider*). Traditional mythology was alive in the counterculture's version of the frontier, which was part parody and part pastiche.

The decade of the 1970s saw the fall of Nixon and Carter, the defeated ERA movement in the US, and a worldwide recession. The political conservatism of the 1980s (Hall, 1988: 39–56), with its emphasis on a romantic nostalgia for the past, and a general effacement of the boundaries between the past and the present, set the stage for a return to a new traditionalism in American life, especially in the arenas of family and work.

American advertisers would begin to apply labels to each decade since the 1950s. That decade is labeled 'childhood.' The 1960s is labeled 'protest', the 1970s 'feminist', the 1980s, 'yuppies,' and the 1990s 'new traditionalists' (Dougherty, 1988). According to this reading, Americans in the sixties and seventies were idealists; the eighties were materialists, and the nineties were realists. The copy for a national advertising campaign for *Good Housekeeping* reads: 'There's a rebirth in America, There's a renewal, a reaffirmation of values, a return to quality of life' (*New York Times*, 1988a: 50). Another version of this ad goes on to define the new traditional woman.

> She has a mission in life – and it could shape your marketing plan . . . A new kind of woman with deep-rooted values is changing the way we live. Market researchers call it 'neo-traditionalism.' To us it's a woman who has found her identity in herself, her home, her family . . . She is part of an extraordinary social movement that is profoundly changing the way Americans look at living – and the way products are marketed. The home is again the center of American life, oatmeal is back on the breakfast table, families are vacationing together, watching movies at home, playing Monopoly again. Even the perfume ads are suddenly glorifying commitment. (*New York Times*, 1988b 46; see also *New York Times*, 1989a)

Statements such as this constitute the postmodern woman as a concrete subject within a set of traditional values. She is given a set of beliefs (old-fashioned, the home as the center of life, commitment to another, and so on). She is anchored in a specific site, the home, doing specific things (caring for her children) which embody *Good Housekeeping*. This woman has a mission, which is to create a more meaningful quality of life for herself and her family. She is the mover of family values, and her daughter is the embodiment of these values. She is a traditionalist, which means work is less important than family and home.

A central marker of the postmodern moment is given in texts like this. This ad provides a new historical reading of sexuality and gender in American culture. Ideological productions like this reify the gender stratification system. They suggest a return to an earlier time when women were also urged to return to their homes (post-World War II) and take care of their husbands and children.

The Crisis in Ideology

As postmodernism pushes itself into everyday life, old political ideologies (democracy, communism, socialism, conservativism, liberalism: Laclau and Mouffe, 1985) are collapsing. The boundaries and borders between national states are being redrawn. Traditional meanings of health, illness, AIDS (Treichler, 1987), the human body (Frank, 1990b; Turner, 1984; Kroker and Kroker, 1987), reproduction, medicine, sexuality (Balsamo, 1987, 1988, 1990), the family, intimacy, love (Malhotra-Bentz, 1989), education, work, leisure (Featherstone, 1987), science, religion, art (Lyotard, 1984a), entertainment (Jameson, 1983, 1987; Morris, 1988a), and the private and the public (Baudrillard, 1988a) are being swept aside. Even as this occurs, fits of nostalgia for the past lead to its reenactment and effacement in contemporary popular culture.

This postmodern world is characterized by the cultivation of conspicuous consumption consumer lifestyles (Featherstone, 1987), already established under early capitalism (Veblen, 1899; Baudrillard, 1970; Wiley, 1967), which stress the prestige and exchange value of appearance, civility, and personal pleasure and desire (Elias, 1982; Finkelstein, 1989, 1991). The public self and its masks are increasingly defined by a media-oriented mass culture in which youth, health, and sexuality have taken on premium values. The popular culture of the past, especially film (*film noir*, grade B films) and pop music (1950s and 1960s rock), now define the present. Noisy, brightly colored TV advertisements are interrupted by the soft nostalgia of an old black-and-white film, as film stars from the fifties sell eighties products. Cultural eclecticism has become a way of life, 'the degree zero of contemporary culture: one listens to reggae, watches a western, eats McDonald's food for lunch and local cuisine for dinner, wears Paris perfume in Tokyo and "retro" clothes in Hong Kong; knowledge is a matter for TV games' (Lyotard, 1984: 76).

A New Cultural Subject

The most salient dimensions of the contemporary postmodern social order have been defined by the New Right. The rise to power of the conservatives and the radical right. America and Europe, which reflected a new worldwide 'anti-statism,' coupled with a vigorous rhetoric of law and order and human rights, was in part a 'backlash to the revolutionary ferment of 1968' (Hall, 1988: 39). It also reflected a conservative, late-capitalist response to the worldwide economic crises of the 1970s, and the emergence of contradictions in social democracy, communism, and the international labor movements.

Throughout the 1980s the New Right constructed conceptions of who its ideal subjects were and how they personified the sacred values of religion, hard work, health, and self-reliance. This new ideology redefined the meaning of an 'ordinary, normal, commonplace' individual, as it put in place a politics of health and morality that 'centered debates around abortion, child abuse, sex education, gay rights and AIDS' (Hall, 1988: 282), family violence, drug and alcohol abuse, the war on drugs, homelessness, and the general social health and moral hygiene of American (and British) society. A new, repressive politics emerged in the decade of the 1980s. This legacy will now be worked through in the 1990s.

During the 1970s and the 1980s the New Right in Europe and America attempted to undo the radical civil and human rights impulses of the late 1960s. These two decades were defined by 'Just Say No' drug programs, romantic nostalgia for the past, an authoritarian populism, and the rise in popularity of televised religion. The New Right seized control of American popular culture by centering discourse on the family, the body, sexuality, desire and a patriotic individuality that made the military a new employment site for the underclass.

The Right, through 'a series of ideological, religious, philosophical, political and juridical polemics' (Hall, 1988: 146), maintained its control over American society. It generated and participated in a series of economic and political crises (the crash of Wall Street, the Panama drug scandal, the Savings and Loan crisis, Grenada, the Middle East). These crises shifted attention away from civil and human rights and made being patriotic the most important identity an American could hold (see Kroker et al., 1990). At the same time, the underclass, the homeless, and the drug addicts were defined as morally unworthy persons who were out of work because they chose to be.

Like Thatcherism, Reaganism (and now Bushism) played on common sense and ordinary American values. It did this by creating multiple fields of discourse where these common values were celebrated. In the field of education 'it has made itself the guardian of the "return to standards" and [the] authority in the classroom' (Hall, 1988: 144). Here, as Hall noted, it helped create the figure of the worried parent, 'facing the harsh realities of a competitive world . . . aiming to secure . . . an education that will help his or her children to "get on and compete"' (1988: 144). The New Right's attacks on the liberals and their proposals to teach the literatures of racial and ethnic minorities was thus justified, because these 'radical' individuals were undermining the patriotic agenda of the American school system. Hard work and family once again became central cultural values. Women who worked outside the home were frowned upon because they were letting their children down. The housewife was defined as the moral center of American society. Abortion was defined as a crime against nature. The American woman was no longer safe on the streets of America. If she was a college student she was under constant threat of being raped or mugged by a minority group member, or an irresponsible 'wealthy' white male.

In the area of crime a series of moral panics were produced. These centered on minority youth gang members, addicted to or dealing crack and using guns randomly in the large cities, to kill upright, white citizens. Delinquent teenagers who disrupted schools were attacked in popular films (*Stand and Deliver, Lean on Me*).

The welfare system was also attacked. The 'spendthrift' state was scrutinized. The concept of recklessly giving money away to the needy was mocked and seen as an act which depleted the wealth of the nation (Hall, 1988: 144). The welfare system undermined self-confidence and perpetuated poverty. The welfare mother who drove a Cadillac was singled out as an example of the abuses this system produced. The plight of the ordinary man who worked to support his family was contrasted to the morally unfit black male who sold drugs. Here, as Hall notes, the 'Protestant Ethic makes a late return' (1988: 145). A new cultural racism thus joined all of the above moral panics under a single term, the non-white male who was a threat to the core values of American society.

In academia and higher education it has created a conflictual discourse surrounding the canon and what is to be taught to American students. Controversies surrounding the politics of leading postructural and postmodern theorists undermine their works by suggesting that the postmodern agenda leads to fascism. These attacks from the Right come at a time when previously excluded voices are starting to be heard in the American classroom.

In each case, the moral panic took the shape of cultural texts. These texts attempted to capture the crisis in question, represent it over the media, and show how the New Right was containing these threats to the traditional order.

Thus this historical period, extending for nearly fifty years, contains tensions and contradictions within itself, which are continually worked and reworked in the popular culture. With the recent political changes in East Europe, the partial dismantling of the Star Wars Program, the reductions in the huge budgets of the Soviet and American military, and the concentration of the telecommunications, film, print, and music industries into a handful of multinational corporations (for example Warner-Time), an even greater spread and homogenization of American postmodern culture throughout the world will be seen.

Representing the Real

We are now in the third stage of the sign.[5] The sign has become reality, or the hyperreal (see Baudrillard, 1983a: 11); the sign, that is, masks the fact that there is no basic reality. The cool communication forms (satellite and cable TV, telex, fax machines, instant electronic communication [electronic mail]) have produced a global village predicated, not on a shared humanness, but on marginality, and on cultural and racial differences. Controlled by multinational and state corporate structures, a satellite communications system connects the First and Third Worlds (McLuhan's hot and cold countries). This system articulates a set of popular culture ideologies which value family, sexuality, work, and leisure. These are pro-Oedipal stories (Barthes, 1975) marketed, distributed, sold to, and consumed by Third World, Soviet, and European audiences. These narratives and myths are communicated through (and in) the popular press, (*National Inquirer*, *Reader's Digest* and so on), advertisements, popular cinema, and neo-(or recycled) popular American television including sitcoms, crime dramas, family melodramas, and soap operas. They involve the telling and retelling of a very small number of stories, contained and recontained within the above genre forms.

Visual Literacy
These visual discourse structures are producing a new 'videocy,' or language of the visual, video image. This language displaces the earlier forms of literacy based on orality and the print media (Ulmer, 1989). It introduces a new set of media logics and media formats (Altheide, 1985). These new formats alter the person's relationships to the 'real' and the technologies of the real. They maintain a narrative and epistemological commitment to the simulational logic of the third stage of the sign. They serve to turn the individual into a new cultural object; an object who produces cultural knowledge and cultural texts via the new informational formats. At the same time they become new vehicles for the production and reproduction of official ideology. In the hands of the powerful they become tools for 'the perfection of a utilitarian attitude and the indefinite expansion of the administrative mentality and imperial politics' (Carey, 1989: 171). (The data banks are now controlled by the state – Lyotard, 1984a.)

The new information technologies turn everyday life into a theatrical spectacle; into sites where the dramas that surround the decisive performances of race, ethnicity, gender, sexuality, and age are staged. These dramas are staged against the backdrop of compelling, newsworthy events which are shaped by uncertainty, unpredictability, and natural disaster (for example a tidal wave in Pakistan). The *faits divers*, or the diverse fact connected by the bizarre, is also a favorite news story (for example a wounded reindeer in Alaska tripped a railroad turn signal causing the mayor of Anchorage to miss his daughter's wedding: see Baudrillard, 1981: 175 on these stories). Such stories tell heroic tales of life and death, courage and survival. They reaffirm the cherished values of community, family, and individuality.

These events and their meanings are coded within a system that allows nothing to escape interpretation. The interpretive code of the media contains everything, including the message and the receiver (Baudrillard, 1981: 179). The code excludes all communicators, except those frozen within the communicative frame itself. The result is an over-abundance of meaning; an ecstasy of communication (Baudrillard, 1988a) which delights in the spectacle itself and finds pleasure in the pornography of excess that flows from the media's desire to tell everything.

To summarize, a complex set of cultural logics defines postmodernism. These logics turn on the meanings brought to five terms: the cultural object, the individual, family, sexuality, and work. Conservative, consumer oriented, cinematic and visual to the core, the postmodern culture, in its many contradictory forms, is a masculinized culture of Eros, love, desire, femininity, youth, and beauty (see pp. 14-16). The postmodern person is a restless voyeur, a person who sits and gazes (often mesmerized and bored) at the movie or TV screen. This is a looking culture, organized in terms of a variety of gazes, or looks (tourist, investigatory – medical, social science, television, religious, political – artistic, photographic and so on: see Urry, 1990: 135).

The myth of Oedipus is alive and well, and continues to argue that the path to happiness and fulfillment is sexual, and lies in the marital, family bond. The contemporary yuppie family formation has become a valorized consumer purchasing unit, and its consumption needs now drive the political economies of everyday life. The raw racial and sexual edges of contemporary life produce anxiety, alienation, madness, homelessness, ressentiment, and anhedonia (Lyman, 1990). Large cultural groupings (the young, women, the elderly, racial and ethnic minorities, gays and lesbians) are unable to live out their ideological versions of the American dream, or to experience personal happiness.

The New Historians
Journalists, politicians, and advertisers are the new intellectuals; the new historians who have no sense of history, only meaning. The challenge to academics, artists, and intellectuals is clear (see Carey 1986, 1989; Meyer, 1990a, 1990b; Schudson, 1988). These cultural intermediaries, who play to the market-oriented consumer culture, must be challenged, and their messages deconstructed (Featherstone, 1989a, 1990). These specialists in symbolic production constitute the new ruling class, or power elite (Mills, 1956). They have turned news into entertainment (Altheide, 1985), and their commentary into instant analysis. They perpetuate a hegemonic control over popular culture, defining in every instance proper images of the American dream and the inheritors of that dream. They provide the cultural readings of class, race, gender, protest, revolution, success, and happiness.

The dependence of these symbolic specialists on a world economic system which requires their presence cannot be underestimated (Featherstone, 1989a). The two parties go hand in hand. Excess finance capital (such as junk bonds on Wall Street) permits gross indulgences in postmodern lifestyles, which require the presence of prized cultural artifacts (BMWs, expensive artworks, architecturally designed, postmodern homes and hotels, pristine Caribbean beaches for Club Med members), whose prestige, exchange, and symbolic values are announced in the expensive weekly and monthly magazines (*GO*, *New Yorker*, *Architectural Digest*, *Rolling Stone*, *Ebony*), often alongside ads for expensive alcoholic beverages, which are consumed by embodiments of the postmodern aesthetic (see Denzin, 1987a).

It is tempting to praise the anti-aesthetic, anti-institutional, anti-intellectual impulse which runs through many postmodern productions. But such praise must be tempered by the earlier discussion of the *Good Housekeeping*/Wall Street/*New York Times* interpretations of the contemporary woman and her family. Here the anti-aesthetic values of postmodernism are turned back against the contemporary woman as she is confronted with two competing images of herself – modern and postmodern. The postmodern images are denigrated (non-commitment, me generation and so on), as a mythical picture of the deep-rooted, old-fashioned American family is brought back into place. The symbolic producers of meaning on Wall Street will use any technique or device to sell a product, especially when the product is a way of life.

Cinematic Formations

Contemporary cinema perpetuates modernist impulses (auteurism, social realism, genre-driven productions such as comedies, cop-mystery thrillers, musicals, westerns, biographies,) punctuated by periodic postmodern breaks with the past (see Ray, 1985; Connor, 1989: 173–81; Jameson, 1983). Films like *Blade runner* (1982), *Blue Velvet* (1986), *Something Wild* (1986), *Kiss of the Spider Woman* (1985), *Brazil* (1985), *The Man Who Envied Women* (1985), *Hannah and Her Sisters* (1986), *sex, lies and videotape* (1989) invoke a nostalgia for earlier films, while presenting a mix of pastiche and parody of these productions. These films locate the viewer in a perpetual present, where the signifiers from the past (for example shots from *Casablanca* in Woody Allen's 1972 *Play It Again Sam*, or a shot of Jimmy Stewart as Elwood P. Dowd talking about his friend Harvey in the 1989 film *Field of Dreams*), circulate alongside advanced technologies, and modern conveniences (*Blue Velvet*). These films mock contemporary social formations and myths (family, science, love, intimacy, the middle class) by confronting the viewer with 'unpresentable' violent images of sexuality and urban decay.

Self-reflective cinema, which turns back on and critiques the cinematic images that are produced in the contemporary period, is an important variant on the postmodern, 'retro' film. From *Citizen Kane* (1941) to *The Manchurian Candidate* (1962), *The Conversation* (1974), *The Parallax View* (1974), *All the President's Men* (1976) *The Mean Season* (1985), *Salvador* (1986), to *Broadcast News* (1987), Hollywood has periodically deconstructed a demonic version of the cinematic apparatus which comes under the control of a self-serving power elite.

An important variation of this type of film is given in the 1960 cult movie *Peeping Tom*, and its contemporary descendants, *sex, lies and videotape*, (1989), *Bad Influence* (1990) and *Speaking Parts* (1990). In these texts the protagonist is a peeping tom with a camera. Such works cut close 'to the cold hearts of movies that see cameras and monitors everywhere: televisions in every room, videocameras in every elevator, department store and bank . . . [these films] offer a metaphor for the camera's potential to isolate people and destroy lives' (James, 1990, B: 1). The very title of *sex, lies and videotape* stands as a description of this trend, 'capturing the tangled way that taped images shape what we know, how we communicate, even how we love' (James, 1990, B: 4). Reflective postmodern movies issue a warning about film, television, and video-cameras, and affirm the 'genre's potential for depicting' (James, 1990, B: 4) new categories of truth about the cinematic society.

There exists, at the same time, another category of contemporary film which explores the so-called ability of 'classic' Hollywood films to bring positive value into postmodern life. Woody Allen's *Hannah and Her Sisters*, for example, has his character walk away from a botched suicide attempt, watch a Marx Brothers' movie, and decide that such hilarious moments make life worth living after all. The more recent *Cinema Paradiso* extends this romantic line.

Some of these productions, like 'neo-TV' (Eco, 1984), take themselves and their participants as their own subjects, turning the camera on themselves, as when the camera in a TV talk show pans the audience. In some cases a character steps out of the film and talks to the audience (for example *Purple Rose of Cairo*, 1985). The audience, in effect, watches the production of a production, the traditional boundary between film text and viewer is erased in such moments.

A variant on the film which turns inward and makes the audience a participant in the production, is the live concert, where audiences watch huge video screens which project direct images of the performance that is occurring on stage in front of them. Watching themselves watching the performance on stage, the audience engages in an ecstasy of simulated communication (Baudrillard, 1988a) which transforms the real into its simulated image. In some cases audience members at home watch these audiences watching 'an image of themselves on the giant video screen' (Connor, 1989: 153). The audience at home becomes part of the audience on the screen. Not infrequently audiences at home will be shown watching these productions on their own TVs. In such moments 'we are not sure whether it was the audience itself that we were seeing, or the image of the audience projected on the video-screen at the event – whether we were watching them or watching them watching themselves' (Connor, 1989: 153); or watching ourselves watching ourselves watching ourselves watching them.

Thus double and triple reflexivity that 'neo-TV' and the video-text permit, mocked in films yet lived out on a daily basis, reflects just how far the simulational, hyperreal mode of experiencing reality has gone in the contemporary age. It is not enough to call these TV texts intertextual, empty surface productions characterized by fragmentary subject positions, which are 'in-different to differences' (Grossberg, 1987: 41). Nor will it do to call the video-text the 'strongest and most original and authentic form of the logic of postmodernist culture' (Jameson, 1987: 223). Such moves valorize a form of representation which is neither authentic nor original. Intertextual reproductions of reproductions have been present since the beginnings of modern cinema and photography (Ray, 1985). The fraudulent representation of the reproduction as reality reproduces a cultural logic which values a simulational technology of domination which turns captured 'lived experiences' into a new form of manufactured textuality. The supposed realism of these texts, Lefebvre's (1984: 187) 'illusion of immediacy in everyday life,' is only simulational. In Hutcheon's (1988: 229) words, it represents not just 'liberal humanism's assertion of the real but the apocalyptic murder of the real,' for this version of the real is controlled by those who control the cameras, do the editing and write the scripts which interpret what the camera has captured. This technology permits a form of neo-Fascist, state-sponsored, multinational corporate control over the flow of information individuals have about the world they live in. The video-text potentially represents a new form of state-manipulated information control, distortion, repression, and censorship (Jansen, 1988).

Undoing the Present

An interpretive account of everyday life (de Certeau, 1984) in the postmodern period must take account of the cultural practices (Featherstone, 1989b: 134–5) that allow individuals to come to grips with, and find a home in this contemporary world which is part modern and part postmodern. These cultural practices, which turn on pastiche, parody, and the effacement of the boundaries between the past, the present and the future, must be connected to contradictions in late capitalism. But postmodernism, as Featherstone (1989b: 137) notes, involves more than a response to the unfolding logic of late capitalism. It entails a simultaneous collapse and then resurgence in popularity of old metanarratives concerning peace, freedom, communism, worldwide democracy, the 'end of history,' patriarchy, racism, and colonialism (Hutcheon, 1988: 6–7). At the same time that these old myths come under assault, the radical and middle-of-the-road right asserts their primacy. So, at the level of the political, the postmodern is played out in an interactional-global televised war where the enemy becomes you, and I, and 'them.'

Enter Feminist Cultural Studies
A feminist cultural studies approach to the contemporary moment examines three interrelated problems: the production, distribution, and consumption of cultural meanings; the textual analysis of these meanings

and practices; and the study of lived cultures and lived experiences (Johnson, 1986–7: 72).

Each of these problems constitutes a field of inquiry in its own right. The production, distribution, and consumption of cultural meanings involves issues of ideology and the political economy of signs (such as the *Good Housekeeping* ad series on the neo-traditional woman), including how these signs are worded, photographed, where they circulate, who buys them, and so on. The textual analysis of meanings requires the implementation of a variety of reading strategies (feminist, semiotic, hermeneutic, psychoanalytic) which examine how a text constitutes (hails) an individual as a subject in a particular ideological moment and site (Althusser, 1971). At the level of lived experiences, a central problem becomes the examination of how interacting individuals connect their lives, during moments of upheaval and epiphany, to these ideological texts and make sense of their experiences in terms of their meanings.

Interpretive interactionism (Denzin, 1989a) enters the field of cultural studies at the level of lived experiences. The focus is on those life experiences, called epiphanies, which radically alter and shape the meanings people give to themselves and their life projects. This existential thrust calls for an examination of those moments when the individual, in a variety of sites, comes in contact with the terror and repressive taken-for-grantedness of the postmodern (Lefebvre, 1984: 143–4).

In whatever form, bizarre, frightening, dramatic, or mundane, such contact produces a shock of recognition in terms of lifestyle, and personal meaning. At the level of collective lived experiences, the epiphanic approach aims to identify how different social and cultural groupings, for example gays, the elderly, women, youth, racial minorities, yuppies, the media elite, the new middle, service, therapy, knowledge and cultural intermediary classes (Featherstone, 1989a), the unemployed, the rich, the famous, and the fallen attach themselves to and come to grips with those traces of postmodernism that invade and become part of their lives. It seeks, that is, to locate epiphanal moments which mobilize collectivities and individuals in protest as well as reactionary (the neo-conservatives) and defeatist directions. The intent is to connect the lived cultures of these groups with the cultural texts that organize and represent the experiences in them.

At the same time there is a concern for how new cultural lifestyles emerge and come to symbolize adaptations to and celebrations of the many postmodern aesthetics of personhood that now circulate in the popular culture, including body-building, therapy groups for rape and incest victims, recovery groups for sex addicts, alcoholics and drug addicts, children of alcoholics, debtors anonymous, shoppers anonymous, health care consumers, anti-nuclear protesters, animal rights advocates, Native American activists, gay and lesbian liberation members, Vietnam veterans against war and so on.

To speak, then, of a postmodern culture is to make loose reference to a body of understandings which 'go without saying' in this complex, heterodox mass of shifting, conflicting, regional, cultural understandings that make up the cultural fabrics of late twentieth-century America. What-goes-without-saying refers to the *form*, not the *content* per se of the mass-mediated information which permeates and attempts to make sense of the society-at-large. But loosely connected to these forms is a body of cultural myths, which attempt to transcend region and locale. Embodied in the culture's heroes (Rocky, Michael Jordon, Ronald Reagan) these figures speak the voices of freedom, liberty, individuality, family, self-responsibility and so on.

This rather lengthy discussion suggests that there is no single postmodern subject in American society. He or she comes in a variety of shapes and forms. But a single cluster of meanings emerges and these turn on the pervasive effects of the popular culture and its heroes in defining what is important to this culture. There are two categories of the postmodern subject defined by race, gender, and income: those above the poverty line and those below. There is a black-Hispanic underclass, producing a generation of postmodern children who are likely to be unemployed, drug-addicted, homeless victims of violence, yet believers in the fantasy systems surrounding the American dream which are conveyed in such cultural stories as *The Cosby Show* and enacted in the lives of people like Eddie Murphy. Put another way, one out of ten (greater depending on race and gender) postmodern subjects will be one or more of the following: gay, lesbian, alcoholic or drug addicted, ill, elderly, battered, homeless, and unemployed. Yet each type will be electronically connected to the American dream; even if they have to watch themselves on TV sets in shelters for the homeless, while their age, sex, and race are being recorded by 1990 census takers.

Passing on the Postmodern

A key question involves how the cultural logics of the postmodern are passed from one generation to the next. How, that is, does this diverse system of contradictory cultural meanings and practices constitute, over and over again, new versions of the postmodern subject? Which dividing and constituting practices, at the level of the micropolitics of the every-day, do this work? Put another way, how are new versions of men, women, children, youth, the elderly, the middle-aged, the sick, the diseased and infirm, the heroes, the villains, and the fools reproduced by this cultural logic?[6]

Lefebvre (1984: 173) provides one answer. In the bureaucratic society of controlled consumption the everyday life world has taken the place that Marx previously accorded economics and the modes of capitalist production (Baudrillard, 1975). 'Nowadays everyday life has taken the place of economics; it is everyday life that now prevails as the outcome of a generalized class' (Lefebvre, 1984: 197) struggle. A diverse, hegemonic cultural politics stressing consumption now becomes the chief carrier of state ideology. This system of taken-for-granted beliefs (what-goes-without-saying) embodies the traditional patriarchal myths of western culture involving love, beauty, youth, sexuality, intimacy, romance, marriage, and family (see Fiedler, 1966).

This system of beliefs focuses on two classes of subject: youth and women, who constitute two versions of life and love, desire and sexuality for the culture. Childhood and youth are the doors one must open and pass through, on the way to becoming a member of this postmodern world. One must be motivated to open this door into the postmodern. Hence needs and desires, specific to children and youth, males and females, must be created. They must become desiring subjects who desire the needs and gratifications that the culture holds out to them. They are seduced into this system of needs through a youth-consumer-oriented culture. This culture is articulated in and through an ecstasy of communication specific to this age group. It is inscribed in the rock music which flows out of the earphones attached to Walkmans. It comes at them from the television screens in their bedrooms, where MTV, cartoons, and reruns of family melodramas (*The Waltons*, *Little House on the Prairie*, *Father Knows Best*, *The Brady Bunch*) endlessly play. It is present at the movie theaters in the shopping centers where films aimed at the 6–18 year-old are screened. It is in the pages of their comic books, science fiction, romance novels, *Ms* magazine, and *Rolling Stone*.

This system of beliefs is directly translated into the spheres of commodity consumption which are represented and presented in all of these sites. These beliefs are presented under a double logic. They valorize childhood and youth. They speak their language, and argue that they are not understood by their parents. They are presented in the guise of a revolutionary, resistance form of discourse. Yet underneath is a conservative system of meanings which reproduces the cultural meanings of youth, sexuality, love, and beauty which are part of the larger patriarchal myths that circulate in the adult world (See Featherstone, 1987). This commodity system turns youth and women (men too) into consumers of goods which stress femininity, masculinity, youthfulness, health, and beauty. It turns these subjects into symbols of the postmodern society, who even before they enter the youth culture, are socialized into the postmodern way of life in daycare centers (only 7 percent of American households have a stay-at-home mother: Leavitt et al., 1989: 36). In these settings they learn to simulate authentic emotions (after TV), are rewarded for 'performativity' and find that their inner feelings are denied legitimacy (Leavitt et al., 1989: 36). These children quickly become the objects of advertising strategies, and advertising subjects, who in their smiling, coy nakedness, and lithe, muscular bodies 'become living display units of the postmodern person' (Lefebvre, 1984: 173).

Youthful men and women, if family income permits, are given their own operational physical and electronic environments (TV, bedrooms,

cars, street corners, clubs, schools, sports, hobbies, make-up, drugs) where
they are then encouraged to appropriate the existing symbols of happiness,
eroticism, taste, power, and individuality which are uniquely theirs. They
express this new-found individuality through the hair styles, clothing
(Bugle Boy jeans), perfumes, aftershave lotions, and jewelry they put on
before they leave the house, through the gifts they buy and exchange with
one another, in the women and men they date, and in the 'trances, ecstasies
(simulated or sincere)' (Lefebvre, 1984: 171) these pleasures give them.
Their dances, close moments together, and phone calls which last for hours
signify that their lives are both work and pleasure, and constitute provinces
of meaning to which adults are outsiders.

'In this loveless everyday life eroticism is a substitute for love' (Lefebvre, 1984: 172), and youth a measure of joy and freedom. The cult of
Eros and Youth (Love and Death) reduces sexuality to a commodified
myth which stifles desire, intimacy, and love. Patriarchy rears its ugly
head, and sexual harassment and sexual violence are soon translated into
the arrangement between the sexes. By late adolescence and early
adulthood two sexual cultures are in place, and women are once again
transformed into the objects of male possession. Over wine and roses the
two sexes blend into coupled units, who will now become conjoint
consumers of the postmodern culture's symbols of electronic adulthood:
TV, VCRs, tape decks, compact disk players, video-disks, and intercom
systems.

In this way the postmodern culture, in all its forms – joyful,
narcissistic, nostalgic, erotic, playful, ambiguous, harsh, repressive, and
liberating – reproduces itself.

A sociology of the postmodern (Featherstone, 1990; Bauman, 1988;
Turner, 1990) can best be accomplished by fitting a concern for the
postmodern, in all its variations (aesthetic, art, religious, technology,
literature, film, architecture, TV, photography) and formations (class
group, collectivity, individual) inside a broader cultural studies
framework. This must, however, be a feminist-based cultural studies, for
feminist theorists were doing postmodern analyses before it became
fashionable (see Richardson, 1990a, b). I turn, then, to the feminist
response to postmodernism.

Feminism Reading Postmodernism

It is clear that the primary theoretical texts on postmodernism
(Baudrillard, Jameson, Lyotard) have excluded feminist theory, or
relegated it to the sidelines. Arac (1986, xi), for example, observes that,
'almost no women have figured in the debate, even though many analysts
include current feminism among the features of postmodernity.'[7] Morris
(1988a: 11) argues that this judgement 'reflects the work of male critics
referring primarily to each other.' She asks, not rhetorically, 'under what
conditions [can] women's work figure . . . in such a debate,' and suggests

that this will occur only when such work is properly framed within the metanarratives that now define postmodern discourse (see also Hutcheon, 1988: 16, who notes that the voices of blacks have also been excluded from this discourse; and Suleiman, 1986: 268; also Richardson, 1990a, b). While Morris (1988a: 11, 16) proposes to neither salvage feminism for postmodernism, nor to situate feminist theory as postmodernist, she does offer a bibliography of feminist work which fits the altered postmodern frame and runs to over 175 items.

This silence on women, Connor (1989: 229) suggests, 'projects the female as the place of patriarchy's Other, identified with the dark and discredited side of every polarity, as body to mind, nature to culture, night to day . . . madness to reason.' Writers like Kristeva (1985: 150) have attempted to undermine this position which defines women as marginal in the first place. As Connor (1989: 230), notes, this concern for marginality should align feminist thought with the postmodern concern with difference. Owens (1983: 59, 65–6, 77), for example, argues that feminism's concerns with sexual difference, its refusal to theorize totalizing metanarratives, and its critique of patriarchy and theories of representation, forces a reconsideration of what postmodernism had previously ignored; namely the persistent presence of a master narrative which legitimizes Western man's self-appointed mission of transforming the entire planet in his own image. Yet Owens (1983: 59) recognizes that postmodern theory has been 'scandalously in-different' to sexual difference.

A feminist, postmodern, cultural studies program can only be hinted at (see Balsamo, 1990). Informed by Fraser and Nicholson's (1988) discussion of the uneasy encounter between feminism and postmodernism, such a program would seek to avoid essentialist, functional categories and dichotomies (public/private, mothering/fathering functions, reproduction, biology/culture, fixed gender identities and so on). It would be historically and situationally specific, grounded in the particular class–race–gender–economic–ideological configurations that operate in a particular time and place. It would posit a multiplicity of subject positions, not just the 'unitary notions of woman, or female gender identity, treating gender as one relevant strand among others, attending also to class, race, ethnicity, age and sexual orientation' (Fraser and Nicholson, 1988: 391). It would study how gender is enlivened through sexuality (Lacan, 1982), as it examines how the master narrative of patriarchy is woven through the reinforcing myths of Eros, Youth, Beauty, and Love. It would study how these narratives are implemented in everyday life through a political economy of signs and differences which turn women into commodities, desire into sexuality, and erotic love into pornography. It would examine how sexual ideology, at the material level of popular culture, recruits sexually gendered subjects through a process of interpellation. This hailing of the sexual subject presumes that individuals are 'always-already [gendered] subjects' (Althusser, 1971: 176), constituted in and through the interactional-ideological practices of every-day life. This involves, in part, the analysis of the social texts of and about gender that come into play in the popular culture when the master myths of partriarchy are represented, gazed at, listened to, and learned. It also includes the study of the textual construction of sexual subjects in advertisements, film MTV, and popular music.

In a parallel manner, consistent with a cultural studies approach to epiphanic moments and lived experience, studies must be organized around how the worlds of patriarchy are lived into existence. How domi-nant and subordinate sexual codes (homosexual, lesbian, male, female, love, sex, intercourse) are represented, acquired, and enacted must also be studied. The guiding question in such inquiries becomes how the lived experiences of sexuality depart from, yet articulate and amplify, the mythical beliefs that operate in the popular culture about love, family, eroticism, and the relations between the sexes in late twentieth-century America.

The interactionist, feminist, postmodern approach to these phenomena, presumes that gender inequality is a given. It moves, at all times, between three levels of cultural analysis: the production, distribution, and consumption of cultural texts; the reading and analysis of these texts; and the relationship between these texts and the everyday world where gender inequality occurs. Stressing the violent, erotic side of gendered, postmodern life, this perspective argues that a systematic deconstruction of the cultural myths and beliefs about men, women, sexuality, love, and marriage must occur before inequality will begin to disappear. The emphasis is always on the worlds of lived experience where men, women, and children together produce sexuality and gender, under conditions specified by a patriarchal system of domination and control.

In such a world all too often 'the self is confused with its image' (Finkelstein, 1991: 193). When such reductions occur, the postmodern self is defined in terms of its surface reflections which are shaped by race, gender, and class. When the picture becomes the reality, and when that reality is ideologically coded, then the essential humanity of human beings is reduced to a code. That code strips each of us of our dignity and pride. It reduces us, in the end, to signs which bear the traces of racism and sexism. This is the dilemma of the postmodern self: to find an essential humanity in a forest of signs which deal only in reflections.

Notes

1. After 1946, television, of course, begins to displace cinema as the main carrier of cultural values and meanings.

2. See the analysis of *Blue Velvet* (Ch. 5, and Denzin (1991, Ch. 1; also Hall, 1980) for a discussion of how films such as these may be read.

3. See Featherstone (1990: 2–10) for a review of this term and its history. The term was first used by Federico de Onis in the 1930s to indicate 'a minor reaction to modernism' (Featherstone, 1990: 7). It was used again in 1942 by Fitts to describe contemporary Latin-

American literature, in 1947 by Toynbee to designate a new cycle in western civilization, and again in 1959 by C. Wright Mills (1959: 166) to describe the Fourth Epoch in world history. It then became popular in the 1960s in New York 'when it was used by young artists, writers and critics such as Rauschenberg, Cage, Burroughs, Barthelme, Fiedler and Sontag to refer to a movement beyond the "exhausted" high modernism' (Featherstone, 1990: 7). In the 1970s and 1980s the term 'gained wider usage in architecture, the visual and performing arts, and music' (Featherstone, 1990: 7). By the mid-1980s postmodern social theory began to emerge (Featherstone, 1990: 7). Within postmodern theory (Jameson, 1988a: 110; Hassan, 1985: 122) there are multiple positions (pro-and anti) defined by the terms modernist and postmodernist (pro-modernist, anti-postmodern [Habermas], pro-modernist, pro-postmodern [Lyotard], etc.). By the late 1980s and early 1990s books (Harvey, 1989; Eagleton, 1989; Featherstone, 1990; Morris, 1988a; Connor, 1989; Grossberg, 1988a; Kellner, 1989a, 1989b; Berman, 1988; Kariel, 1989; Hutcheon, 1988; Ross, 1988), entire issues of journals (see Connor, 1989: 266) and professional scholarly societies, from the regional, to the national and international levels, would devote special sessions to the topic (*Theory Culture & Society*, 1985, 1988; *Amerikastudien*, 1977; *Cultural Critique*, 1987; *New German Critique*, 1984; *New Literary History*, 1971; *Screen* 1987; *Salmagundi*, 1985; *Triquarterly*, 1973, 1974, 1975). A plethora of journals, some new, some old, would enter this discourse (i.e. *Social Science Journal, Theory, Culture & Society, Diacritics, New Left Review, October, Canadian Journal of Political and Social Theory, Ideology and Consciousness, Semiotext (e), New German Critique, Media Culture and Society, Cultural Studies, New Formations, Textual Practice, Feminist Review*), as would philosophers (Habermas, Lyotard, Derrida, Foucault, Baudrillard), sociologists (Bell), anthropologists (Marcus, Clifford, Fischer, Tyler) literary critics (Jameson, Kristeva, Eagleton), and geographers (Soja): See Featherstone (1988: 196), Huyssen (1984). According to Arthur J. Vidich, Veblen may have been the first person to use the term in the twentieth century. Veblen used the term postmodern in *The Vested Interests and the Common Man* (1919: 11).

4. Laurie Anderson's performance art, for example, mixes literature, theater, music, photography, stand-up comedy, storytelling, film, architecture, poetry, fantasy, and dance. Her multimedia arrangements of text, image, movement, and musical sounds exploit, while mocking the new high-tech equipment which permit the perfect reproduction of sounds and images. Anderson's performances 'relentlessly circle around and even poke fun at issues central to postmodernism: the slipperiness of language, the way our alienation and confusion are produced by Big Science and the media, how words and images are created in today's world – and how we are inundated and affected by them' (McCaffery, 1990: 27).

5. In the first stage, realism, the sign mapped concrete objects in the world. In the second stage the sign becomes arbitrary and no longer refers to a thing with a fixed presence, i.e. a religious icon (see also the discussion of Baudrillard in chapter 2).

6. It must be remembered, as argued in the Preface, that reactions to postmodernism can range from complete acceptance, to rejection, to mid-way positions which take part of the postmodern while ignoring its other features.

7. In some cases the feminist voice has been ignored altogether, only to be heard later (i.e. Owens, 1983). For some, feminism has not figured in the important postmodern debates of the day (Arac, 1986: xi). Some contend that 'feminist issues' are better fitted to the problems of class, or race (Jameson, 1981: 84) and others argue that Freud was right, 'there is only one single sexuality, one single libido – masculine' (Baudrillard, 1979: 16). It is even implied that patriarchy no longer functions as an oppressive principle in contemporary culture (i.e. Lyotard, 1984a, b; Fraser and Nicholson, 1988: 390). The feminist, cultural studies approach to sexuality, gender, and patriarchy refuses the above positions (i.e. Daly, 1980; Coward, 1985; de Lauretis, 1984, 1987; Morris, 1988a).

2
Postmodern Social Theory

> The status of theory could not be anything but a challenge to the real.
> (Baudrillard, 1988a: 98-100)

Not surprisingly, because of their commitments to a 'modernist foundationalist project' (Frank, 1987: 295; Seidman, 1990: 1) the major contemporary American (and British) social theorists have turned their backs on postmodern social theory. Giddens (1987: 195), for example, declares that 'structuralism and post-structuralism are dead traditions of thought'. Alexander (1985, 1987a, 1987b, 1988a) and the neo-functionalists make no reference to either the term or the historical period it marks. Collins (1988a, 1988b, 1989: 131) reduced the poststructural concern for discourse and textual analysis to the level of 'a professional ideology [which is useful for] elevating literary theorists' own field' and subsumes Foucault's project into a neo-Weberian-Durkheimian theory of modernity. The widely acclaimed new theory book, *Social Theory* (Giddens and Turner, 1987) contains no index entry to postmodernism, nor to the key postmodern theorists (Baudrillard, Lyotard, Jameson). Only Foucault gets notice, and this negatively (Giddens, 1987: 209–10). Joas, in his contribution to *Social Theory* (1987: 111), expresses the most favorable position, and this is borrowed from Rorty, 'In my view, James and Dewey . . . are waiting at the end of the road which, for example, Foucault and Deleuze are currently traveling' (Rorty, 1982: xviii). The picture is clear: the major contemporary American (and British) social theorists want to either absorb postmodern theory into existing 'modernist' frameworks, or ignore the perspective entirely. These theorists remain preoccupied with writing modernist micro–macro theories of contemporary society (Alexander, 1987a; Collins, 1988a, 1988b, 1989; Giddens, 1984, 1987; see also Frank 1989 on Habermas's project).

As a consequence, with few exceptions (Denzin, 1986; Lemert, 1979, 1989; Manning, 1990; Maines, 1989b; Katovich, 1990; Richardson, 1990a, b; Clough, 1988a, 1988b, 1990a; Agger, 1990; Pfohl and Gordon, 1986) the poststructural–postmodern project has not occupied the attention of the American Sociological Establishment. Even in those areas, like the sociology of science, where it has had a presence (see Ashmore, 1989 for a review of this literature), that presence has been discounted by mainstream social theorists (see Collins, 1989: 131–2). Likewise the American sociological version of cultural studies (Bellah, Bell, Wuthnow, see Denzin, 1990e for a review), while conducting readings of such theorists as Barthes, Foucault, and Derrida, has mapped this work into existing structural-functional models of society and culture. Similarly,

American sociological feminists (see Wallace, 1989; Deegan and Hill, 1987) have by and large attempted to assimilate feminist concerns into existing sociological theory (that is, functionalism, conflict theory, sociological psychoanalysis, symbolic interactionism, rational choice), thereby refusing to take up the challenge of formulating a poststructural–postmodern feminist agenda that theorists like Clough (1988a) Balsamo (1987), Richardson, (1990a, b), Treichler (1987), Morris (1988a), and Fraser and Nicholson (1988) have called for (but see Smith, 1989).

Hence, while the Canadian sociologist J.N. Porter can write in 1990 (p. 323) that the publication of a work like *Postmodernism*, edited by Mike Featherstone and published in 1988, 'makes it no longer possible for sociologists to claim that postmodernism is unintelligible, irrelevant, or inaccessible,' the sad fact remains that most American sociologists remain ignorant of the postmodern challenge. Current work in postmodern theory is marginal to mainstream American sociology, finding its expression in only a handful of journals (*Theory, Culture & Society*, the *Canadian Journal of Political and Social Theory, Current Perspectives in Social Theory*), and either in fields next to sociology, for example anthropology (Clifford and Marcus, 1986), and political science (Kellner, 1988), or in the interdisciplinary spaces provided by film theory and cinema studies (Ray, 1985; de Lauretis, 1987; Doane, 1987; Mulvey, 1989), literary criticism (Derrida, 1972, 1978, 1986), communications (Grossberg, 1988a), British cultural studies (Hall, 1986b) and philosophy (Lyotard, 1984a, b; Rorty, 1986). This is a paradoxical situation, for as Bauman (1988: 234) observes, '*the task of providing men and women with that 'sociological imagination' for which C.W. Mills . . . appealed years ago, has never been so important as it is now, under conditions of postmodernity*' (italics added).

In this and the following chapters I take up this task. Here I will briefly review the state of current social theory, beginning with a deconstruction of ordinary, everyday mainstream sociology's micro–macro dilemma concerning the 'reality' of this thing called the social. In this struggle to develop a theory which would reach from the top (macro) to the bottom (micro) of contemporary societies sociologists reflect an attempt to keep the grand sociological theories of the past alive in the present (Collins, 1988a, 1988b; Alexander and Giesen, 1987; Giddens, 1981, 1984; Hall, 1987; Maines, 1982; Lyman, 1989; Huber, 1989; Prendergast and Knott-nerus, 1990; Ritzer, 1988; Wiley, 1988).

The Current State of American Social Theory

A critical reading of the recent dialogue and debate within American social theory would echo Mills's (1959: 21) observations, now over thirty years old, that 'many practitioners of social science . . . are curiously reluctant to take up the challenge that now confronts them,' namely to develop a sociological imagination relevant to the times. Instead theory has become the focus of theorists, as they have withdrawn 'into systematic work on conceptions' (Mills, 1959: 48) about society and the social order. Such focus, Mills reminds us, 'should only be a formal moment within the work of social science . . . only a pause . . . [not something] which seems to have become permanent. As they say in Spain, "many can shuffle cards who can't play"' (1959: 48).

The blindness to the postmodern moment is evident in the battles which go on between the various proponents of conflict theory (Collins, Dahrendorf, Coser), microstructuralism (Blau, Giddens), exchange theory (Homans, Blau, Emerson), rational choice theory (Coleman, Becker, Burt, Hechter), symbolic interactionism, ethnomethodology (Garfinkel, Schegloff), neo-functionalism (Alexander) Marxism (Miliband, Wright, Buraway), world-systems, and historical-comparative theories. Each theorist theorizes a specific terrain, protecting a turf which is insulated from the surrounding social world.

Recent efforts to transcend these local debates have shifted attention to the micro-macro level (Huber, 1989; Alexander and Giesen, 1987; Frank, 1989), wherein some version of a yet to be discovered grand theory will solve sociology's puzzle concerning the classic question, 'How is society possible?' Such efforts display commitments to conceptualize societies as totalities, to form models which connect the micro and macro levels of experience, as if by fiat, or a stroke of the pen, within a science called sociology, which while conflict oriented, stresses individualism, the voluntary basis of interaction, a social order based on moral consensus, incremental proposals for social change, and an enduring optimism (see Smelser, 1989: 421 on these trends within American sociology) about capitalism, democracy, and the American way of life. At the same time there is an under-theorizing of language, the human subject, the mass media, commodity relations in a consumer society, the legitimation crisis surrounding science and sociology, (Bauman, 1988) and the general failure to produce a sociology which would make a difference in today's world.

A recent past President of the American Sociological Association phrased American sociology's problem this way: 'The macro/micro relationship is a problem that in one way or another most of us confront daily . . . Yet there is little consensus as to its implications' (Huber, 1989: 2). Alexander and Giesen (1987: 1) phrase the issue thus: 'The micro–macro problem transcends paradigmatic boundaries and in so doing fosters communication between different theory traditions and disciplinary integration.' The same authors argue that while 'we are not suggesting that the widespread acceptance of a new theory of micro–macro articulation is imminent . . . It is our view that only by establishing a radically different theoretical starting point can a genuine inclusive micro–macro link be made' (p. 37). It is clear that they think they have offered this starting point.

The postmodern deconstruction of ordinary (mainstream) sociology's micro–macro dilemma rests on three assumptions. First, society as it is lived, known, felt, and written about goes on behind people's backs; people, that is, as Marx (1852) reminded us, make history, but not under conditions of their own making. Secondly, ordinary sociology's society, society-at-large, is a sociological fiction; society in the abstract is neither visible nor countable. It exists only in the texts that sociologists and others write about it. Thirdly, this fiction of a society-out-there is important, and apparently necessary, for it allows ordinary sociologists to invent problems about how their discipline confronts this 'thing's presence.' Hence the micro–macro dilemma. Sociology's most prominent practitioner tells us over and over again that while scholars 'agree on the definition of macrosociology,' microsociology is so variously defined as to 'make the debate on the macro/micro relation less productive than one would like' (Huber, 1989).

Creating a problem – too many definitions of microsociology, and no ability to handle macro problems – sociology's esteemed macro-theorists presume to tell micro-practitioners, those afflicted with various versions of symbolic interactionism, ethnomethodology, and phenomenology, how to correct their diseased condition. Alexander (1988b) sets a research agenda for Garfinkel. Collins (1988b), in yet another essay on the micro–macro problem, writes on how the macro tradition can shape the micro position, while noting how the micro constraints of everyday life filter larger macro forces. Giddens (1984) offers a theory of structuration to account for the structural regularities of interactional processes. Ritzer (1988) proposes a metatheoretical levels solution to the problem. Wiley (1988) offers a theory of levels, moving from self to interaction, structure, and culture, and inserts the concepts of emergence and feedback as devices which connect each level. This framework deconstructs the simplistic micro–macro dichotomy that organizes much of the discussion in this area, and clears a space for a theory that would connect all four levels. Prendergast and Knottnerus (1990), in an exhaustive review of interactionist attempts to resolve their so-called 'astructural bias,' conclude that interactionist metatheory remains wedded to a threefold dualism of subjectivism, humanism, and idealism and can only handle the macro problem when it adopts a systems-centered paradigm. And so on. The list is endless.

On the other side of the playing field, micro-sociologists and interactionists from Couch (1984), to Hall (1987), Farberman (1981), Strauss (1978), Becker (1986a), Maines (1982), and Lyman (1989), have offered closely knit, tightly argued historical, comparative, interactionist treatments of traditional macro problems, including race relations, mesostructures, the worlds of work, the political economies of everyday life and the construction of civilizations. These works exist alongside, but remain uninformed by, the problematics of the postmodern condition (for example Featherstone, 1983).

Neither side speaks to the opponent, or when it does, it typically

misreads the other's theory. It is clear that what is occurring here has
little to do with the development of sociology as an empirical discipline
which might have something to say about what goes on behind people's
backs in the world out there. What's at issue is hegemony and control
of a theoretical paradigm that would speak for all of sociology. Beneath
this search for power are individual careers, prestige, publications, and
the power to determine what passes as knowledge within a discipline.

Enter Postmodern Social Theory

Postmodern social theory may be read as a response to the above situation. Refusing the modernist agenda to theorize societies as totalities
interpreted from within the grand metanarrative theories of Marx,
Weber, and Durkheim, postmodern social theory has the following
characteristics. It shuns the positivist and post-positivist attempts to build
a science of society. It seeks to produce theoretical-interpretive analyses
which illuminate the social world through the close-up analyses of
selected social texts (see Chapters 3 and 4). This anti-totalizing stance
stems from the belief that terror resides in any attempt to conceptualize
societies as coherent, integrated entities. It derives from Lyotard's
(1984b: 81) argument that 'The nineteenth and twentieth centuries have
given us as much terror as we can take. We have paid a high enough
price for the nostalgia of the whole and the one.'

Postmodern theory has no desire to wed the micro and macro levels
of analysis. It argues, following the interactionist tradition (Blumer,
1969), that society in the here-and-now, society-at-hand, is best
understood as an interactional accomplishment which is shaped by pre-
existing and emergent political, economic, ritual, and moral structures of
crystallized social experience. These crystallized structures assume taken-
for-granted meanings, yet they constrain and control the individual and
shape, as well, the ensembles of social relationships that the person
inhabits. Mediated by localized, interactional practices, these structures
manipulate human experience, calling forth in specific situations
overdetermined forms of subjectivity, meaning, and interpretation (such
as gender identities). These localized practices (dining out, making love,
shopping, watching the evening news, doing work) involve the exercise of
power, influence, and authority, often with physical, emotional, and
moral consequences. Localized practices translate power in the abstract
into power-in-use. Such practices will force a President out of office,
produce the destruction of Berlin Walls, and place the homeless out on
the street.

The exercise of power involves the control and manipulation of
knowledge, and quickly translates into the control and application of
knowledge structures at the level of micro, situational, local politics.
Under the cultural logic of late capitalism, knowledge is progressively
centered in modes of scientific discourse which focus on a bio-politics of

control (Foucault, 1982). This regime of power turns each postmodern subject into an object to be manipulated by the state and its various control apparatuses. In the postmodern world these systems of control work through a computerized, data-bank system which stores information on each individual, including age, marital, health, financial, residential, work, and legal history.

Postmodern social theory orients itself to this modern, computerized, mass-media-dominated world where information technologies define what is real. It connects the crises of understanding which have invaded the postmodern university and its scientific structures to the emergence of a paralogical system of legitimation which values new knowledge for its own sake, while it undermines previous understandings in the process (Lyotard, 1984b: 3–5). It understands that the current crisis in knowledge reflects the shift from a modernist, rational, *discursive* system of representation, to a postmodern, *figural*, paralogical system of representation which asks, 'not what a cultural text "means," but what it does' (Lash, 1988: 314; Lyotard, 1971).

The conflict between the discursive and figural regimes of signification inserts into postmodern knowledge systems (e.g. the university) new modes of representation (figures, images, tables, charts) which, as they replace and supplement words and statistics (printed texts), create conflicts in understanding. The traditional referents of a text have come to be signifiers themselves, cut off from any firmly established concrete object, event, or person (see Lash, 1988: 332; 1990: Chapter 1). This symbolic representation of natural facts as cultural facts has created a situation where 'cultural facts [have] become so pervasive that they [now] challenge "natural facts" for hegemony' (Lash, 1988: 333).

At a certain juncture in modernism, as Lash (1988: 333) notes, cultural facts (figural representations, simulations of the real) accumulated 'to a point at which they could no longer be considered solely as representations, and the whole problem of their proper materiality and hence character as representations' had to be taken seriously. What started as a colonization of representations by the commodity form (that is the ideological commodification of objects) has now turned into a situation where the postmodern culture colonizes the commodity. Advertisements, for example, began as 'bits of information to help market commodities' (Lash, 1988: 334).

With the advent of ad agencies advertisements became commodities. Images rather than information soon became the content of the new commodities (Ronald McDonald for McDonald's, the *Good Housekeeping* photographs of the New Traditional Woman and her family). The next move was to attach 'already existent cultural representations' (Lash, 1988: 334), for example pop music, to these images of the commodity (The Beatles 'Revolution' coupled with tennis shoes, 'I heard it Through the Grapevine' matched with kitchen appliances and breakfast food, and so on).

The consequence is the recommodification and revival in popularity of the earlier form which is now attached to the new object (for example soul music from the 1950s and 1960s). This process of circling back to an earlier cultural form and attaching it to a new commodity produces a new form of signification. In a complex process of doubling it invokes the cultural nostalgia for an earlier form, resurrecting the cultural memories of that form and its moment while attaching a 'purified' cultural ethic to the new object. It places the newly advertised object in a seamless present which extends, unbroken, into the past. It extolls all that was good about the past in the present. As the Berlin Wall was being torn down, ads for Pepsi and Coca-Cola were produced and used to frame the historical moment, suggesting that the political act of tearing down the wall was inspired by these two commodities, and the lifestyles associated with them.

The figural logics of simulation and paralogy have undermined the Enlightenment myth concerning science and truth as liberators of humanity, for the enactment of this myth has created the current crisis in representation outlined above. Predictably, as one myth dies, another emerges to take its place. A new system of discourse derived from the structures of narrative knowledge lodged in everyday life, the realms of folklore, myth, ideology, and folk heroes (Lyotard, 1984b: 27–31), now replaces an older objective discourse predicated in reason, science, and truth. Biographies, autobiographies, and films which celebrate the private lives of scientists, their conflicts, failures, successes, and tragedies keep alive the myth of the scientist, which recasting this figure as a folk hero who has ordinary, human failings (the Watson and Crick story in *The Double Helix* (1968); the Tom Wolfe story-film *The Right Stuff* (1983) which cast the real Chuck Yeager in a cameo role as a bartender, and told the story of the birth of America's space program; *Torn Curtain* (1966), *The China Syndrome* (1979), *E.T.* (1982), *War Games* (1983), *Silkwood* (1983), *2010* (1985), *Star Trek II, III,* and so on).

In these new narratives, biographies and lived experiences serve the larger purposes of legitimizing the mythical story about America's role as a leader in space-age, atomic technology. Audiences are taken up to the brink of disaster and annihilation, and then brought back to safety through the actions of well-meaning scientists and ordinary citizens, sometimes children. A hyperreal logic of representation, deterrence, and control is embedded in these texts. It regulates (mollifies) the organization of a horrifying cultural experience in the face of a nuclear holocaust (Krug, 1989a). Science and politics now appeal to these structures of narrative knowledge in their attempts to achieve legitimation. The politics of truth in the postmodern age is now cast inside a narrative model which sees figural representations replacing older, literal models of truth and knowledge. The real, to use Baudrillard's phrase, has become the hyperreal.

To summarize the above discussion, postmodern social theory is characterized by the following eleven features:

- A departure from theorizing in terms of grand systems which conceptualize the social as a totality.
- A turn away from formal, positivistic conceptions of social theory and the belief that the sociological classics speak to the current moment.
- An intense preoccupation with the crises of representation and legitimation that characterize the modern computerized, media-dominated world cultural systems.
- A critique of scientific knowledge and realism coupled with a profound distrust of reason and science as forces which will produce a utopian society based on consensus, rational communicative action, and human freedom (Lyotard, 1984b: 64–7, 79–82).
- A radical conceptualization of language, semiotics, and theories of representation leading to the analysis of social texts which represent society and social experience.
- A return to the commodity and the commodification of experience as central theoretical preoccupations.
- An attempt to periodize the postmodern moment, to separate it from the modern period, and to disclose the continuities and breaks between the old and the new (Kellner, 1988: 256).
- The attempt to formulate a feminist, cultural studies agenda which would give a voice to the 'silenced' minorities and speak to the technologies of repression and representation which dominate the current historical moment.
- The development of a politics of resistance which would deconstruct the repressive features of postmodern culture while developing a local and global politics predicated on new rhetorical forms of expression, representation, and protest which enact and simulate the real in the name of human freedom and dignity (Guattari and Negri, 1988; Ryan, 1988: 575–6; Ulmer, 1983: 107).
- The beliefs that the personal is political, the political is personal, and social theory must always move from the one to the other.
- Radical experimentations with the writing of theory and interpretation, including poetry, performances, and multi-media 'mystories' (Ulmer, 1989: Part 3; also Richardson, 1990a).

In Conclusion

A certain nostalgia pervades contemporary social theory, a longing for a past which postmodern social theory says is over. Unwilling, for whatever reasons, to confront the postmodern challenge, current theory is in danger of being passed over by a new generation who now suspect

that the classical conceptual and epistemological apparatus of Marx, Durkheim and Weber, of Mead and Parsons, has outlived its half-life. This apparatus, which we call 'sociological theory,' can still educate students when we teach it, can still give us insights when we read it, but more and more contemporary experience eludes it. The world being described has changed (Frank, 1991: 97–8).

How these changes have been perceived by three leading postmodern theorists is the topic of the next chapter.

3

Takes on the Postmodern: Baudrillard, Lyotard, and Jameson

Let us wage war on a totality; let us be witnesses to the unpresentable. (Lyotard, 1984b: 82)

It is not enough for theory to describe and analyze, it must itself be an event in the universe it describes . . . It must tear itself from all referents and take pride only in the future . . . . It would be better for theory to divert itself, than to be diverted from itself. (Baudrillard, 1988a: 98–100)

I believe that the emergence of postmodernism is closely related to the emergence of this new moment of late, consumer, or multinational capitalism. I believe also that its formal features in many ways express the deeper logic of that particular social system. (Jameson, 1983: 125)

So 'post' means, for me, going on thinking on the ground of a set of established problems, a problematic. It doesn't mean deserting the terrain but rather, using it as one's reference point. (Hall, 1986a: 58–9)

Here I critically examine the formulations of Baudrillard, Lyotard, and Jameson, in preparation for a treatment of C. Wright Mills in Chapter Four. I will be asking how these theorists define, make sense of, and address the postmodern self and its social situations. In particular I will examine how race, gender, and class are conceptualized by each theorist.

Enter Baudrillard

Baudrillard has been called France's leading philosopher of postmodernism, one of the most innovative thinkers in the discourses of poststructuralism (Kellner, 1989b: 1).[1] A postmodern event, Jean Baudrillard has been generally derided and misunderstood by American critics, seldom given anything but a superficial reading (but see Kellner, 1989b).[2]

These criticisms cannot be ignored (see pp. 33–5). Still, Baudrillard's theory of the postmodern condition cannot be discounted. He has touched a nerve, which others had exposed before (the Frankfurt School, McLuhan, Barthes, Deleuze/Guattari, Lefebvre). Perhaps the 'first to organize these interventions into a postmodern social theory' (Kellner, 1988: 242), his work may be read as a progressive elaboration of a postmodern critique of social theory, traditional Marxism, cybernetics, ethnography, psychoanalysis, feminist thought, communications theory and semiotics (see Chang, 1986). It is a threat to standard sociology and social theory. His analysis of the 'death of the social' (Baudrillard, 1983b) suggests that contemporary social theorists must seriously rethink how they conceptualize the social and their relationship to it.

An analysis of his work, especially the most recent formulations (1987a, 1988a, 1988b) which take up the topics of sexuality, seduction, and pornography will reveal the sexist limits of one version of postmodern theory as presently constituted. Kellner, for example, (1988: 248; 1989b: 184, 203, 217) finds 'shamelessly racist, sexist and chauvinist passages' in Baudrillard's 1980s metaphysical works which display 'regressive thinking, arguably quite good science fiction [but which are] rather problematical as models of social theory.' These later works display a turn to a conservatism which has no apparent exit (Kellner, 1988: 217).

His theory unfolds in four parts, involving four key terms: the simulacrum, the mass media, the sign, and communication. Underlying his use of these terms is a theory of history that attempts to describe the precise breaks which separate the premodern, the modern, and the postmodern moments. A science fiction, cinematic, cybernetic impulse organizes Baudrillard's theory of the postmodern. (He has, on occasion, described his own work as science fiction: Kellner, 1989b: 236, n. 13, also 203–8. More on this below.)

The Simulacrum, the Stages of History and the Image

The simulacrum, which means an image, the semblance of an image, make-believe, or that which conceals the truth or the real (Baudrillard, 1981: 32–3) is the central concept in Baudrillard's theory of history. He assumes that in the postmodern moment the simulacrum is true; images and signs have come to stand for the objects and commodities that make up everyday life. This has not always been the case.

Western culture has progressed through three historical orders of appearance where images and signs changed their relationship to reality.[3] These orders of appearance are: (1) the *counterfeit*, the 'dominant scheme of the "classical" period, from the Renaissance to the industrial revolution,' where signs reflected and then perverted a basic reality, art imitated life (Baudrillard, 1983a: 83); (2) *production*, the dominant scheme of the industrial age, where signs masked the absence of a basic reality, as in the age of mass reproduction; (3) *simulation*, the reigning 'scheme of the current phase,' where signs now bear no relationship to any reality (Baudrillard, 1983a: 83). In the third order of the simulacra, 'The very definition of the real becomes: *that of which it is possible to give an equivalent reproduction* . . . the real is not only what can be reproduced, but *that which is always already reproduced. The hyperreal*' (Baudrillard, 1983a: 146, italics in original).

Fiction has become truth (1983a: 148). McLuhan's global village has been obliterated by the cyberneticized society (Baudrillard, 1981: 202). This techno-culture (1981: 185) makes Marx's theories of capitalism irrelevant (1975; 1981: 164–5), and reduces the Left's dreams of a media takeover to an impossibility because such a proposition presumes the untenable belief that the media is merely the transmitter of messages about the dominant repressive, capitalist ideology (1981: 169). In fact, according to

Baudrillard, the media is anti-mediatory. It fabricates non-communication and short-circuits history by creating instant meaning, and producing a fictional sense of public opinion which immediately passes judgement on the news of the day (for example the events of May 1968 in France). The medium is the message, but the model that organizes the messages has 'evolved into a total system of mythological interpretation, a closed system of . . . signification from which no event escapes' (1981: 175).[4]

This dreary model presumes that any attempt to change the system by remaining within the structural communication grid is doomed to failure. Members of society are confined 'to fragile manipulatory practices that would be dangerous to adopt as a "revolutionary strategy." What is strategic in this sense is only what radically checkmates the dominant form' (1981: 184). We are all trapped. There is no longer any room for change. All that remains is to play 'with the pieces – that is postmodern . . . And postmodernity is the attempt – perhaps it's desperate . . . to reach a point where one can live with what is left. It is more a survival among the remnants than anything else' (1984: 24–5).

In an age of hyperreality, 'when the real is no longer what it used to be, nostalgia assumes its full meaning' (1983a: 12). There is, Baudrillard argues, a proliferation of myths of origin, and signs of reality. A pre-occupation with authenticity, and an 'escalation of the true, of lived experience . . . a panic-stricken production of the real and the referential' (1983a: 12–13). The hyperreal age works under a strategy of deterrence, as if a surfeit of lived experiences could erase any doubt that the real has ceased to exist.[5] This premium on the real and lived experience only underscores the extent to which the 'aura' that previously surrounded lived experience, like the 'aura' of the 'original' work of art (Benjamin, 1955/1968: 223), has been erased. They have both become reproductions, separated from their original time and place, they have now become commodities which circulate inside the simulational model of communication.

The problems of origin, uniqueness, and authenticity are no longer relevant. Paraphrasing Walter Benjamin (1968: 223), 'what withers in the age of simulation is lived experience and its aura.' Freed from biographical context, lived experience is now confronted by viewers (listeners) in their own particular cinematic situation. This shatters the tradition and personal meaning surrounding the experience, and makes any film clip or sound bite depicting the experiences of 'real people' (also the title of a TV show) functionally equivalent to any other representation.[6]

The postmodern age is governed by a new technology of operational simulation, in which cybernetic systems of binary oppositions organize everyday life. Baudrillard's fascination with this simulational code and its everyday logic leads, as if caught up in a science fiction world of his own making, to endless speculations on the DNA codes, artificial intelligence machines, robotic beings, cyborgs, androids, computers, bubble-children, artificial insemination, and the artificial purification of all 'milieus, atmospheres, and environments' (1988a: 37).[7]

Sexuality and Baudrillard

In this postmodern world seduction, which oscillates between two poles, the masculine (strategy) and the feminine (animality), has replaced production. The feminine version of seduction, which takes place at the level of appearances, surfaces, and signs, is a powerful ritual game (Baudrillard, 1988a: 59). It breaks with and exposes the logics of production and desire which the 'cool' simulational society promotes. It has the potential of unmasking the order of appearances and secrets which are embedded in the 'surveillance and computer processes, [and] the evermore sophisticated methods of biological and molecular control and retrieval of bodies' (Baudrillard, 1988a: 74). Seduction, in its feminist forms, is a

> disguise for survival . . . which is stronger yet than that of the system. The evil forces which it has raised against God, against morality . . . the Evil Demon of dissimulation and absence, of challenge and reversion, which it has always embodied and for which it has been damned: seduction can today reinvent these forces, and raise them against the terrorist seizing of truth and verification, of identification and programming which engulf us. Seduction remains the enchanted form of the devil's share. (1988a: 75)

Women are the bearers of freedom, if they will just play their parts, allowing their own seductive strategies to become the medium that exposes the drama of communication which now captures and seduces all postmodern individuals. A new obscene ecstasy of communication prevails, an obscenity which is not 'confined to sexuality, because today there is a pornography of information and communication, a pornography of circuits and networks . . . . It is no longer the obscenity of the hidden, the repressed, the obscure, but that of the visible' (Baudrillard, 1988a: 22).

Race and Baudrillard

The Third World and blacks do not escape Baudrillard's gaze. In 'What are you doing after the orgy?' (1983d: 46), after a discussion of cannibalism, Playboy pictures, male strippers, female mud wrestling, seductive females, and male erections, the following lines appear: 'Black is the embarrassment of White . . . Marvelous Emperor Jean-Bedel Bokassa eating up little black babies . . . . The west would be hard pressed to rid itself of this generation of simian and prosaic despots, born of the monstrous crossing of the jungle with the shining values of ideology.'

Marx's alienation was from the commodity; Baudrillard's is from the postmodern human condition and the communication process. Sexuality, passion, and desire are dead, replaced by ecstasy and obscenity, a cool world of seductive signs, defined always in terms of the feminine figure, the mistress of seduction. But even her body, like the man's, has been transformed by the age of soft technologies, 'the prostheses of the industrial age' (1979: 233) have turned 'every possible body . . . [into] its immutable repetition – this is the end of the body and of its history: the individual is henceforth only a cancerous metastasis of its basic formula' (1979: 233). In this world Oedipus and his problems are dead: 'The digital Narcissus replaces the triangular Oedipus . . . the clone will henceforth be your guardian angel . . . consequently you will never be alone again . . . "Love your neighbor as yourself": this old problem of Christianity is resolved – your neighbor, *it's yourself*. This love is total. And so is self-seduction' (1979: 235, italics in original; also quoted by Kellner, 1989b: 102).

Baudrillard's alienation extends beyond cool communication, to women, minorities, the Left, to all of the pieces of the postmodern puzzle, to even theory itself, and his own apparent place in this obscene hyperreal world he has created (1987a: 128).

Baudrillard *The Blade Runner*

Turn back on the above discussion. This is science fiction, or negative utopia (Kellner *et al.*, 1984: 6). A nightmare vision of the futuristic, postmodern society. It looks and feels like Ridley Scott's 1982 film *Blade Runner*, which was set in the quintessential postmodern city, Los Angeles, in the year 2019. This is the now of now. (Robots, cyborgs, and androids aren't named by Baudrillard, but they are everywhere present.) As stand-ins for humans, they inhabit *Blade Runner*-like hallucinatory, over-crowded, acid-rain-drenched cities, where futuristic, electronic billboards broadcast obscene sex and unfeeling, narcissistic clones fake orgasms. Gone are individuals, love, families, jobs, and religion. Only romantic nostalgia remains. Not 'What are you doing after the orgy?', but 'What will we do now that reality is gone?' All that remains is living with what is left. And what is left? No pleasure, no desire. Only obscene sex; the pleasures of a cloned body, nothing else. Unlike Mary Shelley's *Franken-stein*, which killed off the monster created by science, Baudrillard's fatalistic, nihilistic science fiction keeps the monster alive. Like Stanley Kubrick's (1963) *Dr Strangelove (or How I Learned to Stop Worrying and Love the Bomb)*, Baudrillard has stopped worrying. He has learned to live with postmodernism and asks that you do the same. He is Dr Strangelove.

For a moment call Baudrillard Deckard, the *film noir* hero of Ridley Scott's film, and compare Deckard's chore, to put replicants into retire-ment, with Baudrillard's self-assigned task of making sense of this mad, contemporary world. What does Deckard's world look like? The Los Angeles of 2019 is a giant, overcrowded, Asian-dominated polluted megalopolis. Punk–Oriental–heavy metal–Krishna–hustler–lowlifes stand on street corners. Air thick enough to walk on rises like fog off the streets. Gravity-defying high-rises for the rich tower over Asians riding bicycles and tending stalls at street level, where garbage is piled high and acid-rain pours down incessantly. Futuristic blimps with huge neon billboards float by advertising products familiar in the present-day USA like Coca-Cola, Atari, Jim Beam, Trident, Michelob, and Shakey's.

Another sign shows a Japanese woman popping pills, and loudspeakers hawk the pleasures of an 'Off-World vacation' where a new paradise and a new life can be found. Ten feet above street level, police cars hover, monitoring the 'future as it molders into chaos' (Corliss, 1982: 68). In this anti-paradise, part Babel and Babylon, where the language is cityspeak, a gutter mixture of Japanese, Spanish, German, and English, time flashes back and forth between the past and the future. A futuristic building is decorated in 1940s *film noir* style.

The simulation has become the real, but it out-distances the real, for what the androids have, no human appears able to find. In this decaying, devastated world, pure nature is presented as the site of salvation. Men still lead (and save) women, racism is everywhere, capitalists control labor markets, which are now genetically programmed, and individualist solutions to society's problems, joined with a liberal, neo-Christian, nostalgic, moral romanticism, and a deep faith in the family prevails, 'while empathy is privileged as the distinctively human trait, the basis of morality, and solidarity with one's fellow beings' (Kellner *et al.*, 1984: 7, 9). The old dominations of white capitalist patriarchy pevail.[8]

Back to Baudrillard. His science fiction doesn't go far enough, yet it goes too far. Unwilling to embrace fully the *Blade Runner* world of 2019, but perversely fascinated by the genetic codes, informational technologies, computer designs, and cybernetic, feedback systems that define a cyborg culture, he refuses either to accept this world or to propose its destruction. Afraid of android creatures, he, like Deckard asks only half-seriously, 'What defines a human in this postmodern world?' Alienated from this electronic world, Baudrillard stands back and mocks it, laughs at it, pokes fun at it. Yet his ironic cynicism displays a failure of nerve. He doesn't want to cut loose from the old world of white capitalist patriarchy. He is afraid of the replicants; if he could he would, like Deckard, retire them. And there is no danger that he will fall in love with one. To him, you and I live in an off-world colony. Our termination dates have been set, and we are illegal on earth. Even if one of us takes the Voight-Kampff empathy test (the device used to spot replicants), and passes it he would write us off as being, like Rachel, a replicant who faked the test. Our emotions would be lies. And if one of us went to him, the genetic engineer of postmodern theory, and asked him to repair what he has made, he would only laugh, and with Tyrell say, 'There is no way. You are doomed to live your programmed life as a simulated human being and your feelings are all false!'

Thus Baudrillard shares a vision and a fate with other male science fiction writers. The visual effects are terrific, but the narrative doesn't work. In becoming what he describes, he ceases to challenge the real. Baudrillard ends up, like the baby in the bubble, a clone of himself, inside a narcissistic text which only takes pleasure in itself. But worse yet, he has become the enemy. Unable, or unwilling to see both sides of the cyborg picture, he remains trapped by his own creation.

There is more going on here of course. Baudrillard never defines his key terms (for example the code). Shunning a grand theory, he writes a three-stage theory of history. His theory of the sign fails to accord with the fact that since the invention of the symbol, dissimulation and simulation have been part of the fabric of all cultures, from the Greeks to the present, and the totalitarian control of information is not unique to the postmodern world (see Couch, 1984: 342–3; Jansen, 1988: 23–59). His postmodern individual is a cultural dope (Garfinkel, 1967b) who can't see through the simulational, hyperreal informational structures presented by the mass media. (This argument runs counter to those investigations which show that individuals can discern fraud when they see it, fakery when they confront it, and ideology when it hits them in the face: Davis, 1989; de Certeau, 1984; Lefebvre, 1984; Hall, 1988).

His reading of the Information Age, which implies that reproduction has replaced production, ignores the fact that 'those computer chips are still produced by factory labor in third-world countries like Malaysia, the material basis of the first world's Information Age. And that labour is predominantly female' (Ryan, 1988: 567). His model, as Ryan (p. 576) observes, reproduces the capitalist displacement of work from the white center to the non-white periphery. At the same time it ignores Haraway's (1985) argument that the 'New Industrial Revolution' is producing a new worldwide working class of Third and First World women trapped in a new 'homework economy' tied to the microelectronic revolution. Baudrillard's discourse, scripted by a nostalgic science fiction longing for the modern age, inserts a white capitalist patriarchy into the new simulational age where information technologies dictate the contours of social life.

Lyotard's Postmodern Project: Long Live Modernism

The failures of Baudrillard's project are partially corrected by Lyotard's 1984a, b; 1989) reading of the postmodern condition. While departing from Baudrillard's fatalism, he still shares a commitment to writing a grand theory of history, a totalizing theory of the postmodern society, even as he contends that such grand metanarrative productions are dead. Politically Lyotard's formulations involve a radical democratic relativism, which is universalized into a vague principle for political action ('silence no voice'). When historicized (Berlin 1953, Budapest 1956, Czechoslovakia 1968, Poland 1980, May 1968; Lyotard, 1988a: 179), the political consequences of the principle too often 'turn proud struggles for independence [into] young, reactionary States' (1988a: 181). Seeking a just society, he ends with no politics at all, a pessimistic conclusion which in his words yields a situation where 'you can't make a political "program" with it, but you can bear witness to it' (1988a: 181).

Presented as an occasional text, *The Postmodern Condition* is a multilayered, controversial work (see Denzin 1986: 198–202; Bennington, 1988;

Honneth, 1985; Connor, 1989: 27–43; Kellner, 1988: 248–57; Fraser and Nicholson, 1988; Rorty, 1985a, 1985b; Toulmin, 1983; Ryan, 1988; Benhabib, 1990; Rose, 1988; Lash, 1988). In it Lyotard attempts to periodize the postmodern moment (since the end of the 1950s), while offering an interpretation of the cultural logics which characterize the computerized societies of the West (see also Lyotard, 1971, 1974, 1984b, 1985, 1988a, 1988b). His operative terms are the legitimation of knowledge through narrative (everyday) and scientific language games, the social bond, performativity, the commodification of science, and the pragmatics of paralogy. Now ten years old, his text reads like an advanced, but benign version of *Blade Runner*, a kind of zen Marxism applied to the contemporary moment (Ryan, 1988: 56).

The analysis unfolds in three parts.[9] Part one of his argument defines the postmodern condition as 'an incredulity toward metanarratives' (1984b: xxiv) wherein the grand interpretive theories of the last two centuries (Hegel, Marx, the Enlightenment ideals of freedom and education for humanity, positivism, phenomenology, existentialism, and psychoanalysis) are dead and no longer serve as anchoring posts for the reading of history, and the legitimation of knowledge claims about society as a totality. The modern period, in contrast, was defined by its appeal to these grand narratives about science, society, and truth (p. xxiii). Put another way, the modern–postmodern conflict reflects the transition and tensions between an aesthetics of interpretation (modern) and an aesthetics of sensation (postmodern).

For the last half-century the major representational models of society have been functionalism (Parsons, Luhmann), and 'critical' theory (he cites Horkheimer, and later Habermas). Of the first model he states, 'the idea that society forms an organic whole . . . was supplied by functionalism; it took yet another turn in the 1950s with Parsons's conception of society as a self-regulating system' (p. 11).[10]

Marxism, the second model of society, rests on the principles of class struggle and a dialectics which should prevent its followers from the allure of a self-regulating picture of society. But in fact 'critical' theory has been absorbed by the functional position. He concludes, with bitterness, that this model, which was 'born of the struggles accompanying capitalism's encroachment upon traditional civil societies' (pp. 12–13) has been a failure.[11]

Capitalism has triumphed, but a crisis in legitimation, centered in science, now confronts the postmodern world. The delegitimation of science has been hastened by the process of commodification, the natural consequence of the industrial revolution which discovered that without technology there could be no wealth, and without wealth, no technology (p. 45). Science has become a commodity. Here is how this happened.

A technical apparatus requires an investment; but since it optimizes the efficiency of the task to which it is applied, it also optimizes the surplus-value derived from this improved performance. All that is needed is for the surplus-value to be realized, in other words, for the product of the task performed to be sold. (p. 45)

The system can now be sealed in the following way, 'a portion of the sale is recycled into a research fund dedicated to further performance improvement. *It is at this precise moment that science becomes a force of production, in other words a moment in the circulation of capital*' (p. 45, italics added).

Several consequences follow from this transformation in science. It no longer becomes a pure enterprise in search of truth; it is transformed into a productive activity judged by its ability to generate money. The performative criteria take over and displace the traditional Enlightenment concept of truth for humanity. The desire for wealth replaces the desire for knowledge. The university becomes a site where capitalism directs and controls research, directly through grants from large corporations (IBM, Du Pont and so on), and indirectly through the state (for example Defense Department contracts funneled through private corporations).

The computerized, self-regulating society has won out.[12] All is not grim. Here we come to the 'driftworks', visionary part of Lyotard's solution, the third piece in his puzzle. Unwilling, for whatever reason, to accept the fact that science has sold out completely, he now argues that there is a side of postmodern science that is characterized by the search for undecidables, instabilities, and paradoxes (paralogies, p. 60) which overturn previously established understandings. Paralogy, the hallmark of postmodern science, introduces dissent and heterogeneity into the language games of science, and this move works against the principles of consensus, performance, and market-value which serve to transform knowledge into a saleable commodity. As if by magic, the very developments that destabilized modern science are now conceptualized as formations which provide an answer to the self-regulating, terrorizing computerized society.

Now the last part of Lyotard's picture. Rejecting functionalism and Marxism, for their failed attempts to formulate totalizing theories of postmodern society, he offers a pragmatic, conflictual theory of the social bond. Disposing of Baudrillard's suggestion that the social bond has dissolved and disintegrated into a 'mass of individual atoms, thrown into the absurdity of Brownian motion' and claiming that 'nothing of the kind is happening' (p. 15), he suggests that the self 'exists in a fabric of relations that is now more complex and mobile than ever before', and that these relations can be understood as a network of conflictual language games which structure the social bond, 'the human child is already positioned as the referent in the story recounted by those around him' (p. 15). A pragmatic theory of communication and social games 'which accepts agonistics as a founding principle' (p. 16) provides the framework for the interpretation of these games.

Failing to develop a symbolic theory of communication (Manning, 1988: 234), he confuses the transmission of knowledge (information), with the rituals of the communicational process which involve a complex interactive semiotic where the truth and credibility of a message are always judged 'on the spot' by a receiving agent. Institutions become arenas for the playing out of diverse language games (see Manning, 1988), in which local narratives, stories, fables, poetics, and scenarios can be performed (Lyotard, 1984b: 17). Such performances stretch the boundaries that institutions impose on knowledge, these 'limits are themselves the stakes and provisional results of language strategies, within the institution and without' (p. 17).

Establishing agonistics as the final link in his argument, he now makes the logical connection to dissent and paralogy in postmodern science. Communicational theories resting on consensus, like their counterpart in science where consensus is the criterion of validation, are now inadequate. This permits his final confrontation with Habermas and Luhmann. Habermas's search for universal criteria of truth and consensus works outward from the outmoded grand narrative of emancipation (Lyotard, 1984b: 60) for a universal, collective subject called humankind. Postmodern life, he wants to argue, has abandoned the belief in traditional narratives of legitimation; the ideologies of the system, with pretensions of a totality, are attempts to hide this cynicism. Accordingly it no longer becomes possible to follow Habermas in 'seeking out treatment of the problem of legitimation in the direction of a search for universal consensus' (p. 65). Speakers can never come to complete agreement on which rules are universally valid for language games, which by their very conflictual nature are heteromorphous and heterogeneous (p. 65). There is no universal subject. Attempts to conceptualize societies as totalities organized in terms of either emancipation or self-regulating, cybernetic principles must be regarded as projects which only produce terror.

Luhmann is treated even more harshly. His self-contained, self-reflexive system requires 'clear minds and cold wills' (p. 63), and produces a morality in which the

> needs of the most underprivileged should not be used as a system regulator as a matter of principle: since the means of satisfying them is already known, their actual satisfaction will not improve the system's performance, but only increase its expenditures . . . In this sense the system seems to be a vanguard machine dragging humanity after it; dehumanizing it in order to rehumanize it . . . such is the arrogance of the decision makers – and their blindness. (p. 63)[13]

Lyotard's Failures

So ends the story. Science becomes a double-edged sword; in its cybernetic, functional versions it threatens to destroy postmodern society. In its antimodel, paralogical version it becomes society's saviour; both metaphor for the agonistic, conflictual theory of language games and a tool for the opening up of the gates to knowledge that are stored inside the Big Computer. Lyotard wants the best of two worlds, and he has created both of them. Like a utopian he embodies paradox. The grand narratives of the past are not dead, nor are they exhausted. From the university to the state, they are everywhere present and firmly in place. Marxism, functionalism, Big Science, positivism, cybernetics, artificial intelligence systems, robots, cyborgs, Oedipal myths, conflicts and consensus, pragmatic paradoxes, and catastrophe theories exist alongside one another in this world he has labeled postmodern. He has written a version of the postmodern that conforms to his own nostalgic longing for an era where language in fact captures reality. He wants to be a modern postmodernist. He wants to grit his teeth and put 'forward the unpresentable in presentation itself' (Lyotard, 1984b: 81), without nostalgia, or a sense of taste grounded in consensus. His postmodern modernist takes pleasure in the pain of the unpresentable; his business is not to supply 'reality but to invent allusions to the conceivable which cannot be presented' (p. 81). Death to nostalgia. Let go of the grand narratives about totalities, 'we have paid a high enough price for the nostalgia of the whole' (p. 82).

Lyotard refuses to endorse a set of universal principles which create spaces for the voiceless. Nor does he articulate a plan of justice that goes beyond the call that no voice should be silenced, or excluded from participation in any given language game (1984b: 63–4). The 'line between truth and deception, consensus and coercion disappears in Lyotard's agonistics' (Benhabib, 1990: 116); that is the social bond which contains speaker and receiver seldom, if ever, positions the two subjects as equals. Furthermore, while Lyotard wants to bring an end to all grand narratives, including psychoanalysis, as legitimizing principles of the social, 'the loss of the psychoanalytic dimension leads . . . to the foreclosure of any sexual politics from the account . . . he cannot dispense with the naming of the infant – it is always a sexually differentiated naming – as the most fundamental narrative of all' (Rose, 1988: 244). Lyotard throws the gendered baby out with the bathwater. Only by separating language games from enunciation, 'the naming of the infant from the sexual trajectory of the child [can he] avoid any consideration of what might be the implications of paralogy, heterogeneity and catastrophe for the postmodern ordering and disordering of the sexual realm' (Rose, 1988: 244). A similar argument could be made for the inability of Lyotard's model to provide the conditions for the critique of patriarchy and racism in contemporary society (see Fraser and Nicholson, 1988: 380–1). His agonistic theory fails to serve as a 'basis for a post-Marxian radical democratic politics' (Benhabib, 1990: 122).

Lyotard promotes a kind of neo-liberal pluralism (let each interest group and social movement have its say), with overtones of Rorty's (1985a) 'contextual pragmatism' and liberal irony (1989). But he abandons the metanarratives of emancipation, letting 'the local narratives which hold our culture together do their stuff' (Rorty, 1985a: 164). There is a great risk in these formulations. Not conservative on the surface, in the wrong hands they can be. They falter on a single premise, the very term he uses to define the postmodern moment, 'an incredulity toward metanarratives.' Nowhere, as argued above, is there any evidence that the metanarratives of freedom and emancipation have died. Post-Marxism is still alive (Laclau and Mouffe, 1985; Hall, 1988). Psychoanalysis as a metanarrative has not disappeared (Rose, 1988). Nor is there any evidence that postmodern science works the way Lyotard says it does (see Ashmore, 1989; Rorty, 1985a: 163; but see Toulmin, 1983). By asserting the death of the grand narratives (see Kellner, 1988: 253 on the diverse types of master narratives Lyotard glosses), Lyotard can then write a theory which ignores the very structures of oppression other meta-narratives, including feminism, make problematic. In his desire to erase Marxism from the postmodern moment Lyotard is left with a 'polytheism of desire' (Benhabib, 1990: 120) which wages its particular war against its version of a radical, post-Marxist democratic politics of freedom.

Appropriately fearful of cybernetic, functional theories of the totality, scornful of those who lament 'the "loss of meaning" in postmodernity' 1984b: 26), Lyotard mistakenly contends that this condition 'in post-modernity boils down to mourning the fact that knowledge is no longer principally narrative' (p. 26). The loss of meaning comes not from the fact that knowledge is no longer principally narrative. All knowledge is narrative. Today, more than ever in the history of western civilization, multiple, local narratives, framed within larger interpretive patriarchal frameworks, daily circulate through the currents of popular culture, from film to soap operas, comic books, popular music, and romance novels. No, the loss of meaning and the mourning come from the very conditions that Jameson and Baudrillard have identified. The cultural logics of late capitalism keep the unattainable (the real, the past, romantic love, true happiness) alive, attempting over and over again to reconcile the image with its referent, the concept with the sensible, the transparent with the communicable experience. 'The mutterings of the desire . . . for the realization of the fantasy to seize reality' (1984b: 82) will not go away. Wars against Marxism and computerized societies won't stifle these mutterings.

To conclude with a paradox: Lyotard rejects metanarratives, yet his own metanarrative account of the collapse of metanarratives is a metanar-rative (Bennington, 1988: 114–17; Connor, 1989: 36). In fact, as Connor (1989: 36) observes, Lyotard's project is doubly totalizing. It depends on a vision of the total collapse of metanarratives 'everywhere and for always,' and it presumes the 'absolute dominion of metanarrative before the arrival of the postmodern condition' (Connor, 1989: 36). Equally crucial, this anti-metanarrative theory cannot theorize, since it has no recourse to universal norms, 'the equal right to coexistence of all everyday cultures' (Honneth, 1985: 155). Indeed Lyotard's own critique of capitalism notes that 'cultural differences are in fact encouraged even more, by virtue of the whole range of tourist and other culture industries'

(1986: 121–2, translated by and quoted in Connor, 1989: 40). Capitalism devours the differences he values; difference is not resistance, it is a 'constitutive condition of the global economic situation' (Connor, 1989: 41).

Lyotard's micropolitics of subversion (paralogy), transforms 'the field of postmodern society into an aesthetic field' (Connor, 1989: 42). This totalizes the postmodern condition under a narrative version of the sublime. It elevates the intellectual to the central, but ineffectual, position of being interlocutor to a plurality of cultural differences. At best this avant-garde anti-hero carries out 'intellectual guerrilla war on the inside of the system, inducing esoterically destabilizing moves in the knowledge-games of authority' (Connor, 1989: 42). This is a postmodern version of Don Quixote. But it is neither wholly benign, nor generous. Such debates about postmodernity repressively reproduce the very conditions of the postmodern that theory must work to expose and overturn. Still, there is an appeal, but with a cost. Lyotard's is an *existential pragmatism* which by making no appeal to a grand narrative, only personal conscience and local narratives, always leaves open the potential of the very reign of terror he (and Sartre, Merleau-Ponty, and Rorty) so vehemently opposes.

Jameson and the Cultural Logic of Late Capitalism

In two articles (1983, 1984b) and one book (1991: 1–55), which have attained near canonical status, and related essays (1984c, 1987, 1988a, 1988b), Jameson has maintained his position as *the* American Marxist theorist of the postmodern condition (Kellner, 1989a: 2–3).[14] His interpretation of the postmodern borrows heavily from Mandel's (1975) three-stage theory of capitalism (market, monopoly, multinational),[15] Althusser's treatment of ideology, and Lacan's discussion of schizophrenia as a language disorder experienced as a temporal disruption in which signifiers do not connect to a material world. Unlike Baudrillard and Lyotard, he is committed to the position (Jameson, 1981: 19) that 'only Marxism offers a philosophically coherent and ideologically compelling resolution . . . to the mystery of the cultural past.' He assumes that 'anyone who believes that the profit motive and the logic of capital accumulation are not the fundamental laws of this world . . . [lives] in an alternative universe' (1988b: 354).

His theory neither articulates the cultural logic of late capitalism, nor fully explains how the postmodern emerged out of the modern. While borrowing his metaphors and examples from the aesthetic and artistic fields (architecture, music, film, painting), recognizing that at one level postmodernism represents a stylistic, aesthetic break from modernism (1984b: 56), Jameson is careful to separate himself from a purely aesthetic, or narrative analysis of the postmodern (such as that of Lyotard). The proper use of the term is as a periodizing concept 'whose function is to correlate the emergence of new formal features in culture

with the emergence of a new type of social life and a new economic order
– what is euphemistically called modernization, postindustrial, or
consumer society, the society of the media, or the spectacle, or multinational capitalism' (1983: 113; also see 1984b: 57). Each of these descrip-
tions of society refers to a specific moment in capitalism. For Jameson,
like Lyotard and Mills, this new moment

> can be dated from the postwar boom in the United States in the 1940s and early
> '50s . . . . The 1960s are . . . the key transitional period, a period in which the
> new international order (neocolonialism, the Green Revolution, computerized
> and electronic information) is at one and the same time set in place and is swept
> and shaken by its own internal contradictions and by external resistance. (1983:
> 113)

When asked to articulate just what happened in capitalism's third stage
he resorts (1984a: xiv–xv) to an extended quotation from Mandel (1975:
190–1): 'Late capitalism, far from representing "postindustrial society",
thus appears as the period in which all branches of the economy are fully
industrialized for the first time; to which one could further add the
increasing mechanization of the sphere of circulation . . . and the increasing mechanization of the superstructure.' He then notes that this explana-
tion is consistent with the work of the Frankfurt School, and concludes
by observing that Guy Debord said 'the image is the last stage of
commodity reification' (1984a: xv). He never provides 'a detailed
narrative of the transitions' (Kellner, 1988: 258–9), between each of
capitalism's three major stages.

A 'dominant cultural logic or hegemonic norm' (1984b: 57) character-
izes this period and can be measured and assessed. The postmodern
culture is American, and the 'internal and superstructural expression of a
whole new wave of American military domination throughout the world'
(1984b: 57). His is not a technological interpretation: 'I want to avoid the
implication that technology is in any way the "ultimately determining
instance" either of our present-day social life or our cultural production'
(1984b: 79).[16] The current crisis reflects a 'distorted figuration of something even deeper, namely the whole world system of present-day multinational capitalism.' (Does he now include other cultures besides
America's in this whole world system?)

The Marxist critique must be kept in place; capital, not technology
causes the problems. Once again (1984b: 77–8) he turns to Mandel (1975:
18). Late, multinational capitalism now becomes the purest form of
capitalism, 'This purer capitalism of our time thus eliminates the enclaves
of precapitalist organization it had heretofore tolerated and exploited in
a tributary way . . . the colonization of Nature . . . the Unconscious . . .
the destruction of precapitalist third world agriculture by the Green
Revolution, the rise of the media and the advertising industry' (1984b:
78). The postmodern machine, organized by the logic of the simulacrum,
reproduces, rather than produces. The aesthetic embodiment of this
process, especially in advertising, film, and television 'does more than

merely replicate the logic of late capitalism; it reinforces and intensifies it' (1984b: 85).

The argument becomes even murkier. 'Everything . . . that we have been calling postmodernism is inseparable from, and unthinkable without the hypothesis of some fundamental mutation of the sphere of culture in the world of late capitalism, which includes a momentus modification of its social function' (1984b: 86). Now culture is everywhere. He asks if postmodernism isn't defined by the destruction of culture's semi-autonomous sphere by the logic of late capitalism? (1984b: 87). The model thickens. Something new has happened:

> A prodigious expansion of culture throughout the social realm, to the point at which everything in our social life – from economic value and state power to practices and to the very structure of the psyche itself – can be said to have become 'cultural' in some original and as yet untheorized state. (1984b: 87)

If this all sounds circular, it is. That which causes the postmodern (late capitalism), has become the postmodern (its culture). There is no analytic division between the two phenomena (see Connor, 1989: 47). Refusing to explain the logic of late capitalism (other than Mandel's three stages of the machine and capital), he now offers a reading of the culture logic of post-modern culture. Mindful that not all 'cultural production today is "post-modern"' (1984b: 57), he insists in seeing the postmodern as 'the force field in which very different kinds of cultural impulses – what Raymond Williams has usefully termed "residual" and "emergent" forms of cultural production – must make their way' (1984b: 57). These characteristics (forms of production, cultural impulses) of postmodern culture, of course cause and are caused by late capitalism. Here's what they are: pastiche, that is imitation without a satiric impulse (not parody, but see Eagleton, 1985: 61–2) in the production of artistic works; schizophrenia or the death of the centered subject as the object of theoretical-artistic analysis; the reification of commodity production in the era of the simulacrum which produces a new kind of depthlessness in the representations of reality; a weakening of history only partially recovered through nostalgia narratives (especially E.L. Doctorow's novels, *Rag Time*, *Loon Lake*), and nostalgia films which recreate the lost past (the innocence of the 1950s – *American Graffiti*, *Star Wars*, *Body Heat*); a new form of emotional intensity (called the hysterical and technological sublime!); the new computer technology; a new world economic system; a commodified past; the mutation of lived space; and a non-political art, which can become politicized through a new aesthetic which attempts a cognitive mapping of the hyperspaces of the postmodern environment (1984b: 89).[17]

Jameson's Postmodern Culture Machine

Thus concludes Jameson's aesthetic reading of postmodernism. What he calls the cultural logic of late capitalism are cultural forms which embody all of those things called postmodern. These forms are not the logic of late capitalism; they are its symptoms. Nor do these forms constitute a cultural logic. Sometimes called cultural impulses, or forms of cultural production, they are 'objective' indicators of what he wants to call the dominant social, economic, and aesthetic motifs of postmodern culture. Deeply rooted in capitalism's most advanced forms of development, these forms express the 'inner truth' of this newly emergent social and economic order. How? Jameson appears trapped within a framework which, while recognizing that it is impossible to get any distance from 'the new space of postmodernism' (1984b: 87), remains committed to an objectivity which allowed Marx to theorize capitalism's development in the nineteenth century (1984b: 86). He never succeeds in expressing a truth that goes beyond Baudrillard's simulacrum, Debord's insight that 'the image is the last stage of commodity reification,' Lacan's arguments about the linguistically decentered schizophrenic self, Althusser's distinctions between science and ideology (experience and knowledge), and Mandel's 'great book' (1984b: 91) about capitalism's three stages.

More importantly, his transformation of the signifiers of the postmodern condition into the cultural logic of late capitalism fails to reveal the inner truth of this new economic order. Signifiers as symptoms are not causes, nor do they constitute a cultural logic. Nowhere does Jameson perform a *cultural* analysis of the postmodern scene. There are no cultural studies in Jameson's cultural logic of late capitalism, only a repetition of what others have said about this historical period. There is no *analysis* of culture, in any of its forms, nor any systematic treatment of how the objectified, externalized features of the feminized-masculine postmodern culture (Simmel, 1984) works its way into the structures of feeling and experience (Williams, 1977: 128–35) of ordinary, interacting individuals (Carey, 1989).

The Empty Image and Lived Experience

Understanding, with Debord and Baudrillard, that the image has been transformed by the simulacrum into the last form of commodity reification, Jameson, like those he borrows from, fails to grasp what the image represents. Jameson's image is empty; like Lacan's endless chain of signifiers, it ends up with no referent in the world of experience. Rephrasing Debord, *Lived experience is the last stage of commodity reification.* Put another way, *lived experience, in terms of its hyperreal representations, has become the final commodity in the circulation of capital.* Lived experience did not die with modernism; nor has it fled the postmodern scene. Baudrillard understands this. Lived experience is everywhere present as the *sine qua non* of the postmodern signifier. From Michael Jordon tennis show commercials (with Spike Lee), to the evening news, where 'real' people suffering 'real' crises zoom into our living-rooms through the window of the TV, lived experience is all around us. It is the last commodity to be reified in late capitalism. Postmodernism's claim to authenticity lies in this ability to capture, in vivid color, life and its meanings. In no other time in world history has the technology for reproducing the real been so effective. The subject is not dead. He or she is still alienated, and while fragmented across a variety of viewing scenes, remains a voice and a presence which the postmodern media requires for its daily productions. It is not possible to allow Jameson's poststructuralist claim that the 'autonomous bourgeois monad, or ego or individual . . . has today [dissolved] in the world of organizational bureaucracy' (1984b: 63). This subject is alive, but not doing particularly well.

To turn Jameson back on himself, 'there is a reality *that one cannot not know*. The ragged edges of the Real, of Necessity, not being able to eat, not having shelter, not having health care, all this is something that one cannot not know. The black condition acknowledges that' (West, 1988a: 277). This is the reality of lived experience which does not get commodified into the images that the postmodern news machine regularly produces. But it is a reality that stands there waiting to be represented and given meaning, and its reality stands outside the 'teflon existence' (West, 1988a: 277) of many upper-class American poststructural, Marxist intellectuals. The postmodern culture has placed a premium on only certain kinds of lived experiences, those which authenticate a particular aesthetic picture of the world out there.

Writing lived experience out of the picture, Jameson's cultural analysis fails to show how the objectification of cultural values turns these authentic values of the postmodern period ('real' lived experience) into instrumentalities with utilitarian value. As this objective culture expands, its 'cultural artifacts become increasingly inaccessible to the subjective culture of the individual' (Oakes, 1984: 19). A new pseudo-subjective consumer culture arises in which 'the personality of any given consumer is qualitatively indistinguishable from that of any other' (Oakes, 1984: 21). This process of postmodernization perpetuates the objectification of a masculine set of cultural ideals which reifies the white male point of view.[18] Individuals who stand outside this preferred reality are doomed to experience alienation, resentment, detachment, strangeness, depersonalization, commodified sexuality, blocked desire and continual estrangement from the 'objective' worlds of postmodern cultural values which cease to embody their subjective life situations. And many of these persons 'live a life of living death, of slower death . . . of walking nihilism . . . a nihilism that is lived' (West, 1988a: 286). Where are these people and their lived experiences in Jameson?

Jameson needs a model which joins objective and subjective culture and which is attentive to race and gender as structuring forces which mediate between these two forms of the cultural experience. Granted, the instrumentalization of culture describes a general process of commodity fetishism, involving a cultural logic which is grounded in the late phases of capitalism. How do the objective conditions of postmodern culture-out-there work their way into the subjective culture of individuals and their social relations of consumption (Oakes, 1984: 20)? The cultural logic of late capitalism involves a logic of social relations mediated by larger cultural codes concerning gender and the arrangements between males and females in the dominant, residual, and emergent cultures of the hyperspaces of postmodernism. The logic of these relations is missing from Jameson's theory.

Back to Jameson and the Nostalgia Film

Jameson's invocation (1984b: 57) of Raymond Williams's (1977: 122–3) concepts of residual and emergent culture suggests that a Williams-like analysis is forthcoming, but it never appears. Treating the postmodern cultural logic as the dominant, not emergent, cultural logic of the times, as a logic that erases all boundaries between past and present, he fails to note how the residual cultural meanings of the 1950s, which are incorporated into nostalgia films, become emergent critiques of the present. That is these films (for example *Body Heat*, *Blue Velvet*, *American Graffiti*), and others more radical, which I called self-reflective in Chapter One, and which Lash (1988: 326–8) terms mainstream, and transgressive postmodern cinemas of the spectacle, do more than colonize the present in a way that symbolizes an inability to 'focus on our own present' (Jameson, 1983: 117). Rather, as Lash (1988: 328–9) observes, such non-discursive, figural texts problematize and make unstable the very ability to represent, hence capture the 'real.' They are not a symptom of 'a society that has become incapable of dealing with time and history' (Jameson, 1983: 117). They reappropriate the residual past through pop images which simultaneously mock the past and the present. Films like *Blue Velvet* state that the present only makes sense in terms of the past, and it will remain forever out of touch if it is not compared to the way things used to be.

Such moves, which reflect the pervasive tendency of human beings to reinvent the past, mythical and otherwise, to suit present purposes, are interpreted by Jameson as peculiar features of the postmodern moment. They are not. They implement a pragmatic theory of the past (Maines *et al.*, 1983; Mead, 1929; Katovich, 1990), in which an 'objective-structural,' mythical past is always symbolically reconstructed in the present, through the workings of interaction and memory. Yet the present structures what is remembered, represented, and made real. This pragmatic view of temporality is well suited to the postmodern cinematic apparatus, for now the past and the present can be symbolically reconstructed and represented in ways which simultaneously efface and valorize the real and its representations. As Lash (1988: 324) notes, 'cinematic signification . . . in the age of high technology and the 30 million dollar film, comes closer than other forms of signification to resemblance of reality.'

Thus it is necessary to reject Jameson's argument (1983: 118) that these films condemn us 'to seek the historical past through our own pop images and stereotypes about that past, which itself remains forever out of reach.' Believing that the 'real' past, where repressions and injustices have occurred, can be uncovered, Jameson thus rejects all literary (Doctorow) and cinematic (Lucas) efforts which attempt to recover the past as mere 'stereotypes about that past' (1983: 118). Will the real past, wherever it is, please stand up and be represented? By reifying his indicators, by holding to a paradoxical position that there is a reality outside the text lodged in real, objective history, and by insisting that everything be fitted to his grand Marxist narrative, Jameson contributes to the capitalist postmodern machine he wants to dismantle. At the same time, like the Frankfurt critics, he derogates popular culture and its representations. Does he cling to a high modernism which will somehow guide us through this mess called postmodernism?

His aesthetic reading of the cultural forms of postmodernism, which attempts to renarrativize the past in terms of a grand Marxist narrative, dates the crisis of modernism to the postmodernist understanding that the older models (Picasso, Proust, T.S. Eliot, D.H. Lawrence, Rilke, Hitchcock, Jean Renoir) of representation 'do not work any more (or are positively harmful), since nobody has that kind of unique private world and style to express any longer' (1983: 115). Says who? Even more drastically, he proposes that nothing unique can any longer be represented: 'they've already been invented; only a limited number of styles and worlds are possible; the most unique ones have been thought of already' (1983: 115). This means that postmodern art can only be about 'the necessary failure of art and the aesthetic, the failure of the new, the imprisonment in the past' (1983: 116). Of course this indictment applies to his theorizing of the postmodern, for he is imprisoned in a Marxist past, where all the unique thoughts have already been thought. His 'social cartography' of the postmodern hyperspace (1984b: 91) is a feeble attempt to map the prison that traps all of us.

His Marxist narrative, not unsurprisingly, excludes women and minorities, except in the following ways. In *The Political Unconscious* (1981: 86), as noted in Chapter One, he calls for the 'reaudition of the oppositional voices of black and ethnic cultures, women's or gay literature, "naive" or marginalized folk art and the like.' Equating these marginalized voices, women especially, with 'folk art' (Owens 1983: 62), he quickly offers a disclaimer: 'The affirmation of such non-hegemonic cultural voices remains ineffective' if they are not rewritten in terms of 'their proper place in the dialogical system of social classes.' No patriarchy here. The master Marxist will give women, blacks, and gays a voice! Five years later (1988b: 355) he will bow in the direction of women once more, but again within the Marxist narrative (and in response to a feminist revolt at the conference where these comments were generated):

> Historically, all forms of hierarchy have always been ultimately based on gender hierarchy and on the building block of the family unit which makes it clear that this is the true juncture between a feminist problematic and a Marxist one – not an antagonistic juncture, but the moment at which the feminist

project and the Marxist and socialist project meet and face the same dilemma: how to imagine Utopia.

In a subversive way he inserts women into the model, for the traditional family form has been patriarchal.

Baudrillard, Lyotard and Jameson: Postmodern Dilemmas

Our three theorists of the postmodern all define postmodernity in ways which make it impossible to untangle the social from the cultural and the economic. Each 'conjoins the cultural/aesthetic realm . . . with the socio-economic realm . . . by aestheticizing the latter, reading the social as a species of the cultural' (Connor, 1989: 44). Each becomes implicated in a descriptive process which struggles to separate theory from the reality it describes (Connor, 1989: 61). Narrative is alive and well in each theory. Each theorist works from or against a grand Marxist narrative of history. Baudrillard has his Code, Jameson his Marxism, and Lyotard his local narratives grounded in an existential pragmatism; a local politics of resistance which has many similarities to both Foucault and Derrida's projects. Each neglects gender and race, although Baudrillard, in his early work, comes the closest to connecting the structures of capitalism with these categories of oppression. He states (1975: 138), 'In order to function capitalism needs to dominate nature, to domesticate sexuality . . . to relegate ethnic groups, women, children and youth to genocide, ethnocide and racial discrimination.' Each understands that 'we are *within* the culture of postmodernism ·to the point where its facile repudiation is as impossible as any equally facile celebration of it is complacent and corrupt' (Jameson, 1988a: 111).

The Young Conservatives?
What to make of this condition is what separates these theorists from one another. They are nostalgic romantics, longing for some version of Utopia. Lyotard presents an aesthetic, pragmatic, narrative theory of language games which rests on a simplistic theory of communication and interaction in society. Jameson offers an aesthetic reading of modern and postmodern art, where theory and culture dissolve into one another. Baudrillard produces a nihilistic interpretation of the hyperreal world where theory simulates the simulated. Each theorist has a politics: Jameson's socialist, didactic, political cartography, Lyotard's praise of difference, and Baudrillard's nihilistic desire to push the system to its absurd limits.

Habermas (1983: 14) calls these theorists the young neo-conservatives. While he only applies this label directly to Lyotard, it is clear he would attach it to Baudrillard as well, but perhaps not to Jameson (and see Jameson's 1984a: xvi–xviii apparent refusal to take a stand on the Habermas–Lyotard controversy). It is not clear why the label of neoconservative can necessarily be applied to those who give up the universalistic criterion of rationality. An existential pragmatics which refuses to endorse the 'positive' power of rationality and consensus and which works to undermine and expose the micropolitics of control that pervade everyday life is not conservative (see Rorty, 1985a: 174–5).[19]

The conservatives are the mainstream sociological theorists of the micro and macro order, who interpret the crises of the post-industrial societies (Habermas, 1985: 79–84), in terms of a perceived loss of authority in the family, the polity, and the state. Such theorists then criticize postmodern culture for its failure to hold society together and call for a return to a form of religion or tradition which will reintegrate the social and the cultural (for example Bell, Berger, Shills, Alexander; see O'Neill, 1988). Habermas's criticisms are better directed to these theorists then to Lyotard and Baudrillard.

Back to the Features of Postmodern Social Theory
Return to the characteristics of postmodern social theory outlined in Chapter Two. The three theorists present, in unique ways, all but two (absence of a grand narrative, and a feminist agenda) of the eleven points that I said should characterize postmodern theory. Each turns away from positivism, deals with the crises of representation in the postmodern period which they attempt to periodize, offers critiques of scientific knowledge, coupled with a radical conception of language, a return to the problem of commodification, and the development of a politics of resistance.

Each offers a grand narrative, or overarching theory, connected in every instance to the three phases of capitalism, the sign and movements in art and literature (realism, modernism, postmodernism). For these theorists the attempt to periodize the postmodern requires a larger narrative which separates this period from those that have come before. Always in the background lurks capitalism, the economy, and a theory of social structure and social relationships which presumes some connection between experience, consciousness, and the material world (Hall, 1986a: 57).

But it is surely possible to develop an interpretation of the postmodern and the postmodern self without recourse to a grand narrative. Each historical moment can be taken on its own terms, and situated within its particular cultural, sexual, racial, social, moral, economic, and political order of things (see Foucault, 1970, 1977, 1980a, 1980b, 1982, 1986). Just as we lack concrete, detailed cultural readings of life in America up to and through the 1950s (Mills, 1959), so too do we lack similar readings for the post-1950, contemporary period. We have broad brush-stroke pictures (Baudrillard, 1988b), but little else.

In the rush to periodize the postmodern within an evolutionary theory of capitalism, postmodern theorists have glossed life in the historical epoch it supposedly surpasses. More importantly, unexplained in each theory is the way in which human beings, in and through interaction and communication with one another, make sense of and connect themselves to the dominant, residual, and emergent features of postmodern life (see Carey, 1989: 67; Blumer, 1969: 76; Hall, 1988). A grand narrative is not needed to explain the postmodern, especially one which displaces the performances of gender, race, and ethnicity, in the name of social class.

Missing in the above formulations is a critical, feminist cultural studies approach, as outlined in Chapter One. Such a perspective would inter-rogate the ethnically gendered subject positions, the structures of temporality, selfhood, character, violence, desire, sexuality, self-destruction, racism, addiction, and commodity consumption that now circulate in the multiple cultures that make up the fractured spaces of postmodernism. It would examine the media and mediated representations of childhood, youth, love, marriage, family, and individuality that flow in and through the lives of the men, women, and children who live in this historical time (see Denzin, 1990a). It would analyze how the Oedipal myth, in its various hetero and homoerotic forms functions to reproduce the idea that human subjectivity is sexually realized in the bonded, love relationship (Fiedler, 1966; Clough, 1988a; Foucault, 1980b, 1986). If a major defining characteristic of postmodernism is the loss of 'aura' that is attached to lived experience, then the cultural logics which structure how such experiences are represented (CNN, TV, MTV, film) require serious attention. It is also necessary to examine how these representations (the effacement of the real) contribute to a nihilistic, flattening of affect which too often turns into self-destruction (West, 1988a).

Notes

1. He has also been called the theorist of the death of modernity. Entire journals and books have been devoted to his work (e.g. *Semiotext(s)*, *Telos*, *October*, *Artforum*, *The Canadian Journal of Political and Social Theory*, *Thesis Eleven*, *Z/G*, *On the Beach*, *Theory, Culture & Society*; Kellner, 1989b).
2. For example, Robert Hughes, art critic for *Time*, reviewing Baudrillard's book *America* in the *New York Review of Books* ('A pop guru's America', 'The patron saint of neo-pop', Hughes, 1989: 32), calls him the 'patron saint of those who wish to turn affectlessness into a commodity.' Calling Baudrillard's prose an impenetrable prophylactic, a compound of snobbery, overgeneralization, oracular pronouncements, with a pervasive tone of apocalyp-tic hype, and extravagant rhetoric, Hughes compares this French theorist to Walt Disney, *le grand simulateur* (pp. 29–30). See also Vidich (1991: 143–4) who suggests that Baudrillard's 'lament for Kennedy and his hatred of Reagan and Yuppies seems to me to express his broader lament for and hatred of a world that took an unexpected turn away from the youthful expectations and optimism of young and middle-aged middle class radicals of the sixties'. See also Ryan (1988: 565–8) and Morris (1987: 28) who calls him the 'professional *enfant terrible* of French sociology who is now playing hard at being the Disappearing theorist.' Hall (1986a: 45) suggests that 'Lyotard, and Baudrillard in his celebratory mode, have gone right through the sound barrier. They are involved, not simply in identifying new trends . . . new cultural configurations, but in learning to love them.'
3. See the earlier discussion of this point in Chapter One (pp. 7–8).

4. Any attempt to subvert this system, to put the press in the hands of the people, or to promote the 'mass ownership of walkie-talkies, or everyone making their own cinema: a kind of personalized amateurism, the equivalent of Sunday tinkering on the periphery of the system' (Baudrillard, 1981: 182) is doomed to failure because the code still prevails.

5. Hence the preoccupation with the live event, the on-site news broadcast, the immediate interpretation of an event after it has occurred, the replaying of newsworthy events, the simultaneous broadcasting of an event and its reproduction on a screen that audience members can watch, in case they missed what they just witnessed.

6. See the currently popular TV shows *Unsolved Mysteries, America's Funniest Home Videos*, and *Night Court* all of which present real people in real life situations.

7. His science fiction world also includes the following: genetic and mental software (Baudrillard, 1979: 233); 'prostheses [which] infiltrate the anonymous and micro-molecular heart of the body' (1979: 233); the displacement of sexuality into pornography and instant, obscene sex; the seduction of signs; violence turned to terror; fashion transformed into simulations which colonize sexuality; history reduced to 'instantaneous memory without a past' (1988b: 103–4); the electronic miniaturization of energy circuits; the transistorization of the environment; life in micro-satellite homes in electronic orbit; humans as computer operators at the helms of these moving spaceships called home and car (1983c: 127–8); and even sex turned into a short-lived obscene experience, periodically disrupted by a 'ridiculous type of feminist' (1983d: 45) who turns the tables and attempts the seduction which is rightfully the male's to perform.

8. But another level of critique operates in the film and this is its playful, yet tragic treatment of the android which is pure simulation, part human, part machine and cyborg, but genetically programed and made from organic materials. These android/cyborg-like replicants stand on the borderline between human, animal, and machine. They have transgressed boundaries, like Haraway's (1985) cyborgs; programed to kill, they want to live and love and be loved. They live in a post-gender world, are still tied to Oedipal complexes (Tyrell), but want to be free of these bonds. Without innocence, the replicants dream, unlike Haraway's cyborg, of the Garden of Eden. They are still the offspring of 'militarism and patriarchal capitalism' (Haraway, 1985: 68). Haraway's cyborg challenges this model.

9. The first and last parts rest on dubious grounds, the second (pp. 13–17), which articulates an interactionist, conflictual theory of the social bond, appears sound and has parallels with the statements of Blumer (1969) and Lyman and Vidich (1988), although he aligns this part of his theory with Goffman, Gouldner, Touraine, Bateson, Watzlawick and other pragmatic theorists of communication, including his version of Wittgenstein (pp. 16–17, 52, n. 63).

10. Cybernetics, he suggests, after World War II, supplied a missing link in Parsons's system, making the computer the model of a self-regulating system. This model, and the principle behind it, he contends, organizes the current welfare state, and in the work of contemporary German theorists (Luhmann) becomes technocratic, 'the true goal of the system, the reason it programs itself like a computer, is the organization of the global relationship between input and output – performativity' (p. 11).

11. In the socialist and liberal countries the struggles of labor have been 'transformed into regulators of the system' (Lyotard, 1984a: 3), and in communist countries, 'the totalizing model and its totalitarian effect', while making a comeback in the name of Marxism, have 'simply been deprived of the right to exist'. Everywhere Marxism has failed, 'the Critique of political economy . . . and its correlate, the critique of alienated society, are used in one way or another as aids in programming the system . . . we cannot conceal the fact that the critical model in the end lost its theoretical standing and was reduced to the status of "utopia" or "hope"'.

12. This means that society now needs professional and technological intelligentsia (computer scientists, linguists, mathematicians, logicians, statisticians, p. 48) who can program the machines, and a laboring class who can enter data into them. The focus of higher education becomes one of continuing education (retraining an adult labor force), and instruction in informatics and telematics. The goal is to create skills, not ideals (p. 48). This

. mercantilization of knowledge asks not if knowledge is true/false, or just/unjust, but whether it is saleable (p. 51).

13. Theorists like Luhmann identify themselves with the system conceived as a totality 'in quest of its most performative unity possible' (p. 63). 'Such behavior is terrorist and delusionary,' for no true scientist, Lyotard wants to believe, identifies with the system as a totality, or neglects the 'needs' of a research project 'on the pretext that they do not add to the performance of "science" as a whole . . . to the extent that science is differential, its pragmatics produces the antimodel of a stable system' (pp. 63-4).

14. According to Kellner (1989a: 2) Jameson's essay, 'Postmodernism or the cultural logic of late capitalism' (1984b) 'presents one of the most illuminating analyses of postmodern culture and is probably the most quoted, discussed, and debated article of the last decade' (for critical readings, see for example Connor, 1989: 43-50; Eagleton, 1985; O'Neill, 1988; and essays collected in Kellner, 1989a).

15. This includes three corresponding stages of the sign, which are also aesthetic periods (realism, modernism and postmodernism – the pure play of the simulacrum), and of space (Jameson 1988b: 348-9) and its experiencing (as a grid, as contradiction, as over-saturated, hyperspace).

16. Such a move would apparently align him with those post-industrial, anti-Marxist theorists (Bell, 1976) who interpret the contemporary moment and its crises in terms of the primacy of science and technological invention, and the exhaustion of modernism (and postmodernism).

17. Cognitive mapping becomes an essential aesthetic part of 'any socialist political project (Jameson, 1988b: 353), because it permits a totalizing conception for a 'total transformation of society' (1988c: 360) as an 'integral part of a socialist politics' (1988b: 356).

18. Simmel (1984) would call this the iron cage of postmodernity.

19. But see the critical reading of Rorty's politics in Denzin (forthcoming b: Ch. 9).

4

Learning from Mills[1]

The Modern Age is being succeeded by a post-modern period . . . . Will there come to prevail, or even to flourish, what may be called The Cheerful Robot? (Mills, 1959: 166, 171)

C. Wright Mills. His *Sociological Imagination* gave American sociology its first systematic treatment of the postmodern condition. Every generation of sociologists has its book, that text which captures the imagination of newcomers to the field. In the 1960s that book was C. Wright Mills's *Sociological Imagination* (1959). Long regarded as the penultimate statement by America's foremost critical sociological theorist, it represents a rejection of American positivist, functional social theory in favor of a critical sociology of the European, Frankfurt variety (see Gouldner, 1970: 12; Horowitz, 1983; Collins, 1981: 315; Coser, 1978: 300; Tilman, 1984).

Set Baudrillard, Lyotard, and Jameson aside for the moment. Consider another set of questions, those raised over thirty years ago by Mills (1959: 8–13). They follow from Mills's distinction between the personal troubles which occur in the immediate worlds of experience of interacting individuals and the public issues of social structure. Troubles have to do with the self, its emotionality, its life-projects, its relations with others. Troubles are personal matters which spill over into families and groups. They occur in the immediate milieux of the person. Public issues transcend personal troubles. They have to do 'with the organization of many such milieux into the institutions of an historical society' (Mills, 1959: 8). They involve the social, economic, moral, and cultural fabrics of a society and the ways in which these fabrics 'overlap and interpenetrate to form the larger structure of social and historical life' (Mills, 1959: 8). Issues are public matters, often involving a perceived crisis in current institutional arrangements, which threatens cherished values.

What are the key personal troubles and public issues of the postmodern moment? Consider the major news stories involving the heroes, villains, and victims of the last decade in American society:[2] AIDS, the homeless, alcoholism and drug addiction, unemployment, child sexual abuse, environmental destruction, terrorism, women in the labor force, the plight of African Americans. What values and meanings are threatened by these perceived 'social problems', which are major issues for the American media and key troubles in the private lives of individuals in this time?

Notice that these are not the problems identified by Baudrillard, Lyotard, and Jameson. There is no mention of the crisis of legitimation in scientific knowledge, no concern for the hyperreal and its distortion of the real, no preoccupation with the death of modernism, or the centered, middle-class subject. There is no focus on a past which has been lost, or a present which cannot be properly represented. No, the concerns of the American public, as represented in the media, are not those of the postmodern theorists. Their concerns turn, instead, to paraphrase Cornell West (1988a: 277) on the 'ragged edges of the realities of postmodernism which one cannot not know': death by AIDS and drug addiction, violent sexuality, abused children, women at work, no fathers at home, homelessness, racism, and the black underclass.

These are existential concerns, living and dying in the postmodern moment, making do, being free, bad faith, lies, deceptions, connecting dreams to realities, living lives that are more real than the hyperreal. These concerns do not involve indifference, or the waning of affect represented in a depthless superficiality. The emotions of modernism – anxiety, alienation, self-destruction, radical isolation, anomie, private revolt, madness, hysteria, and neurosis – which Jameson (1984b: 63) claims are dead, are still present. These emotions are reflected in the increased incidence of alcoholism and drug addiction, homeless isolation, African American alienation, and self-destruction. To these emotional forms of being are now added anger and fear; fear of the unknown and the inability to control it, anger at the disenfranchised by those on the Right; anger in the underclass towards those in power. Anger and fear, coupled with existential anxiety, unite the Right and the Left, the ethnic underclasses, all men, women, and children who feel threatened by a postmodern world that promises more than it can deliver. Powerlessness is all-pervasive. This world, out there and in here, is out of control. The media's ceaseless flow of images and commentary on everyday life attempts to make this world appear controllable, but it clearly isn't. Tensions and fears flood into an anxious, often drug-induced euphoria. This euphoria promises to blot out the fears, in return for a moment of peace. But in this hyperstrange world, where nearness is so real it overwhelms, the only safe place is inside one's head. Here, where reality no longer crowds in, fantasy reins, closure occurs, and a meaninglessness 'so well understood' is experienced as 'a walking nihilism' (West, 1988a: 286).

Ressentiment as the Postmodern Emotion

Ressentiment (Denzin, 1984: 224–8), the self-poisoning form of self-hatred which arises from the systematic repression of certain emotions, including envy, pride, anger, and the desire for revenge and self-conquest, is the predominant postmodernist form of emotionality. It molds all of the above emotional states into a pervasive view of the world. Although Scheler (1961) and Nietzsche located ressentiment at the heart of the early modernist experience, it clearly transcends modernism, and has become part of the contemporary scene. This emotion, which builds on revenge, hatred, malice, and joy at another's misfortune, reflects an underlying self-hatred and lack of self-worth. It is an emotional mood systematically produced by those social structures, including the social democracies, which espouse the equality of rights for all, but permit wide gaps between expectations and what is in fact received. These social structures 'engender ressentiment on the part of the young, the elderly, women, the handicapped, the sexually and morally stigmatized, and members of racial and ethnic minorities' (Denzin, 1984: 226). Ressentiment is greatest when self or group injury is experienced as destiny and beyond one's control. When powerlessness and hopelessness are great, ressentiment increases. In such moments the other is transformed into an object deserving of revenge and violence.

The cultural logics of late capitalism amplify and increase ressentiment for the above groups. The continual circulation of commodified fantasies stressing erotic beauty, wealth, masculinity, achievement, happiness, successful love relationships, and joyous, free selfhood make it clear that for many these states can never be attained. Existential anxiety, fear, and hatred feed on these conditions; violence towards self and other are thereby produced.

For over half of the African American population an overwhelming part of the postmodern condition consists of these conditions (West, 1988a: 277). Treating each postmodern subject as an universal singular (Sartre, 1981: ix–x), universalized by this historical moment, but unique in the reproduction of it as an individuality, postmodern theory must uncover how, in epiphanal moments, each person lives this time of history into existence. So far this theory, in its many forms, has failed to address this problem.

Mills's Postmodern Sociological Imagination

Now over thirty years old, *The Sociological Imagination* asked of sociologists trained in the 1960s a politically informed sociology, methodologically sensitive to human experience and based on the work of the classic social theorists (Marx, Mosca, Schumpeter, Veblen, Michel, Pareto, Weber, Durkheim, Freud). It challenged sociologists to develop a sociological imagination that would nurture a form of self-consciousness capable of comprehending biography, history, world politics, and particular societies as intertwined totalities. It would make sense of the traps and personal troubles of ordinary, little people. The relationship between personal troubles and public issues was central to Mills's position (1959: 8–13).[3] He did not examine how troubles are both created and transformed when they become public issues. Biographical, first-person accounts of life in the United States in the 1940s and 1950s are not present in Mills's texts. Instead, these consist of summaries of novels, popular films, newspaper stories, government statistics, and historical works on the American class structure. Mills did open up a postmodern theme, already noted by the Frankfurt School and subsequently elaborated by Baudrillard: the erasure of the divisions between public and private life.

Yet, like other 'high culturalists' (even Jameson today), he took a disparaging stance toward popular culture and its representations of contemporary life.

The Sociological Imagination is a work of Mills's imagination. In it he thinks and writes vaingloriously. He constructs images and pictures of society, men (seldom women), and history real only within his ten chapters.[4] The book summarizes his earlier works on the American class structure, *The White Collar* (1951) and *The Power Elite* (1956), studies executing his self-appointed task, after Balzac, to cover all the 'major classes in the type of society in the era he wished to make his own' (1959: 200).

Like all theory, it is a rhetorical work. It uses all of Hayden White's (1973) tropes of discourse and modes of writing metahistory (see also Marcus and Fischer, 1986: 14–16).[5] Mills speaks in multiple voices: in places as Weber; in others as Marx urging people to change, not just understand history, and in the Appendix as 'the intellectual workman [who] forms his own self as he works toward the perfection of his craft' (p. 196). These oxymorons clearly establish the point that although supposedly one of the workers, he is an intellectual worker, and hence not one of the workers after all.[6]

The interplay of three conversations and four texts structures the work. The former comprise Mills's interactions with himself, the influential theorist who looks over his shoulder, and the discourse between the reader and Mills's book (see Mills, 1956: 363).[7] The latter include Mills's biographical history with himself as a sociologist, as well as his interpretations of the texts of his sociological contemporaries, the texts of the classical social theorists he emulates, and the text of American society he hopes to understand.

Mills converts these texts and conversations into a system of discourse which invariably allows him (like Baudrillard, Lyotard, and Jameson) to have the final word on how his imagination will bring about the kind of sociology (and Marxism) he has constructed. In this double-play on imagination. Mills creatively imagines and constructs the very texts he criticizes from the vantage point of his sociological imagination. He thus turns the sociological imagination into a force that can change history. But this force is the product of his imagination and his imagined readings of the classical theorists whom he respects. It is nowhere present in current sociological work. It is present only in his work. He is the sociological imagination. This textual transformation of self allows Mills, as it does the postmodern theorists, to locate himself outside history and outside sociology and to become the objective observer of world history and America's place in that history (see Merleau-Ponty, 1964: 109 on the impossibility of this). He is the hero of his own text and the reincarnation of those dead theorists he so admires.

Thus established as America's self-proclaimed, preeminent 'classical theorist' of the contemporary age, he is released from empiricism. (He states, [p. 205] 'I do not like to do empirical work if I can possibly avoid it.') He has displaced Parsons and Lazarsfeld. With this identity he can read the social structure through the lens of his heroes, as they, in their turn, were read through his lens, or sociological imagination. Accordingly, what he imagines to be (like Baudrillard), is, for his imagination is real, verified by his experiences. He will surpass even Balzac. Having already 'covered' the class structure, he will write *the* book on how he did it. Readers need only come and reason with him to participate in a dialogue about 'the higher circles of America' and sociology (1956: 364).

How does Mills do this? He creates a spurious dialogue with the reader. In fact what we have is a monological tirade on the state of mid-century American life; a harangue cloaked in the languages and grand 'metanarratives' of the classic age: reason, freedom, democracy, enlightenment, and positive knowledge about men and their troubles.

Mills's Modernist Text
Mills's dialogue is modernist (see Denzin, 1986: 194–5). It is carefully molded, just as the texts of Baudrillard, Lyotard, and Jameson are, by the language of classical social theory: alienation, anomie, totalitarian, capitalist and feudal societies, class, status, power, key variables, quantifiable indices (see his discussion of variables and quantifiable indices, 1959: 207–9). The words are carefully chosen. Mills has the classical social theorists in his head. Their voices direct him to write a totalizing theory of early postmodern American society that would wed the micro and macro levels of experience and yield yet another version of the *gemeinschaft–gesellschaft* myth. He pursues a verifiable science of society that positions conflict and crisis at the center of the emerging late postcapitalist social structures. Despite his nods toward relativism; biographies and personal troubles; power, knowledge, and the legitimation crisis surrounding modern science, Mills is trapped inside the rhetoric of the theories he so values. He fails to follow his own sociological imagination.

How does he fail? I, flesh-and-blood reader, sit holding Mills's book; he, the flesh-and-blood writer, peers at me from the dust jacket. Here he is: in black shirt, thumb hooked over his belt, staring off into the distance, presumably contemplating the sociological imagination. His book intrudes into my extra-narrative life: I want to believe Mills, be like him, have his sociological imagination. He is describing the early postmodern moment, that even I in the 1990s can identify with. What does this moment look like? He must conflate the moment with its men and women.

The Postmodern Condition for Mills
Here is how this happens. A single sentence, the first in his book, exemplifies this process: 'Nowadays men often feel that their private lives are a series of traps' (1959: 3). I come to Mills's book as a believing reader. By the end of the first sentence I am on his side. Who wouldn't

be? Little men (and women, elsewhere called 'darling little slaves' and 'suburban queens': 1963: 344) are Mills's foil.

Mills purportedly speaks to their existential traps; to the lack of meaning in their everyday lives (1959: 197); their failed marriages; their unemployment (1959: 8–10); the woman's nun-like, low-paying job in white-collar offices (1951: 204); their robot-like work; their drug and alcohol abuse; the fraudulent inspirational literature and popular films that they watch (1951: 282); and the horrible, ugly cities where they live. He predicted that life in the postmodern period would be characterized by drift, increased alienation, indifference, oppressive bureaucratic controls, cheerful, cultural robots made to be 'happy in this condition' (1959: 171) by a combination of 'chemical and psychiatric means . . . by steady coercion . . . controlled environments . . . random pressures and unplanned sequences of circumstances' (1959: 171). This age threatens freedom and reason, and these threats produce apathy (1959: 173).

But nowhere in the pages of his work(s) do these little people and their personal troubles speak. Mills speaks for them; or he quotes others who have written about them, usually novelists, like Sinclair Lewis, Booth Tarkington, Christopher Morley, or James Cain. Hence his 'nowadays' sentence reflects either what he imagines men (and women) nowadays feel about their lives, or what others have written about men nowadays. It cannot be that he writes of his own sense of being trapped, and without meaning, for Mills the intellectual craftsman finds meaning in his theorizing about these lives his texts neither touch nor allow to speak. His use of the 'nowadays' line is pure rhetoric designed to immediately align the reader with his populist, emancipatory text.

The *Imagination* is a hypocritical text. It employs dubious ethics. It is filled with both upward and downward hypocrisy (on these terms see Booth, 1988: 253–6). Mills pretends that he and I (as reader), because of the current state of sociology (and society), are worse off than we really are. This is downward hypocrisy. He wants me to believe my life really is a series of traps; he even suggests that his has been (1959: 201). At the same time, he wants to move me by altruistic moral indignation about the way sociologists like Parsons and Lazarsfeld do sociology. This is upward hypocrisy. Mills plays games with me, moving me first one way, then another, without care for my welfare. He will sacrifice me for his larger aims.

This is tragic, for it diminishes my former or potential relationship to Mills's text: his project can no longer ennoble me. I no longer trust him. His manipulation of me, flesh-and-blood reader, to his own ends erases my trust. His book is unethical, totalitarian, manipulating me and all 'nowadays' persons to his own ends. I can no longer dwell, befriended in his text, sharing his moral vision of how the sociological imagination works. Our friendship is neither full nor reciprocal (see Booth, 1988: 223). Having written us out of Parsons and led us back to Dewey, pragmatism, and symbolic interactionism, Mills emerges, from this reading, a tarnished hero.

Baudrillard, Lyotard and Jameson
Apply the above framework to the postmodern texts examined in the last chapter. Each theorist creates his own trap for the reader: Who can question Baudrillard's world of the hyperreal, Lyotard's crisis in narratives, and Jameson's postmodern condition that no one can escape from? Each articulates a downward hypocrisy; this postmodern world is horrible, out of control, and filled with too much terror. At the same time an upward hypocrisy, predicated on a self-righteous indignation prevails; social theory must do something about the current state of affairs. In each instance the theorist manipulates the reader toward a preferred ideological conclusion.

The Company we Keep
As sociologists, the company we keep (Wayne Booth's [1988] phrase) and the books we read and write tell a great deal about who we are. Most sociologists since Mills have kept company with the 'great' social theorists and empirical researchers who together reproduce the idea of social science that many have come to value. The list of 'greats' (nearly all male) depends on your allegiances;[8] those who carry them forth fill the pages of our prestigious journals with positivist and post-positivist versions of news about society (Maines, 1989a). But as Mills notes, society seldom, if ever, fills the pages of these texts, for here theory, method, and ideology determine subject matter. Mills kept the best of company – where did it get him?

Mills, like Baudrillard, Lyotard, and Jameson, produced a dishonest text, unresponsive to the very needs and demands he (and they) deemed central to the truthful workings of the sociological imagination. His (and their) project failed (and fails) for four reasons: he (and they) kept the wrong company; created the wrong version of the sociological imagination; failed to listen to the little people; and, most importantly, formed an ethical bond with me, the reader, which was later broken. The same harsh judgement applies to Baudrillard, Lyotard, and Jameson. Their dishonest texts have opened up the postmodern in self-serving ways, and in so doing have failed to further the workings of a postmodern sociological imagination.

Coming Full Circle

It is now possible to return to the beginning and reconsider the sociological imagination more clearly. Mills spoke to an earlier generation. His text affected sociological lives and set in motion versions of the postmodern sociological imagination that are now turning back on him. The mark of good sociological narrative is its ability to raise questions and create challenges. Mills did this, but today we must go beyond him, just as we must transcend the other theorists of the postmodern.

Mills's imagination was produced under the banner of a 'reverse orientalism' (Said, 1978): he saw ordinary people as 'the other' whose life he could objectively describe and explain through the tools of the classical theorists.[9] His *imagination* served to legitimize a version of institutionalized sociological practice that interpretive sociologists today wrestle with. It cast American society as a giant theater where the performances of ordinary people could be read from the privileged perspective of a bourgeois sociological aesthetic. Its legacy legitimizes theory and celebrates the virtuoso readings of the social text offered by this or that theorist.

But this legacy no longer works in the late-capitalist, postmodern period. The grand metanarratives of classical theory, reason, rationality, logic, and order, have died. They have been replaced by a 'pastiche' of neo-classical theories primarily derived from pre-World War II European theorists, who wrote, not unlike their postmodern counterparts, from within a colonialist, racist, sexist agenda (See Clifford, 1986: 10). This nostalgia for the past, a characteristic postmodern attitude, flies in the face of the fact that today our social texts no longer, if they ever did, refer to a fixed reality. Our theoretical signifiers have lost their signified referents. They now refer only to other texts, which in turn refer to yet others (see Rabinow, 1986: 250). There is no longer a world out there that can be objectively mapped by a theory or a method.

As argued earlier, we've entered an era where nothing is any longer hidden. The dividing line between public and private lives has dissolved: anyone's personal troubles can now serve as a front-page story couched as a banal morality tale with a happy ending. Here the legacy of the classical theorists and Mills still speaks, for they anticipated the erasure of this division. But as this erasure occurs, groups like ACOA (Adult Children of Alcoholics), AA (Alcoholics Anonymous), NA (Narcotics Anonymous), Adult Children of Sex Addicts, Child Abusers Anonymous, and Adults Recovering from Incest appear and take their place within the fractured fabrics of the American social structure. In these groups members attempt to take back their lives and make sense of the experiences they encountered while being raised in their particular familied version of the American dream.[10] They thus make public, in a limited way, the very secrets they felt the public order had held against them. But along with releasing talkers from an oppressive morality that had previously trapped them in a private hell, the very moment of their talking turns their stories into commodities sold in the public marketplace. Late twentieth-century America is producing cohorts of members who no longer accept things as they used to be. But these persons risk being trapped in a space where nothing is any longer private or sacred. Their new found freedom lies in a gray area where the older moralities no longer pertain and the centers of personal existence, which have been decentered, are no longer holding firm. There is no zero point of personal meaning that readily translates into the public realm, nor is there a zero point in the public realm.

So Mills was wrong in his predictions concerning the postmodern moment. The darling little slaves, the suburban queens, and the alcoholic robots have not settled for indifference, drift, and apathy. They have turned ressentiment into action, even when this involves actively (and publicly) hating their parents. Their fraudulent inspirational literature, their popular films, novels and other cultural texts have told them to seize the day and to no longer accept things the way they are. In small and large groups, and in social movements, they have taken on the American family and its incestuous, violent structures. They have challenged sexism and racism, environmental pollution, and the threat of nuclear annihilation. And in these moves, which are more than symbolic, they have attempted to fit their biographies to an historical social structure which has yet to learn how to accept them.

Alongside these subversive social groups persists a counter-centering logic which canonizes nostalgia, pastiche, romantic beliefs in patriotism, true character, surface images, imitations, simulations, instant information, frauds, and replicas (see Baudrillard 1988b: 101). 'Reality, as it was once known, has been plunged into a world of hyper-communication. History is instantaneous memory without a past' (Baudrillard, 1988a: 103–4). In this America, which Mills could barely glimpse, a thing has only to appear credible in order to be credible. So it is with sociology. While long ago it should have lost its credibility, it did not and has not, because the new masters of sociological thought have learned how to reproduce themselves within the hyperreal world of sociological texts where the real no longer exists, except in the words in which they write about it.

Mills, Politics, and the Postmodernists

Here, at the end, is where Mills engages Baudrillard, Lyotard, and Jameson. He saw, before these theorists, the alienation and hyperrealities that would come to be called the postmodern. He engaged the 1950s and tried to stop history, to turn it back, perhaps to a Habermas-like modern state. He attempted to merge biography, lived experience, and history and to make these terms his windows into the postmodern. Failing to connect to the world of lived experiences, because he never took stories seriously, he ended up writing his version of history. Untroubled by poststructural problems with texts and 'real' subjects, he too, like the postmodernists, forsook the world of the real for theoretical reasons. Fighting what he perceived to be the moral drift in the 'mass societies' of the immediate postwar period, he sought to create informed publics where free and rational human beings were able, with the assistance of sociologists with the sociological imagination, to translate personal troubles into public issues (1959: 186–94).

Seeing himself as a man of reason, who directed his work '*at* kings as well as *to* "publics"' (1959: 181) not an advisor to kings, or a

philosopher-king, he clung, like Habermas, to a master narrative involving reason and rationality as the ultimate tools for creating that moment
when men and women 'freely make history' (1959: 181). The sociologist's
task was clear for Mills: 'deliberately present controversial theory and
facts, and actively encourage controversy' (1959: 191). He saw nothing
wrong with trying to 'save the world – a phrase which I take here to mean
the avoidance of war and the re-arrangement of human affairs in accor-
dance with the ideals of human freedom and reason' (1959: 193). He
clearly did not want to abandon his position as an intellectual:

> The role of reason I have been outlining neither means . . . that one hit the
> pavement, take the next plane to the scene of the current crisis . . . buy a
> newspaper plant [or] go among the poor . . . Such actions are . . . admirable
> . . . but for the social scientist to take them [up] is to abdicate his role, and
> to display his . . . disbelief in the promise of social science and the role of
> reason in human affairs. (1959: 192)

Mills's version of the intellectual, then, has the ability to know that 'what
men are interested in, is not always what is to men's interests' (1959: 194).
But he *does* know, and like Habermas he shares in the Enlightenment
narratives about reason and science being the liberators of humanity. And
like Rorty (Lyotard too?), he holds out hope for a democratic society in
which men and women reason freely over the vital topics which define
personal troubles and public issues.

Mills was not totally blind to the realities that threatened his idea of a
democratic society. He saw such a structure being undermined by a
postwar corporate economy guided by a power elite which had fused its
interests with the military machine. But failing to anticipate the transformations that late capitalism would bring (the electronic revolution, the
commodification of experience, the simulacrum), he did not see how a
new technocratic elite would come to challenge the place held by the old
plutocracy (Carey and Quirk, 1989: 193). He did not anticipate how
knowledge would become a commodity, 'monopolized like any other
commodity' (Carey and Quirk, 1989: 193). Nor did he see how these new
arrangements would further atomize society, to the point where the
masses-transformed-into-publics find it increasingly more difficult to have
a voice, or to be represented. Nor did he see how these conditions would
erode any sense of political or social community in America (Carey and
Quirk, 1989: 193).

Nonetheless, he held out for a kind of radical democratic politics that
has certain similarities with the hegemonic socialist strategies of Laclau
and Mouffe (1985). For example his call for the creation of publics
organized around troubles and issues has parallels with the Laclau and
Mouffe (1985: 153) emphasis on the creation of the discursive conditions
for collective action which emphasize not negative demands on the social,
but the 'positivity of the social and the articulation of diverse democratic
demands' (1985: 189), within 'a radical and plural democracy' (1985:
176).

Mills, like Habermas, is nostalgic for a future where reason prevails. Baudrillard, Lyotard, and Jameson are nostalgic for a past (the 1950s and 1960s) where things were real, politics tasted good, freedom was in the air, a new frontier was on the skyline, and protest was everywhere. Each of these theorists (except for Mills) locates the past 'not in a fixed historical location' but always two generations removed (Carey and Quirk, 1989: 198). The future of the postmodern for Mills was now – 1959. For Jameson, Baudrillard, and Lyotard the postmodern constitutes, to borrow a phrase from Carey and Quirk (1989: 198), a 'continuously receding horizon . . . always just beyond one's grasp,' but close enough to be felt and seen, and apocalyptically real enough to be taken on its own grounds. But any attempt to read the postmodern present from the perspective of the past is to be dismissed as pure nostalgia (Jameson), as conservative, totalitarian, and reactionary (Baudrillard, Lyotard).

For these theorists the future of the postmodern has displaced the past 'in rhetoric and politics without altering the social import of these contrasting images' (Carey and Quirk, 1989: 198). However, the future of the postmodern, which Mills wanted to change, and Baudrillard, Lyotard, and Jameson find unacceptable, cannot be pushed forward into an ever-receding landscape where at some moment everything collapses and a new day reigns. It must be confronted now, on its own terms. Controversial theories like Baudrillard's yes, but it is not enough to be controversial, to mock and ridicule. The postmodern self must be written from the inside out. This is what Mills attempted to do. That he failed makes his challenge today even greater.

One avenue for reading the postmodern self involves the attempt to trace its public contours as given in mainstream Hollywood cinema (see Ryan and Kellner, 1988). Such texts dramaturgically enact the epiphanal moments of postmodernism. They center their texts on larger-than-life persons. The biographical experiences of such individuals represent attempts to come to grips with the existential dilemmas of postmodernism. These dilemmas, as argued earlier, center on the decisive performances of race, ethnicity, gender, and class which define the postmodern self. In the chapters that follow I examine how Hollywood has inscribed this self.

Notes

1. Earlier versions of portions of this chapter are given in Denzin (1989d, 1990b).

2. This list is taken from the *World Almanac and Book of Facts* (1990).

3. However as David Altheide and Raymond Schmitt (in conversation) suggest he neglected troubles that never became issues and issues that were never troubles.

4. The titles are 'The Promise,' 'Grand Theory,' 'Abstracted Empiricism,' 'Types of Practicality,' 'The Bureaucratic Ethos,' 'Philosophies of Sciences,' 'The Human Variety,' 'Uses of History,' 'On Reason and Freedom,' 'On Politics,' and the famous Appendix, 'On Intellectual Craftsmanship.'

5. It is comedy, parody, romance, and tragedy. He makes a comical parody of Parsons and Lazarsfeld, while he laments the tragic decline of reason and freedom in the early postmodern age (see Chs 1, 9, 10). A similar rhetorical analysis can be applied to the postmodernists; comedy and parody prevail in Baudrillard; romance and tragedy in Lyotard and Jameson.

6. This point is underscored by Rose Goldsen's account of Mills's involvement on the *Puerto Rican Journey* (1950) project, where he 'did not interview migrants or try to share their views. He interviewed English-speaking officials and intellectuals' (Goldsen, 1964: 90).

7. In fact six, not three persons converse: Mills, the immediate teller of his story; Mills, the implied teller who knows this is a made-up version of the imagination; Mills, the flesh-and-blood writer; and alongside these, three counterparts for the reader (see Booth, 1988: 125, and Broyard, 1989: 31).

8. Take your pick: Marx, Weber, Durkheim, Simmel, Mead, Cooley, Blumer, Parsons, Homans, Merton, Goffman, Garfinkel, Strauss, Becker, Baudrillard, Lyotard, Jameson, Lacan, Barthes, Sartre, de Beauvoir, Derrida, Blau, Coser, Collins, Giddens, Habermas.

9. The same injunction applies to Baudrillard, Lyotard, and Jameson.

10. *The Utne Reader* (1988) offers both a critical and sympathetic reading of these groups. The telephone directory of any averaged-sized US city contains listings for upwards of 20 self-help groups (for a caustic reading of these groups and their texts see Kaminer, 1990).

PART II
LEARNING FROM CINEMA

5

Wild about Lynch: Beyond *Blue Velvet*[1]

'It is a strange world, isn't it?' (Sandy, in *Blue Velvet* 1986)

There is no more fiction that life could possibly confront. (Baudrillard, 1983a: 148)

The Postmodern would be that . . . which searches for new presentations . . . in order to impart a stronger sense of the unpresentable. (Lyotard, 1984b: 81)

They can sew hands back on these days. (Hotel Clerk in *Wild at Heart*)

Blue Velvet (1986) is a quintessential postmodern film, and David Lynch is one of America's leading makers of postmodern cinema.[2] *Blue Velvet*'s representations of 'astral'[3] woman, sexuality, violence, and the gaze are my topics. However, I do not restrict my discussion to just *Blue Velvet*. This text spread its effects into Lynch's 1990 film, *Wild at Heart* and his 1990 ABC, Gothic soap opera *Twin Peaks*. These productions purport to map a postmodern terrain which is defined by wild sexuality, violence, and a nostalgia for the past where *film noir*, lurid melodrama, cliffhanger endings, and misogynism define the relations between the sexes (see Ebert, 1990b). I speak, then, to that contemporary postmodern phenomenon called David Lynch. I begin with *Blue Velvet* and end with *Wild at Heart* and *Twin Peaks*.

Gazing into *Blue Velvet*

The violent visual surfaces (and interiors) of *Blue Velvet* and *Wild at Heart* reflectively reference Lynch's cinematic eye (and ear), while celebrating the voyeur as postmodernism's penultimate, iconic figure. From its flagrant treatment of the Oedipal drama, to its parody of traditional family values, to the presentation of repressed homosexual desire, the castration complex, the multiplication of mother and father figures, to the symbolic focus on the separation of a mother and her male child, and other primal scenes, Lynch's blatantly Freudian, hysterical text recodes the positions of male and female within an oppressive postmodern family scene (Creed, 1988: 95, 113). It elevates the look and the gaze to new voyeuristic levels (see also the discussion of *Peeping Tom* in Chapter One). Its alarming visual and narrative text violates the usual boundaries between the real and the fantastic, the seen and the heard. The many subject positions it ascribes to woman (Creed, 1988, 112–13) make her the object, the subject, and the victim of a sado-masochistic tale which by now is all too familiar in contemporary Hollywood cult films where the boundaries between *film noir*, melodrama, soft pornography, horror, and the avant garde are constantly transgressed (see Ross, 1989: 155; Creed, 1988: 95).

The multiple positions of woman are given in the film's title, *Blue Velvet*, which with its several meanings quickly alerts the viewer to the fact that more is going on here than a story about the figure of the woman in blue (Dorothy, Blue Lady), who sings the song ('Blue Velvet') about first love. From the opening credits, which play over the surface of crushed blue velvet, to the clear blue skies, and blue water in the film's initial scenes, to the first sight of Dorothy at the 'Slow Club', shot in blue, in a blue velvet gown, singing 'Blue Velvet' ('bluer than velvet were her eyes, lonely as a blue blue star'), to her appearance in her apartment in her blue robe, it is evident that Lynch is playing with the sexual meanings of blue and velvet. In rapid succession we encounter the film's playful treatment of each term, including Dorothy the depressed Blue Lady, blue as signifier of the indecent and the obscene (Dorothy's robe, the strip of blue velvet Frank puts in his mouth), blue as dark and sinister (Dorothy's apartment), and true blue (Sandy's unswervingly faithful love for Jeffrey, Dorothy's love for her child).[4] Velvet is similarly given numerous meanings, which range from the lining of Dorothy's womb and the vagina (where the blue velvet goes), to the source of life, as umbilical cord (when Frank growls, 'Baby wants Blue Velvet,' and gets between her legs and reenacts a primal birth scene), to gentleness, a soft and smooth surface, when Dorothy first caresses Jeffrey, as she holds a knife directed at his penis.

In flaunting his title Lynch challenges the viewer to go beyond the pornographic into his subterranean world of violence through the 'ear' of the other ('Do it for Van Gogh!'). The viewer along with Jeffrey burrows into a vast space (the cut ear first) which becomes the 'interior of woman [and] her hidden places, ultimately into the womb' (Creed, 1988: 110) where the images of the mysterious and the dark (velvet) are opposed to the erotic and the sensual (blue velvet, the liquid velvet womb). In this journey Lynch-as-voyeur turns the viewer, and the women (and men) in his text (Dorothy and Sandy, Jeffrey, Frank) into voyeurs. They are seen as occupying shifting positions in the triangles of Oedipal desire (Dorothy–Little Donny–Don; Dorothy–Frank–Jeffrey; Dorothy–Jeffrey–Sandy; Dorothy–Frank–Donny; Sandy–her father–Jeffrey; Jeffrey–his father–and his mother, etc.) that move the narrative toward its conclusion which is to 'fulfil the child's wish for the mother to give up the father' (Creed, 1988: 111).

These Oedipal structures are embedded in three primal scenes (Creed, 1988: 96): birth (Frank's exist from Dorothy's womb, 'Baby wants to fuck!'); the origins of sexuality (Jeffrey's seduction by Dorothy); and the castration complex (Dorothy's holding the knife close to Jeffrey's penis; Frank's attack on Jeffrey). Lynch invites the viewer to enter each of these primal scenes, and in so doing manipulates the positions of male and female spectator-voyeur. As Creed (1988: 101–3) observes, Lynch produces, through *mise-en-scène*, a sequence of gendered spaces where male and female subjects are free to take up the passive and active forms of the feminine and masculine gaze. Masochistic and sadistic gazes move back and forth between Dorothy, Frank, and Jeffrey. This is evident not only in the scene where Jeffrey spies on Dorothy, but also when she controls his gaze, after discovering him in the closet ('Don't look at me'). It reappears when Frank tells her 'Don't you fucking look at me!', as the camera focuses on her face and the obvious sexual pleasure she is experiencing. By allowing Dorothy to control Jeffrey's gaze, Lynch increases her power by relegating Jeffrey to the position of the powerless figure. In contrast, the looks of Sandy, Jeffrey's detective partner in this little story, are neither masochistic nor sadistic. They lack the power accorded Dorothy. Sandy's gaze, as Biga (1987) observes, is used, in two ways. Her looks are investigative, as she spies for Jeffrey and serves as his look-out. Secondly, they affirm his project, underlining her admiration and love of him. While she remains an enigmatic figure (Biga, 1987), Lynch never has her turn around and look at herself; in refusing her this reflective gaze he keeps her framed within the traditional feminine position, the object of the male's gaze.

Contemporary films like David Lynch's *Blue Velvet* and *Wild at Heart* may be read as cultural statements which locate within small-town America (Lumberton, USA, Big Tuna, Texas, Twin Peaks), all the terrors and simulated realities that Lyotard (1984b), and Baudrillard (1983a) see operating in the late postmodern period. A reading of such films should provide a deeper understanding of the kinds of men, women, and cinematic biographical experiences the late postmodern period makes available to its members (see Corliss, 1986, for a discussion of this film as well as *True Stories* (1986), and *Peggy Sue Got Married* (1986). *Something Wild* (1986), *Raising Arizona*, (1987), *Blood Simple* (1984), *sex, lies and videotape* (1989), *Do the Right Thing* (1989), *Crimes and Misdemeanors* (1989), *Brazil* (1985), *The Fly* (1986), *The Man Who Envied Women* (1985), and *Speaking Parts* (1989) could also be added to this list).[5] Such readings should serve to further clarify the various cultural, aesthetic, everyday, and sociological meanings of the term postmodern in the early 1990s. They should also contribute to further conceptual and interpretive refinements within postmodern cultural theory, including postmodern film theory (Connor, 1989: 173–81; Lash, 1988; Lyotard, 1984b; Jameson, 1983; Grossberg, 1988a: 46–7; Featherstone, 1987, 1989b; Elias, 1987: 223; Games, 1987). At the same time, analyses like this should help to illuminate the discursive languages and figural images of the postmodern that are now being connected to the filmic experience. In elevating the voyeur to a position of authority these films suggest that looking, seeing and hearing are now the principal ways of knowing and making sense of the contemporary, cinematic, visual world. Texts like *Blue Velvet* transgress the postmodern, while they reaffirm certain mainstream cultural values (see Lash, 1988).

I shall first discuss the narrative structure of this film, and then turn to a reading that elaborates the interpretive points to be developed below.[6] (This reading will build upon the reviews of the film in the popular culture press.) I will argue, after Grossberg (1986: 86) that 'the meaning of a text is always the site of a struggle.' And so it is with this film. Reviewers have been divided over its meanings. Robertson, writing in *The New York Times*, observed:

> The movie – one of the most talked about of the year, seeming to divide audiences into those who love it and find it brilliant and bizarre, and those who hate it and find it sick and disgusting – has been drawing around-the-block lines in New York for the last three weeks. (1986: 11)

Doing *Blue Velvet*

Films like *Blue Velvet* simultaneously display the two features of postmodernist texts that Jameson (1983: 111–13, 125) has identified: an effacement of the boundaries between the past and the present (typically given in the forms of pastiche and parody), and a treatment of time which locates the viewing subject in a perpetual present. These films, which I shall call late-postmodern nostalgia, bring the unpresentable (rotting, cut-off ears, sexual violence, brutality, insanity, homosexuality, the degradation of women, sado-masochistic rituals, drug and alcohol abuse) in front of the viewer in ways that challenge the boundaries that ordinarily separate private and public life (Baudrillard, 1983a: 130). The wild sexuality and violence that these films represent signify, in the Bataille sense (1982), modes of freedom and self-expression that the late-postmodern period is both fearful of, and drawn to at the same time.

Blue Velvet, and the other films in this emerging genre, have been read as denigrating women (see McGuigan and Huck, 1986: 67). These are not pro-feminist social texts. Women are treated as traditional sexual objects, and in *Blue Velvet* they are the recipients of sexual and physical violence. Women are contained within one of two categories: respectable, middle-class marriage, or disrespectable occupational and sexual categories (see Gledhill, 1985). These cultural texts maintain images of the gender stratification system that are decidedly pre-postmodern.[7]

These films do not just return to the past in a nostalgic sense, and bring the past into the present, as Jameson suggests. They make the past the present, but they locate terror in nostalgia for the past. The signifiers of the past (e.g. 1950s and 1960s popular music, including rock-'n-roll and rhythm and blues) are signs of destruction. In Lyotard's sense, (1984b: 81), these films wage a war on nostalgia. In so doing they identify two forms of nostalgia: the safe and the unsafe. By creating the comfortable illusion that adult middle-class life is connected to the past in an unbroken chain, these films argue that the rock-'n-roll music of youth, if carried into adulthood, will lead to self-destruction and violence. By moving two versions of the past (the sacred and the profane) into the present, *Blue Velvet* pushes the boundaries of the present farther and farther into the future where the unreal and the hyperreal (Baudrillard, 1983a) are always real, and not just possibilities. In the process, films like *Blue Velvet* expose the margins of the social and bring them to the center of safe society (see Hall, 1986b). These violent margins (dope fiends, sexual perverts), are now placed in small towns, next door to middle- and lower-class Americans who are attempting to live safe, respectable lives. These late postmodern films locate violence and the simulacrum, not just in Disneyland (Baudrillard, 1983a), MTV, or in television commercials. They locate these phenomena within the everyday and give to the simulacrum a violent turn that it never had before (see Featherstone, 1988). It is these arguments that I shall explore in this chapter. I turn now to the narrative of the film.

The Narrative

Blue Velvet's narrative is straightforward (see Ansen, 1986). It is set in Lumberton, USA. The hero, Jeffrey Beaumont, is the son of a middle-class hardware store owner who suffers a stroke as the film opens. Jeffrey, home from college for the summer, takes over for his father at the store. Walking across a vacant lot he discovers a severed ear. He takes the ear to a detective and becomes involved in a mystery to discover who the ear belongs to, and how it got in the field. He is aided by the detective's sweet blonde daughter, Sandy. Jeffrey and Sandy stake out a disturbed nightclub singer, Dorothy Vallens, who lives on the seventh floor of an apartment building. Jeffrey sneaks into Dorothy's apartment and hides in her closet. He is discovered by Dorothy, who commands him at knife-point to strip. She begins to seduce him, but is interrupted by Frank, an obscenity-spouting, drug-inhaling, constantly drinking, local drug dealer. Jeffrey witnesses a bizarre sexual ritual between Frank and Dorothy. Dorothy is the sexual slave of Frank, who has kidnapped her son and husband Don. Frank cut off Don's ear. Jeffrey is subsequently drawn into Dorothy's world of wild, sado-masochistic sexuality, and is seduced by her. At her request he beats her. Discovered by Frank, Dorothy and Jeffrey are taken to one of Frank's clubs where Frank's cronies hang out. There they confront Dean Stockwell, a 'suave', mannequin-like nightclub singer who sings 'Sand Man' to Frank and his friends. They leave the club, and go to the edge of town where Jeffrey is beaten up and left. He makes his way back to town to Sandy's. They go to a high-school party, and dance, cheek to cheek, like lovers. Driving home they are confronted, on the steps of Sandy's house, by a naked Dorothy, who proclaims her love to Jeffrey ('Your seed is in me'). Sandy's mother covers up Dorothy, and offers solace to a shocked Sandy. They send Dorothy off to the hospital. Jeffrey leaves for Dorothy's apartment and there he finds two dead men: Don and a corrupt policeman. Sandy's father, the detective, comes and takes Jeffrey home. The film closes with Sandy and Jeffrey married, having a barbecue dinner with both sets of family relatives. The viewer gazes past a 'mechanical' robin which has landed on the window sill, a plastic worm in its mouth, to the cozy family scene in the backyard.

The Realist Reading

How has this film been read at the hegemonic, realist level? I now examine the hegemonic readings that have been given in the 'mainline' American popular culture texts.[8] *Blue Velvet*'s morality story is simple. A young man takes on evil in the world. He succumbs to this evil, but is ultimately redeemed, and finds his place back within the safe, sexual confines of married middle-class life, with a beautiful young bride. This simple rite of passage story, however, locates all of the unpresentables in everyday life (cut-off ears, murders, wild sexuality, alcohol- and drug-related violence, sado-masochistic rituals) within a nostalgia for the past that includes a soundtrack full of 1950s and 1960s rock-'n-roll songs with singers who croon 'Mysteries of Love,' 'In Dreams,' and 'Blue Velvet.'[9] These unpresentables are seen as existing next door to and just below the surface of small-town, homespun American life.

Blue Velvet as Parable of Sin and Redemption

Nearly every review read the film as a coming-of-age parable. The following statements are representative. David Ansen of *Newsweek* wrote: '*Blue Velvet* is a guilty parable of sin and redemption and true life in which Betty and Archie and Veronica archetypes are set loose in the hallucinatory world of the id' (Ansen, 1986). He continues, '*Blue Velvet* unfolds like a boys' adventure tale of the 1940s and 1950s, but it's as if a Hardy boy has wandered into a scenario devised by the Marquis de Sade.' Pauline Kael of the *New Yorker* wrote:

> A viewer knows intuitively that this is a coming-of-age picture – that Jeffrey's discovery of this criminal, sadomasochistic network has everything to do with his father's becoming an invalid and his own new status as an adult. It's as if David Lynch were saying, 'It's a frightening world out there, and' – tapping his head – 'in here.' (Kael, 1986: 99)

Blue Velvet as Religious Art Portraying Evil

The coming-of-age parable, connected with sin and redemption, is further elaborated by those readings which locate the sin elements within a religious text that deals with evil. James M. Wall, writing in the *Christian Century*, called it the best film of 1986 because of its sensitive probing of evil as an ugly reality in life. Wall (1986: 7) calls the film a contemporary metaphor of one of Paul's letters to the church at Rome. In his letter Paul described sinfulness as a condition of all creatures (1986: 7). The film, Wall argues, clearly communicates Paul's point that all of God's creatures are inventors of evil, disobedient to parents, foolish, faithless, heartless, and ruthless (Romans, 1:29–30). Still, he states that he can't recommend the film as must-seeing for everyone, because its scenes of brutality and violent sex are so realistic and ugly. Nonetheless, he compares the film to the work of the fifteenth-century artist, Hieronymus Bosch (Wall, 1986: 9). Lynch's film, like Bosch's paintings, goes to the heart of a work of art: it realistically portrays the unpresentable, so as to make its point about ultimate human values. Wall's realist reading is to be contrasted to John Simon's, which sees the film as pornography.

Blue Velvet as Pornographic Cult

Here is Simon (1986: 54):

> How long has it been since an American movie has garnered a harvest of laurels like the one being heaped on a piece of mindless junk called *Blue Velvet*? . . . True pornography, which does not pretend to be anything else, has at least a shred of honesty to recommend it; *Blue Velvet*, which pretends to be art, and is taken for it by most critics, has dishonesty and stupidity as well as grossness on its conscience.

Simon, contrary to Wall, sees the film's treatment of sado-masochism, voyeurism, latent homosexuality, and fetishism as an attempt to shock, titillate, and sexually arouse the viewer. He sees Lynch's efforts to comment on small-town American mores as pretentious, and suggests that 'this trash' has been raved about because of a decline of intelligence on the part of those critics who write for sophisticated magazines and family newspapers (Simon, 1986: 56). Simon goes on to criticize the film's cinematography and acting (poster colors and amateurish). Reed (1986), calling attention to what he saw as the presence of 'violence, graphic sex and nudity, sado-masochism and every perversion known to man' in the film, describes it as 'one of the sickest films ever made' and places it in the 'brain-damaged garbage department,' stating that it 'gives pretentiousness new meaning,' and 'should score high with the kind of sickos who like to smell dirty socks and pull the wings off butterflies, but there's nothing here for sane audiences.'

Playboy (Williamson, 1986: 25) reads the film, not so much as pornography, but as a text that continues Lynch's reputation as a builder of cult films. Focusing on the film's surreal, bizarre, hypnotic, and sex-charged scenes, Williamson suggests that the film 'lapses into gratuitous violence and vulgarity' and that Lynch has gone overboard 'while testing how far a maverick moviemaker can go' (Williamson, 1986: 25; see also Reed, 1986). Gelmis (1986) echoed these lines, suggesting that it appeals to 'the same constituency as *Mona Lisa* and *The Fly* – moviegoers tolerant of disturbing sex and violence for the sake of artful filmmaking.' Denby (1986) stresses the film's cult-like characteristics: '*Blue Velvet* isn't a classic, but it's the cult movie of the year and perhaps the decade.'

Locating Blue Velvet within a Film Genre

In their attempts to give the film meaning, critics have sought to locate it within a genre. As the foregoing reactions indicate, it has been called both pornographic, and a cult film. Those who call it a cult film speak of Lynch as a director who has produced earlier cult classics: *The Elephant Man* and *Eraserhead*.

Other critics (Kael, 1986: 102) have called it 'Gothic,' a 'comedy,' 'a coming-of-age' film, and 'surrealistic.' Rabkin (1986: 53) suggests that it is eighties *film noir* in having 'a person getting involved with something over which he has no control.' Corliss (1986: 10) locates *Blue Velvet* within the 'small-town' films genre-tradition, and reads it as an extension of the Frank Capra movies of the 1940s. Gelmis (1986) connects Lynch with Hitchcock, calling it a 'Hitchcockian mystery,' and Benson (1986) sees parallels with 'the comforting small-town homeyness that Hitchcock sketched in *Shadow of a Doubt*.'[10] Hoberman (1986) hints at Lynch's postmodern overtones, stating that the director 'is basically a non-narrative filmmaker,' and his film is 'hallucinated and hyperreal.'

Biga (1987: 44) calls the film a 'reworked fifties crime thriller/horror/ Gothic film.' She reads it through Mulvey's theory of the cinematic gaze. The positioning of Sandy and Dorothy, and the variety of looks (investigative, erotic, affirmative) attached to them, are interpreted as instances of the film's patriarchal, psychoanalytic, Oedipal commitment 'to understand the formation of the male while ignoring, or grafting on in an unlikely way, the formation of the female' (Biga, 1987: 47). Lash (1988: 329–30) locates *Blue Velvet* in the figural, transgressive, postmodern category, arguing that Lynch is pushing back boundaries and making the concept of hero (and anti-hero) problematic, especially by having Jeffrey engage in the same sadistic behavior as Frank. This parallel in the two characters, Lash (1988: 330) argues, underlines the 'instability of [the hero's] subjectivity.' He observes: 'Is not the problem of sadistic behavior toward women made deeper and more urgent through this portrayal than through, say, the simple moral condemnation of a villain who beats a woman?'

The inability of critics to agree on what genre the film belongs to speaks, in part, to its contradictory text and to its arresting sexual and erotic images. By locating a film within a genre, pre-established meanings can be brought to it, and it can be judged by the canons of the genre. Clearly Lynch's film resists classification. Hence it is read in multiple ways. But it is clear that at least some critics lean toward the negative (pornography) in their interpretations.

Lynch on Blue Velvet
What does Lynch say about his film?

'In a way this is still a fantasy film. It's like a dream of strange desires wrapped inside a mystery story. It's what could happen if you ran out of fantasy.' (Lynch in Chute, 1986: 35)

'*Blue Velvet* is a trip beneath the surface of a small American town, but it's also a probe into the subconscious or a place where you face things that you don't normally face.' (Chute, 1986: 32)

'*Blue Velvet* is a very American movie. The look of it was inspired by my childhood in Spokane, Washington. Lumberton is a real name.' (Chute, 1986: 32)

'It's like saying that once you've discovered there are heroin addicts in the world and they're murdering people to get money, can you be happy? It's a tricky question. Real ignorance is bliss. That's what *Blue Velvet* is about.' (Lynch in Rabkin, 1986: 55)

Asked to locate his film with a genre, Lynch comments: 'It's not a genre film in my mind. It's *Blue Velvet*'.

On genre, he states, in response to the interviewer (Rabkin, 1986: 55), who pushes him to locate the film within a category:

'You're saying it like you find a genre to fit every film into. But you don't have to obey the rules of a genre. There are many things in *Blue Velvet* that are against some sort of rules or this normal setup.' (Rabkin, 1986: 56)

Asked to discuss the meaning of his film, Lynch remarks:

'it doesn't make any difference what I say. It's like digging some guy up after he has been dead for 400 years and asking him about his book. His book is what's there, and what he's going to say about it isn't going to change it I think if you're really allowed to be honest then it could be understood little by little at different levels and still hold true. I think that life is like that, that you can work it down lower and lower and it will always make some kind of fantastic sense.' (Rabkin, 1986: 56)

Lynch, like a reader-response theorist, locates the meaning of his film in the viewer's experiences with its text. For him the film is fantasy, a dream, an exploration of the subconscious, a study of what goes on just below the surface in American small towns.

Viewer Reactions
Viewers, as would be expected, have been divided in their reactions to the film. McGuigan and Huck (1986: 66–7) provide a sampling of these reactions:

- In Chicago two men fainted during the film.
- Outside a Los Angeles movie house, a woman who hated it got into a fight with a stranger who loved it. They settled the dispute by going back in to see it again.

- Elsewhere people have demanded their money back.
- Viewers are shocked by certain images: a severed ear, a scene of sadomasochistic fetishism, a naked woman who's been beaten. Or they're repelled by the outrageously evil bad guy (Dennis Hopper) who violently inhales helium through a face mask.
- 'I felt like a pervert watching it.'
- 'I wanted to wash as soon as I got out of the movie.'
- 'I was thrilled. I was completely absorbed.'
- 'When people hear I've seen it six times, they say I'm a sick person.'
- 'Wow, I think I might have hated it.'
- 'I don't know what was weirder – the movie or the people watching it.'
- 'It's like Norman Rockwell meets Heironymus Bosch.'

A local film critic (Champaign-Urbana, Illinois) stated:

> I love it. I watched again last night. It's got everything: mystery, film noir, Hitchcock, horror, outstanding soundtrack, lighting, atmosphere, the way they changed the melodic structure of the song, 'Blue Velvet,' how it builds tension.

These interpretations reflect the same contradictory reactions of the film's critics. As one viewer stated, 'You either love this film or you hate it.' Viewers connect the film's meanings back to the feelings they experienced while viewing it: perverted, dirty, sick person. I will argue below that these opposing, conflictual positions speak to contradictions and tensions in late-postmodern American life. *Blue Velvet* awakens desires and fears that expose the limits of the real and the unreal in contemporary, everyday life.

The Meanings of *Blue Velvet*

The following meanings of *Blue Velvet* can now be enumerated: pornography, parable of sin and redemption, like religious art, a cult film, Gothic, coming-of-age film, trash, mindless junk, *film noir*, murder mystery, small-town film, dream film, comedy, surrealism. The most important film of 1986. The many interpretations of the film speak to and support Grossberg's position that 'the meaning of a text is always the site of a struggle.'

At the hegemonic, realist (and negotiated) levels, two clusters of consensual meanings and interpretations emerge: The film is either high cinematic art or it is trash. It is a coming-of-age film and in its portrayal of evil, violence, and wild sexuality it leans toward an expansion of classic 1940s small-town films, or it is perversion and pornography, if not trash.

These two clusters of hegemonic meaning speak, of course, to tensions within the film; but more importantly, they speak to the postmodern desire to see evil, while being repulsed by it. The morally conservative readings thus reify the culture's desire to repress the sexual and violent themes of postmodern life. The morally liberal readings valorize the film's aesthetic qualities, and locate it within the classic film tradition of the

1940s, and earlier religious, symbolic art. As the film evokes these contradictory readings its cult status is elevated. Viewers continue to be drawn to it. This is so because of the opposing emotional meanings that are evoked by its symbolism and by these earlier cultural interpretations. With few exceptions (McGuigan and Huck, 1986), the dominant cultural readings did not dwell on the violent treatment of women in the film's text.

Blue Velvet as a Contradictory Postmodern Text

I return now to the interpretive points developed above: I will show how this film is pastiche and parody, an effacement of the boundaries between the past and the present, a presentation of the unpresentable, derogatory of women, an assault on nostalgia, and a threat to safe, middle-class life. The negative and contradictory readings that postmodern texts receive can be explained, in part, by these features.

Pastiche and Parody, Past and Present
From its opening scenes, which begin with a clear blue sky, and bright, blooming red roses waving in front of a white picket fence, to a classic 1940s fire truck with a dalmation dog on the fender, slowly gliding down a tree-lined street, and the soundtrack of Bobby Vinton singing 'She Wore Blue Velvet' the movie's hyperrealism signals to the reader that this film is going to be a parody of small-town, 1940s movies. Almost immediately the film shows cars from the 1950s, 1960s, and 1980s moving along Lumberton's streets. Sophisticated 1980s computerized medical equipment is shown in a late forties hospital room, and a scene from a 1950s movie flashes across a black-and-white TV screen. High-school students are shown in dress which spans three decades. This is a film which evokes, mocks, yet lends quasi-reverence to the icons of the past, while it places them in the present. The film has effaced the boundaries between the past and the present. Jeffrey, Sandy, Dorothy, and Frank move through the film as if they were dreaming.

The Unpresentable
Within three minutes Jeffrey has discovered the rotting ear in a vacant lot. The viewer is taken inside the ear. It fills the screen. Strange, roaring sounds are heard. In an even earlier scene Lynch takes the viewer into a front lawn where blades of grass 'as tall as redwood trees' (Kael, 1986: 99) are teeming with big black insects. The film quickly moves from this violence in nature to the sado-masochistic rituals between Frank and Dorothy and Dorothy and Jeffrey described earlier. Violence, and the unpresentable, Lynch seems to be suggesting, are everywhere, not only in nature, but next door to the middle-class homes in Lumberton, USA.

Women
Dorothy's degradation is used as a vehicle for Jeffrey's sexual education.
Sandy's pure sexuality is contrasted to Dorothy's decadence, and her sick
desire to be abused. By locating women within these opposing identities,
and by unglamorously photographing Dorothy in her nude scenes, Lynch
symbolically and simultaneously makes his film pro- and anti-woman. In
so doing he parodies the 'playboy' woman of soft pornography, yet
sustains a traditional view of the 'pure' woman in American life. His
treatment of women contains all the contradictions toward women that
the decade of the 1980s produced.

   Lynch's film celebrates the Oedipal myth and the primal scenes which
define, in the psychoanalytic script, the origins of self, sexuality, and
sexual differences (Rose, 1982; Mitchell, 1982; Creed, 1988). The 'astral'
signs he assigns to Dorothy and Sandy simultaneously give them the
power to satisfy male desires, while depriving them of their own
individuality. He surrounds his women (and men), with blind men,
firemen in blue, drag queens, violent-sick Frank and his crazy buddies,
straight fathers, corrupt policemen, conventional mothers and aunts.
Jeffrey as child-man becomes a sexual-moral responsibility for both
women. The soft, nostalgic songs Lynch brings to them, ('Blue Velvet,'
'In Dreams,' and 'Love Letters') romanticize and feminize their
characters within traditional male signifiers. The colors he attaches to
them (blue and red for Dorothy, peach and white for Sandy) perform the
same function. The sexual scenes they play out (violent sexuality vs teen-
petting, and cheek-to-cheek dancing), the looks they control and receive
(sadistic, masochistic, investigative, affirmative, as sexual objects), and
the subject positions they occupy (victims, sexual slaves, phallic/castrating
mothers, masochistic–sadistic lovers, betrayed women, honored wives)
further underscore the film's anti-woman position. Lynch's final shot,
which is Dorothy embracing her lost son against a sky of blue, seals his
commitment to (as he mocks) the traditional nuclear family, and the
mother–child bond. This symbolic configuration, as Creed (1988: 99)
argues, 'has been reworked many times throughout the narrative in its
parody of Freudian themes.' In mocking these Freudian-psychoanalytic-
Oedipal themes Lynch keeps them alive. In so doing he reproduces the
patriarchal bias that operates in the so-called postmodern woman's films
(*The Morning After*).

Nostalgia
Earlier I argued that *Blue Velvet* locates two forms of nostalgia, the safe
and the unsafe and that the rock-'n-roll and popular music of the film
signify violence and destruction. Lynch parodies 1950s rock-'n-roll in the
character of Dean Stockwell, suggesting that people risk becoming like
Stockwell (and Frank) if they stay too long within this music. Rock-'n-roll
loses its youthful innocence in Lynch's film. But by framing the film with
rock's sounds he appeals to a 1980s adult generation that still venerates

the music of its adolescence. It is as if Lynch were saying this music is not as innocent as it appears to be. But more is involved. By locating the sexual sounds of rock at the center of his film Lynch is arguing that the central illusions of rock-'n-roll (sexuality, true love, violence, terror, boredom: see Grossberg, 1988b: 184–5) have to be lived out before people can find their true romantic and sexual identity in life.

Consider the lyrics from the Roy Orbison song, 'In Dreams,' which is sung in the film's most violent scenes:

A candy-colored clown they call the sandman.
Tiptoes to my room every night
Just to sprinkle stardust and to whisper
'Go to sleep. Everything is all right.'
In dreams I walk with you
In dreams I talk to you
In dreams you're mine all of the time
Forever in dreams.

Jeffrey lives out his wildest sexual dreams with Dorothy, only to return to Sandy at the end of the film, inside the dreams the sandman sings.

Sandy dreams too. Hers is the dream of a world that was dark 'because there weren't any robins, but then thousands of robins were set free and there was the blinding light of love.' Sandy relates this dream to Jeffrey when they are parked in front of a church. An organ plays in the background. Hearing her dream Jeffrey replies, 'You're a neat girl, Sandy.'

The film ends with a slow zoom out of Jeffrey's ear to a mechanical look-alike robin flying to the window sill of the family kitchen. Sandy looks up at the robin; it has a worm in its beak. Lynch closes his film, as he opened it, in one ear and out another, with nature and its violence in front of the viewer. We simultaneously hear and see this violence. Lynch's path into the unconscious is through the ear. 'His sound tracks are ominous and mysterious, full of rushing wind and the roars of animals' (Benson, 1986: 1).

Wild at Heart in *Twin Peaks*

Lynch's project circles back upon itself in *Wild at Heart* and in *Twin Peaks*. *Wild at Heart*, part *Wizard of Oz*, *film noir*, kinky fairy-tale, self-satire, soap opera and sexual exploitation, deals in offensive violence set inside the love-on-the-road movie genre. In a Carolina dance hall Elvis-worshipping Sailor Ripley violently kills a black man. When Sailor comes out of prison, waiting for him is devoted Lula, a sulky sexpot on the run from her jealous mother who wants Sailor killed. As the couple runs from New Orleans to Big Tuna, Texas they are chased by a mobster and a detective and another low-life thug and slick psychopath named Bobby Peru. Encountering fat-lady porn stars, a drug cartel, and the Good Witch, the daring couple come to a happy ending, complete with Sailor crooning 'Love Me Tender.'

Fire is the central imagery of the film. It appears everywhere, in 'huge, screen filling close-ups, cigarette- and match-tips burn like pyres. Flames sprout in burning cars, buildings, and recurring flashbacks of a human torch' (Jahiel, 1990). In between the fire scenes are finger sandwiches, cockroaches and flies on vomit, ritual killers, and Mr Raindeer (the hit man who lives in a whore house).

Being generous, Lynch is exposing the violent psyches that make up American pop culture. The happy ending provided by the *Wizard of Oz* storyline leads to an excessive indulgence in violence toward women. Ebert (1990b) observes, '[Lynch] has a particular knack for humiliating women . . . [for] portraying them in a particularly hurtful and offensive light.' Misogynist to the core, *Wild at Heart* picks up where Jeffrey's violence with Dorothy in *Blue Velvet* ended.

Twin Peaks is soft-Lynch. A dangling soap opera, it is set in a town called Twin Peaks, which is like Lumberton, USA. It has all the ingredients of Peyton Place: soft sex, violence, murders, adultery. All of the needed characters are present: Dale Cooper the FBI agent sent to solve the murder of Laura Palmer; Sheriff Harry S. Truman, who knows more about Twin Peaks than anyone else; Jocelyn Packard, an Asian woman who inherited the Packard Sawmill; Catherine Martell who is locked in a power struggle with her sister-in-law over control of Packard Sawmill; James Hurley, the loner who takes chances; Bobby Braggs who loved Laura; Benjamin Horne, the local mogul; Audrey Horne who has a precocious sexuality; Ed Hurley who runs the local gas station; Norma Jennins, married to Hank, who is in jail, but she loves Ed Hurley; and Dr Lawrence Jacoby, the local psychiatrist who knows Laura's secrets.

Twin Peaks has become a cult phenomenon; a collector's item; a weekly watch by those who normally do not view primetime TV. Laughed at and mocked by its fans, its connections to Lynch are celebrated. Even its weak storyline -- who killed Laura Palmer? - is celebrated.[11] The Gothic text appears to have an appeal grounded in the viewer's inclinations to put down primetime TV. Promoted as a 'quality adult show,' and 'one of the reasons for staying home on Saturday nights' (*TV Guide*, 1990: 7), *Twin Peaks* allows a segment of the TV viewing audience to have the violent world of David Lynch on a weekly basis.

Wild about Lynch: the Postmodern Terrain

Postmodern cultural texts, like *Blue Velvet, Twin Peaks*, and *Wild at Heart*, echo and reproduce the tensions and contradictions that define the late 1980s and early 1990s. The astral signs aligned with the figure of woman still circle in a male-controlled orbit. This circuit is contained within a larger orbiting Oedipal narrative which insists on celebrating the cult of the erotic where the figure of woman is the arch-signifier of desire. Woman as desire entices man, that wild, sexual wayward thing who has to be seduced, captured, and returned to home and hearth. There in the luscious presence of a good woman he is tamed and reined in by family, the final site of masculine safety, and feminine identity. The Oedipal story will not go away. Film-makers like Lynch are trapped, as Foucault might observe, in a sexual prison of their own making, still harnessed 'to the yoke of daddy-mommy and *making no effort to do away with this problem once and for all* (Deleuze and Guattari, 1977: 50, italics in original).

Postmodern nostalgia texts locate strange, eclectic, violent, timeless worlds in the present. They make fun of the past as they keep it alive. They search for new ways to present the unpresentable, so as to break down the barriers that keep the profane out of the everyday. However, they take conservative political stances, while they valorize and exploit the radical social margins of society. Nothing escapes the postmodern eye. But this voyeuristic eye, its visions and its voices, is unrelenting in its unwillingness to give up the past in the name of the future. The postmodern eye looks fearfully into the future and it sees technology, uncontrolled sexual violence, universally corrupt political systems. Confronting this vision, it attempts to find safe regions of escape in the fantasies and nostalgia of the past. Dreams are the postmodern solution to life in the present.

More than the future is looked into. It is the everyday that has become the subject matter of these postmodern nostalgia films. Small-town, any-town, USA is no longer safe. The fantasies of the past have become realities in the present. These realities are now everywhere. By showing this, these films make the global village even smaller. It is now called Twin Peaks, or Lumberton. 'The world that dreams are made of. Our town' (Corliss, 1986: 17). Our town is filled with good people like Jeffrey, Sandy, Dorothy, Frank, Sailor and Lula, Dale Cooper, and Laura Palmer. In Lumberton, Big Tuna, and Twin Peaks their dreams, good and bad, come true. And in these fairy-tale towns individuals meet and confront problems that old-fashioned law and order policemen still help them resolve.

The postmodern landscape and its people are filled with hope. Schizo-phrenic in their vision, these people know that in the end everything will turn out all right. And it does. Villains die, or are reformed. Male heroes transgress moral boundaries but come back home to mother and father with their Oedipal conflicts resolved. In the end these films build their stories around individuals and their sexual fantasies. In so doing they keep alive the middle-class myth of the individual. The postmodern person still confronts the world through the lens of a nineteenth- and early twentieth-century political ideology. Perhaps this is the chief func-tion of the 1980s nostalgia film. As the world political system turns ever more violent and conservative, the need for cultural texts which sustain the key elements of a conservative political economy increases. It seems that postmodern individuals want films like *Blue Velvet, Wild at Heart*, and television series like *Twin Peaks* for in them they can have their sex, their myths, their violence, and their politics, all at the same time.

These, then, are dangerous texts. Politically barren, they reproduce the very cultural conditions they seek to criticize. While superficially calling for a culture of resistance, they 'ARE pop culture' (Ebert, 1990a: 2). They contribute to the creation of 'a culture of indifference' (Connor, 1989: 181). Clearly Lynch's texts appeal to moviegoers and TV watchers who have grown sick of the entertainment they have become addicted to (Ebert, 1990a: 1).

However *Blue Velvet*'s (like Lynch's other productions) distance from and critique of the popular lies too deeply buried in the figural images (and sounds) which are erased by its happy ending. Failing to go all the way, Lynch's parody of small-town violence becomes a slap in the viewer's face. 'Don't stop the presses' (Ebert, 1989a: 85), who didn't know that 'beneath the surface of Small Town, USA, passions run high and dangerous?' (Ebert, 1989a: 85). Stopping short of where Bertolucci took the viewer in *Last Tango in Paris* (Ebert, 1989a: 85) Lynch merely titillates. To be seduced by such texts and to embrace them is not without risk, for just being different is not enough.

Notes

1. This chapter is a revised version of Denzin (1988)

2. *Blue Velvet* was, according to critics McGuigan and Huck (1986), the most talked-about American film in 1986. Lynch was nominated for an Academy Award as best director. The National Society of Film Critics named it the best film of 1986, and Lynch the best director. The award for best supporting actor went to Dennis Hopper, and Frederick Elmes was named the best cinematographer. The film contributed to Lynch's reputation as the most controversial of American film-makers. This view was further secured by his winning the Golden Palm Award, the highest honor at the 1990 Cannes International Film Festival, for his 1990 film *Wild At Heart*. Lynch's 1990 limited television series, *Twin Peaks*, which, like *Wild at Heart*, repeats themes found in *Blue Velvet*, has been renewed for the 1990–1 American television season. In 1990 *Twin Peaks* won three television prizes, including best dramatic series, best television actor for Kyle MacLachlan and best supporting television actress for Piper Laurie. Lynch's vision of postmodern life has found a home in American homes, where viewers fix a good cup of coffee and sit down with ice cream and fresh cherry pie to watch his series. For a repudiation of Lynch's views see Ebert (1990a). Lynch has become a postmodern commodity. Spin-offs from *Twin Peaks* now include T-shirts, and a *Twin Peaks* book, *The Secret Diary of Laura Palmer*, written by Lynch's daughter. Lynch is also now filming perfume commercials and has directed a 25-minute music video. He is scheduled to co-produce a documentary series for the Fox network.

3. *Astral*: Sent from the stars; the American woman revealed in the reflections sent from Hollywood stars.

4. Late in the film Lynch extends the meanings of blue to Frank's preference for Pabst Blue Ribbon beer.

5. Each of these texts uniquely disrupts, through time reversals, and pretend and real violence, the smooth surfaces of everyday middle-class life. They mock and spoof earlier film genres (*film noir*, comedy, family and/or Gothic melodrama, science fiction). Contending that 'anything goes' in today's world, but that certain things will no longer hold, they show a new generation of film-makers (e.g. the Cohen brothers, David Byrne, Jonathan Demme, Steven Soderbergh, Spike Lee, Atom Egoyan) and old (Francis Coppolla, Woody Allen) who are taking the postmodern scene seriously and attempting to make sense of it.

6. See Denzin (1989e, 1991, Ch. 1) for an elaboration of this method. I will contrast my interpretations to Lynch's meanings of his movie, which are themselves open-ended and inconclusive (see Chute, 1986; Rabkin, 1986).

7. That is pre-ERA, pre-pro-abortion, etc. In the reaffirmation of traditional gender stereotypes and identities for women, these texts (see Mellancamp, 1987) become conservative reflections of the traditional gender ideologies that circulated in America in the 1980s, and continue in the 1990s (see Hochschild, 1989).

8. These texts include *Newsweek, The New Yorker, The New York Times, New York, Christian Century, Dissent, Fangoria, National Review, Playboy* and the more specialized cinema text, *Film Comment.*

9. Gil Rodman (in conversation) disputes my use of the label of rock-'n-roll for the film's music. He suggests that the soundtrack is better described as mainstream, popular, 'crooning' music of the 1950s.

10. Lauro (1989: 10) elaborates the Hitchcock themes, seeing in Jeffrey's name a direct connection back to one of film history's best-known voyeurs, L.B. Jeffreys of *Rear Window.* Another Lynch twist is given in Dorothy's address, 'Lincoln Avenue.' Who is better associated with the 'word "Lincoln" . . . than a man named Booth?' [Frank's last name] (Lauro, 1989: 10). Of course Jeffrey kills Booth.

11. For the European video release of *Twin Peaks*'s two-hour première Lynch didn't use the pilot's cliffhanger: 'So he added 15 minutes footage; we needed a killer in an alternate ending for the pilot,' recalls Joan Chen, who plays the owner of Packard Sawmill (Carlson, 1990: 23). The show has now become quite popular in Europe.

6

Nouveau Capitalists on *Wall Street*[1]

'Money itself isn't lost or made, it's simply transferred from one perception to another. This painting here. I bought it 10 years ago for 60 thousand dollars. I could sell it today for 600. *The illusion has become real and the more real it becomes, the more desperately they want it.*' (Gordon Gekko, in *Wall Street*, 1987, italics added)

Reality no longer has the time to take on the appearance of reality; it captures every dream even before it takes on the appearance of a dream. (Baudrillard, 1983a: 152)

Another 'astral' Oedipal tale. Released on 3 December 1987, just 44 days after the worst day (19 October) in the history of the New York Stock Exchange (Glaberson, 1987: 1),[2] Oliver Stone's movie *Wall Street*,[3] set in 1985, portrays the heyday of Wall Street's frantically bullish market in 1985–6.[4] The villain in the story, Gordon Gekko,[5] is loosely modeled after real-life investor, arbitrager Ivan F. Boesky who was convicted of insider trading violations in late 1986. As the film begins, its protagonist, Bud Fox, the hero who falls, is employed as a broker in a second-tier Wall Street firm, yet yearns to make it to the big time. From a working-class family,[6] he sells his soul, so to speak, to become an employee of Gekko's. In the process he learns how to commit securities frauds and is easily persuaded to pass along illegally acquired information obtained from his father about the operations of 'Bluestar' airlines. These moves very quickly make him very rich, but lead to his arrest for conspiracy to commit securities fraud and for violating the insider trader's sanctions act; tricks he learned from Gekko. In the film's final scene he is taken to the courthouse by his father and mother, to whom he has repented and from whom he has sought, and received forgiveness.

Wall Street is a postmodern morality tale; according to many critics, a story of seduction, corruption, and redemption (Ebert, 1987: 21). A tale fitted to the actual doings of real-life people in America's premier capitalist marketplace. Interpreted as a 'radical critique of the capitalist trading mentality' by one film reviewer (Ebert, 1987: 21), the movie in fact is a conservative apologia for the very social structure it purports to critique. The following argument organizes my reading of this text.

On the surface the movie appears to be a hard-hitting, realistic treatment of a corrupt market structure, built on ethical contradictions in late-postmodern, multinational capitalism. However, contrary to appearances, the film resolves its ethical dilemmas in a traditional capitalist fashion. It aligns the forces of rugged individualism and family (Carl Fox, Bud's father), on the side of the young man who capitulated to the unethical, illegal desires of fraudulent commodity trading. It turns Bud's story into a moral fable and suggests that if your family stands behind you, and if you seek forgiveness, then all's well that ends well.

By failing to seriously interrogate the inner market structures that produce unethical commodity trading, and that fuel the desire for money and fame, the text leaves unexamined the ethical contradictions that lie at the heart of late market capitalism. In so doing the text narrativizes the fictional morality that underlies the late postmodern age. It resorts to the Oedipal logic of competing father figures, one evil, the other good, and resolves its tenuous ethical position through a nostalgia which returns the wayward son to the family hearth. It thus implements the primary cultural logics of the contemporary age.

A subversive reading of the film's text suggests that the stories Hollywood tells the members of the popular culture about the problems its capitalist social structures are having are just that, fictions. These tales have become valuable commodities in a nostalgic age that has lost its footing, morally and aesthetically, in a swirling system of avarice and greed which knows only one ethic, the profit motive. By keeping alive the myth of the repentant son who returns to the values of family and individualism, this film, and others like it,[7] creates for the members of the popular culture a sublimating fantasy structure which represses the 'real' destructive forces of a world economy gone wild and out of control.

In order to establish these points it will be necessary to examine in some detail how the film tells its story, which falls into three parts: the seduction of Bud, his corruption and fall, and his redemption. I will examine the various readings the film received by popular culture film critics, and then return to my subversive interpretation.

Seduction

Stone immediately plunges his viewer into the world of *Wall Street*. Frank Sinatra's 'Fly Me to the Moon,'[8] another astral signifier, is heard over opening credits, as a New York City skyline, filmed in grainy, muted orange and amber colors, emerges in the foreground, to slowly dissolve into close-up, hand-held camera shots of people jostling on Manhattan streets, crowded into elevators, shouting bids on the floor of the Stock Exchange, talking to clients with necks cupped against the telephone, eyes staring at the green screens of computer monitors, young brokers hawking clients for five minutes of their time while they explain the international debt market and the hope of a quick sale of a stock on the rise. Out of this jungle of voices and people, captured in an electronic world, emerges young Bud Fox, who has just been shorted on a deal. Turning to his young friend Marvin, he moans, 'American Express's got a hit man out looking for me. My dream is one day to be on the other end of that thing.' Along walks Lou, an old broker, 'Jesus you can't make a buck in this market . . . Too much cheap money sloshin' around the world . . .

Putney drug, you guys might want to take a look at. They got a good new drug. Stick to the fundamentals. That's how IBM and Hilton were built. Good things sometimes take time.' Marvin replies, 'The big game hunters bag the elephants, not guys like us. Gordon Gekko. Thirty seconds after the Challenger blew-up he's on the phone sellin' NASA stocks short.' Bud sings Gekko's praise: 'But 47 million he made on the milk order. 23 on the Imperial deal before he was 40. The guy makes 20 times what Dave Winfield makes in a year, and he talks to everybody.' Marvin: 'And he had an ethical by-pass at birth.'

This conversation sets the context for what is to come. Bud is on the make. Gekko is his hero. All that remains is for the two to meet. But first Bud's father, Carl, must be introduced. After work, the same day, at a local bar where the members of his father's airline union meet to drink, Bud and his father have the following conversation.

> Carl: Told ya not to get into the racket in the first place. Ya coulda been a doctor or a lawyer. If you'd started at 'Bluestar' you coulda been a supervisor by now, instead of bein' a salesman.
> Bud: I'm not a salesman. I'm an account executive.
> Carl: You get on the phone and ask strangers for money. Right? You're a salesman. I don't get it kid. You borrow money to go to NYU. Last year you made 50 grand and you still can't pay off your loans.
> Bud: 50 grand doesn't get you to first base in the Big Apple.
> Carl: Come back home and live rent free. Jesus Christ, 50 grand. The whole world's off its rocker. You know I made a total of $47,000 last year.
> Bud: There's no nobility in poverty anymore. One day you're gonna be proud of me.
> Carl: It's yourself you gotta be proud of Huckleberry. How much ya need?

Bud borrows $300. Carl then tells him of a forthcoming FAA (Federal Aviation Administration) announcement. Which will have a positive effect on 'Bluestar''s financial status.[9]

The conflict between father and son established, Gekko must make his entrance. Bud worms his way, (after calling for fifty-nine days in a row), into Gekko's ultramodern office, which is lined with original artworks by Jim Dine, Julian Schnabel, and Joan Miró. He gives him a box of Cuban cigars as a birthday present, and a tip on a 'hot stock.' Gekko rebuffs him, 'Tell me somethin' I don't know. It's my birthday. Surprise me.' Bud: '"Bluestar" Airlines.'[10] The next day Gekko calls Bud: 'I want you to buy 20,000 shares of "Bluestar"', Bud shouts, to Marvin, 'I just bagged the elephant.' The camera shifts to a shot of the Statue of Liberty.[11]

Playing handball with Gekko several days later, he is told: 'The most valuable commodity I know of is information.'[12] Bud, who has just lost $150,000 on a deal, pleads with Gordon: 'Give me another chance.' Gordon: 'You want another chance. Then you stop sendin' me information and you start getting me some.' The next day Gordon asks Bud to get him information on his rival, Sir Larry Wildman, a British broker. Bud replies, 'It's not exactly what I do. I could lose my license. If the FCC found out I could go to jail. That's inside information isn't it?' Gordon answers:

'You mean like when a father tells his son about a court ruling on an airline? Somebody hears I'm going to buy TELEDAR Paper and decides to buy some for himself. Is that what you mean? I'm afraid unless your father's on the board of directors of another company you and I are gonna have a very tough time doin' business together.'

Bud answers, 'What about hard work?' Gordon: 'What about it? You work hard. Bet you stayed up all night analyzing that dog shit stock you gave me, Uh. Where'd it get ya? My father. He worked like an elephant pushin' electrical supplies. He dropped dead at 49 with a heart attack and tax bills.'[13] Gordon drops Bud off. 'Nice meetin' you buddy.' Bud comes back to the limo, and knocks on the window. 'Alright Mr Gekko. [voice squeaks] you got me.'

Corruption and the Fall

The story moves quickly from this point. Bud is given Gordon's mistress, Darien.[14] He buys a $950,000 condo.[15] He is given a secret account in the Cayman Islands to pass Gordon's deals through. Gordon begins a takeover of TELDAR Enterprises. At a Board of Directors meeting he makes this speech:[16]

'The new law of evolution in corporate America seems to be the survival of the unfittest. Well in my book you either do it right or you get eliminated . . . . The point, ladies and gentlemen, is that greed, for lack of a better word, is good. Greed is right.[17] Thank you very much' [round of applause. Sinatra's voice begins singing, 'Let me fly you to the moon.']'[18]

Bud convinces Gordon to attempt to buy 'Bluestar' airlines. In a pivotal scene Carl and Gordon meet at Bud's new condo. Gordon makes his pitch for the takeover of 'Bluestar.'[19] Carl rejects it.[20] He states: 'Well, I guess if a man lives long enough he gets to see everything. What else you got in your bag of tricks Mr. Gekko? There came into Egypt a pharaoh who did not know . . . . The rich have been doin it to the poor since the beginning of time.'

The clash between Bud's two father figures is brought to a dramatic head in the following exchange between father and son.

Bud: Congratulations Dad. You just did a great job embarrassing me. Look, save the workers of the world unite speech for the next time. You are gonna get axed, just like Branniff, and if it isn't Gekko it's gonna be some other killer.
Carl: He's usin' you kid. He's got your prick in his back pocket, but you're too blind to see it.
Bud: No, what I see is a jealous old machinist who can't stand the fact that his son has become more successful than he has.

Redemption

In a crescendo of scenes the film moves to its conclusion. Gordon betrays Bud, Carl, and 'Bluestar,' immediately setting in motion plans to liquidate the entire firm. Learning of this, Bud goes to Gordon's rival, Sir Larry, and secures his commitment to buy the firm, which he does, leading Gordon to lose millions of dollars in a single day's trading on the floor of the Stock Exchange.[21] The day after the 'Bluestar' deal Bud is arrested by the SEC (Securities Exchange Council).[22] He and Gordon have a final, violent meeting in Central Park.[23]

> *Gordon*: How ya Buddy? . . . Ya sandbagged me on 'Bluestar'. I guess you think you taught the teacher a lesson that the tail can wag the dog . . . . You could have been one of the great ones Buddy. I look at you and I see myself. Why?
> *Bud*: I don't know. I guess I realized. [*wipes blood from face and hands*] I'm just Bud Fox. As much as I wanted to be Gordon Gekko, I'll always be Bud Fox. [*throws handkerchief on ground, walks away*]

Having rejected Gordon, it remains for Bud to be reunited with his father. The film's last scene provides this reunion. Bud, his father, and his mother are on the way to the Federal courthouse.

> *Carl*: You told the truth and gave the money back.
> *Mother*: You helped save the airline and the airline people are gonna remember you for it.
> *Carl*: That's right. If I were you I'd think about the job with 'Bluestar' that Wildman offered you.
> *Bud*: Dad, I'm goin' to jail and you know it.
> *Carl*: Ya, maybe that's the price, son. Its gonna be hard on ya, that's for sure, but maybe in some kind of screwed up way that's the best thing that coulda happened to ya. Create instead of living off the buying and selling of others.

Bud walks up the steps of the courthouse. A long camera shot pulls up to the courthouse, then the Manhattan skyline, then pans the Wall Street corridor; 'THE END' appears on the screen, with the following lines: 'Dedicated to Louis Stone, Stockbroker, 1910–85.'[24] A Talking Heads song, 'This Must Be the Place,' plays over the closing credits,[25] in stark contrast to Frank Sinatra's 'Fly Me to the Moon,' which opened the film.

The Critics Read the Film

Even before it was released, *Wall Street* was surrounded by a laudatory discourse that was apparently determined by two factors: Oliver Stone's reputation as one of Hollywood's new star directors and scriptwriters, and the subject matter of his new film.[26] Consider the following leads either to reviews of the film, or stories about it: '"Wall Street" takes aim at value system' (Ebert, 1987), 'A Season of Flash and Greed,' (*Time*, 1987b), 'Greed' (Canby, 1987), 'A Bull Market in Sin' (*Newsweek*, 1987), 'Wall Street's gutter ethics' (Newman, 1987), 'In the Trenches of Wall Street,' (*Time*, 1987a), 'Making *Wall Street* Look Like Wall Street' (Cowan, 1987), 'Oliver Stone Easing Out of Violence,' (Bennetts, 1987), 'Wall Street Reviews "Wall Street"' (Fabrikant, 1987), 'A View from the Trenches' (Rattner, 1987).

The subject matter could not have been more timely. Wall Street, the new battleground for yuppie America, and 'Reaganomics' were collapsing, and with the collapse a part of the new American dream was being shattered. History and fiction overlapped in the film, and if history was not passing judgement on what was happening on the American scene, Stone was. How did the critics read his production?

Go back to the leads for the reviews: 'A View from the Trenches,' 'A Bull Market in Sin,' 'Wall Street's gutter ethics,' and read the praise: 'A sensationally entertaining melodrama about greed and corruption in New York' (*New York Magazine*, 1987: 87), 'May not be a work of art, but it's . . . the most enjoyable movie of the year . . . . The psychology of seduction is appallingly convincing' (*New York Magazine*, 1987: 88),[27] 'An upscale morality tale' (Canby, 1987). But underneath these gritty, glittering headlines, the critics found fault, especially in the film's narrative and final moral position.[28] Canby (1987: C3) suggested that it would 'entertain achievers who don't want to lose touch with their moral centers, but still have it all.' *Newsweek* (1987: 78). 'Underneath the shiny, contemporary surface is a musty old Hollywood movie about good and evil, full of stock characters and clichés.' *Variety* (1987):

> Watching 'Wall Street' is about as wordy and dreary as reading the financial papers' accounts of the rise and fall of an Ivan Boesky-type . . . with one exception. Instead of editorializing about the evils of greed . . . it lectures, which is great as a case study in business school but wearisome as a film.

Quarreling with the film's praise for the superior morality of the working class, as given in Bud's last speech to Gekko, Sprinkler (1988: 365–6) argues that 'Herein lies the most acute flaw in Stone's conception . . . the plot finally revolves around a small allegory of class: honesty, fairness, and loyalty are working class values; ruthlessness, cunningness, and selfishness are the preserve of financiers.'

As might be expected, so-called Wall Street experts also reacted negatively to the film. Rattner (1987) argued that 'investment banking is tough, but not nearly as brutal as the film makes it . . . Airlines aren't bought and sold in an afternoon . . . the movie focuses on a distinctly small slice of the Street.'[29] This opinion was echoed by the 130 investment bankers and brokers who watched the film in a private showing, 'The people here do an honest day's work,' was one comment (Fabrikant, 1987: 5). Another broker stated, 'It is upsetting because it makes the excesses of Wall Street look like an everyday occurrence' (1987: 5), and still another suggested that the subject of the film was 'too foreign to be a hit elsewhere in the U.S. You have people on farms in Iowa going to movies. How can they relate to this?' (1987: 5). Finally, 'At the end the movie takes a stern but realistic line on the ethical questions it raises' (*New York Magazine*, 1987: 88), but, 'The movie crashes in a heap of platitudes that remind us that honesty is, after all, the best policy' (Canby, 1987: C3).

Back to the Story

Unnoticed in the seduction, corruption, redemption morality tale motif that structures many of the above reviews is the fact that the seduction occurred before the film began, that corruption was already present in Bud's workplace, and his redemption, signaled by the return to his father's values is under-motivated.[30] Listen again to Bud's first speech in the film: 'My dream is one day to be on the other end of the thing.' In his next speech he recites Gordon Gekko's accomplishments: 'The guy makes 20 times what Dave Winfield makes in a year.' He was seduced before the story began. He was already corrupt. He knew it and his father knew it, as did Marvin and Lou, and Gordon knew it the moment he set eyes on him. He had bought into the value system that Stone wishes to critique in his Boesky–Gekko character. Gordon neither seduced nor corrupted him, for he was a player waiting to become guilty, as soon as the circumstances permitted.

The narrative falters, then, from the very beginning. This being the case, Stone's morality tale never gets off the ground as it seeks to explain Bud's corruption by Gekko's effects. Despite his attempts to locate minor corruption in the workplace, what he never succeeds in establishing is how the broader social-historical moment itself created the conditions for Bud's fall. By never going outside the workplace, except to the pivotal conversations with Carl, Stone is left with a simplistic morality tale which espouses the virtues of hard work over easy money. In the very moment when it rushes forward to redeem Bud, in his final speech to Gordon, the film's simplicity and redundancy become most apparent.

As a result, the film is neither a 'radical critique of the capitalist trading mentality' (Ebert, 1987: 21), nor a telling fictional treatment of a passing moment in American history. But it is more than a conservative apologia for 'Wall Street.' It is a form of myth-making which absorbs into its very center the basic features of a postmodern world which threatens to destroy itself from within.[31] The postmodern moment not only commodifies information, as Gekko teaches Bud, but it commodifies time, individuals, lifestyles, status and prestige, and human feelings. This commodification process turns on the representations that are given to 'real' things. But since the real has become a commodity that is transformed into a thing with a market value, all that is purchased are the illusions of things and the money they cost. As Gekko notes, he creates nothing. He only buys and owns. What he buys are illusions. Money is the ultimate illusion for it signifies nothing but more money, and money no longer resides in a real world of signified things. It refers only to itself (see Simmel, 1978). There is only illusion.

Carl doesn't know this. His old time values reference a time that never will be, the time when people create, instead of living off the buying and selling of others. The film's closing nostalgic move, which inserts a false historical moment into the narrative, is pure ideology. Neither Stone nor his critics understood the structure he criticized; he wants, like they do, a time when things are real, have real value, and when real things reflect the real value of hard-working individuals. That time is gone.[32]

Gekko understands part of the new equation, the illusion part. What he hasn't grasped is the unreality of the things he owns, and the unreality of the process which produces the satisfactions he experiences when he buys, sells, and destroys. That is, Gekko is an ideological illusion, a commodity attached to a conservative Darwinian political belief system which holds that the strongest survive and the weakest die. In fact nothing in this system has any reality whatsoever, not even Gekko. In the endless chain of signifiers that money attaches itself to, persons become commodities who have no referent outside the chain of signification. They differ from one another only in terms of the signifiers they can attach to themselves, but the signifiers only sustain one illusion over another, nothing is permanent.

Carl, Gekko, Bud, and Oliver Stone believe in permanence. Stone's permanence, and the one he transferred to Bud and Carl, is old-fashioned American capitalism. And here is where the myth-making becomes so critical. As long as capitalism can sustain the illusion that there are two types of illusion, one moral, the other immoral, one permanent, the other not, it appears able to sustain the belief that everything is fine (see Marcuse, 1964; Baudrillard, 1975; Lash, 1988; Featherstone, 1988; B. Turner, 1987; Stauth and Turner, 1988). As long as there are Oliver Stones who can tell stories like *Wall Street*, nobody has anything to worry about. Don't worry about the simplistic morality tale he tells, don't worry about whether it will play in Iowa, or if he only describes a tiny slice of reality. All that matters is that there are people who know it won't play in Iowa, and these same people know that only a small number of traders really act like Gekko.

Such beliefs sustain the system and that is why this is an important film. Stone's myth turns attention away from the very structure that is no longer reachable, from the unimaginable; for if the world were really filled with Gordon Gekkos we would all be in trouble. But we are not in trouble because there are the Carl Foxs and the SEC out there and they will police this corrupt system and bring our wayward yuppies back into line.

What if there was no system to be brought back into? What if the illusion has become real, and there is only illusion? What if there is no fallback system? This is the ultimate terror that Stone pulls back from, but then he never saw it. What prevented him from seeing what he thought he saw? Go back to the two songs, Sinatra's 'Fly Me to the Moon,' and The Talking Heads', 'This Must Be the Place.' Compare the lines, the historical moments occupied by the singers, and the positioning of the two songs at the beginning and end of the film. Sinatra, the ultimate signifier of conservative, male, mainstream, middle-class American culture, croons the following words, 'Fly me to the moon . . . Let me play among the stars . . . please be true.' Stone intends these words to be more than a song about a man's love for a woman. They are applied directly to Bud. He wants to play among the stars, be a Gekko, a sixteenth-century Italian entrepreneur. He wants to live life on the other side. He worships money and power. He wants these things to be true and real. Stone wants the viewer to believe that Bud has found these things that he adores not to be true. In fact his text does not establish this, for what Bud learns is that Gekko is not true. There is no support in the film for the conclusion that Bud has rejected all that this thing called money can buy. He will probably accept the corporate position with 'Bluestar' that has been offered. He has simply reinserted himself into the very structure that Stone wants the viewer to think he has rejected.

The vehicle for that re-entry is the Talking Heads' song, with its lines 'Home is where I want to be . . . but I guess I'm already there . . . I'm just an animal looking for a home.' Home is where Bud is at the end of the film. Feeling numb, saying little about what has happened, he has plenty of time for now it's for love, not money. Having drifted in and out (away from home), he's back where he started, with mother and father. The prodigal son, like a tamed animal, has returned home.[33]

Consider the source of these lines. The Talking Heads are widely known as a subversive, 'leading avant garde, post punk, rock-'n-roll group, whose nihilistic images have recently turned to a more romantic celebration of love, community, family and the individual's place in the group.'[34] Yet the music of this group signifies a sound which is quite different from Sinatra's. Hip Stone has used radical rock to offer the final commentary in his critique of American capitalism. This is a surface, glossed reading. Underneath the message, from Sinatra to the Talking Heads, can be read as being equivalent. Both voices celebrate the same values: love and family. The paradox of Sinatra's lines lies only in the fact that Bud, at the end, returns to their original meaning. His journey through the film is simply an exploration of their alternative meaning, the one Stone gives them when he allows them to play over his opening shots of 'Wall Street.' Hence while the Heads' lines appear to offer a radical conclusion to a radical film, underneath they simply stitch together the opening and closing parts of the film into a tightly bound structure which is conservative from beginning to end.

Two problems remain. The first, how Stone created his subject called Bud Fox. The second, the multiple meanings contained in the phrase 'Wall Street.' After Althusser (1971: 171) it can be argued that the capitalist ideology Bud has accepted has constituted him, a concrete individual, as a subject who has been 'hailed by' or called to an ideological site where his subjectivity may be enacted. Stone suggests that he was corrupted by this site; a perfect ideological dupe, he fell into Gordon's trap, learned Gordon's voice and realized himself through the language and material wealth Gordon gave him.

In order for this argument to work the film must have a category of ideologically pure subjects who have not been contaminated by the 'greedy' side of capitalism. But where are they? Carl, the working-class hero, makes over $47,000 a year and believes that real men make real things with their hands, and don't live off the buying and selling of others. His airline buys and sells tickets, routes, and services. Lou, the other spokesperson for purity, gives hot tips on a good stock. Carl and Lou trade in information and commodities, just like Gordon. They are ideological dupes of another version of capitalism, that version Stone wants to maintain and valorize. Indeed their version of capitalism sustains the other version that Stone despises – Gekko's sharks who destroy in the name of greed. One version could not exist without the other. In the end the film is about a simplistic clash between two ideological versions of the same thing. Stone wants to destroy one version in the name of the other; in fact he ends up supporting both. It could have been no other way. Stone, as a concrete individual, has been constituted by 'his' popular culture as a subject who valorizes that culture while criticizing it. In so doing he used all of the ideological equipment the popular culture could make available to him, even up to and including the voices of Sinatra and the Talking Heads.

Now the metaphor 'Wall Street.' The words signify more than a place that points to the world's leading financial center. It points to the ethical doings that go on in that place, and there are two kinds of doings that happen there – ethical and unethical. These are the meanings Stone manipulates in his movie. But there is a third meaning, the one hinted at above, and the one that Stone refuses to touch. This is the meaning that says that 'Wall Street' is a purely imaginary ideological site, which has no concrete referent in the real world. This is the meaning that points to the political economy of signs, not money in the postmodern world (Baudrillard, 1975, 1981). In this political economy only signs, representations, and simulations of the real circulate. In fact this is the reality of 'Wall Street.' Go back to the floor of the Stock Exchange, and reexamine the green computer screens of the young brokers at Bud's firm. Numbers flashing across screens, numbers which can be erased with the touch of a finger, or a loud voice. Numbers which point to imaginary properties or imaginary things. Companies with made-up names, whose productivity is measured by imaginary numbers concerning losses and gains. Money going in and out of hidden accounts. Money attached to nothing but imaginary numbers attached to made-up accounts, built on the transactions and imagined doings of imaginary companies. Careers built on who can best manipulate this imaginary political economy of signs.

This is what 'Wall Street' is. A site where a political economy of signs ceaselessly circulates across an imaginary computerized space where nothing is any longer real. This 'cool universe of digitality has absorbed [and] won out over the reality principle' (Baudrillard, 1983a: 152). 'The illusion has become real and the more real it becomes, the more desperately they want it'.

This is the frightening world *Wall Street* refers to and this is the world Stone pretended to open up in his movie. This cool universe, unfeeling, imaginary, and 'real' in its peculiar, quaint, ideological way will destroy all of us, and when it does it will do so in the name of family, love, hard work, and honesty.[35] In the next chapter I take another look at crime and punishment in America, this time in Woody Allen's 1989 film *Crimes and Misdemeanors*.

Notes

1. This is a slightly altered version of Denzin (1990g).
2. The crash led to a serious reappraisal of the US's marketing system, assertions that the new computer technology was partly responsible for the crash, concerns about global securities markets, and debates over the structure that regulates such trading (see Glaberson, 1987: 20). *The New York Times* ran a five-part series on the 'Lessons of October 1987' (see Glaberson, 1987; Sterngold, 1987; Sanger, 1987; Lohr, 1987). In 1990 the same structure that Stone described in his film seems to be in place. All that has changed is the number of brokers who have been arrested for the kinds of violation detailed in the film.
3. Oliver Stone director, produced by Edward R. Pressman, screenplay by Stanley Weiser and Stone, released by 20th Century-Fox, starring Charlie Sheen (Bud Fox), Michael Douglas (Gordon Gekko), Martin Sheen (Carl Fox), Daryl Hannah (Darien Taylor), Terence Stamp (Sir Larry Wildman), Hal Holbrook (Lou Mannheim), Sean Young (Kate Gekko), John C. McGinley (Marvin), James Spader (Roger Barnes), Sylvia Miles (Realtor), running time 124 minutes, Oscar for Douglas, one of the top money-making films of the 1988 season, and a current top video rental.
4. The film takes its name from a place, Wall Street, a metaphor, and in recent years the place where America's ethical standards, 'or lack of them has been determined' (Newman, 1987). At the same time the real place, Wall Street, refers to a 'seven-block alley of skyscrapers on the seaward tip of Manhattan Island' (Newman, 1987). The movie *Wall Street* stands in this double relationship to a 'real' place and the doings that go on in that place. It captures the importance of money, class, morality, and mobility in the postmodern age, while it punctures the dreams that money can make happen. By collapsing reality and fantasy into a single commercial venture, which also incorporates Stone's own life story, the film opens a window into and dramatizes a version of contemporary postmodern life that is more read about than seen. It capitalizes on the viewer's voyeuristic desire to gaze into the worlds of the rich and the famous. Bud (see below), and his father, become, under this formulation, the viewer's *alter egos*, for they do the gazing, and their reactions become ours.
5. A *gecko* is a lizard that feeds on insects and sheds its tail when trapped. Ivan Boesky was convicted of conspiring to file false documents with the federal government. The case in question involved insider trader violations, connected to Boesky's trading of junk bonds with Drexel Burnham Lambert Inc. In 1985 Boesky won the top money-making award on Wall Street ($100 million earnings). His former aide, Michael Milken, was convicted of similar violations in 1988. As part of a sentencing agreement Boesky was granted immunity from federal criminal prosecutors, as was Milken (see *Wall Street Journal*, 1987).
6. His father is an airline mechanic and the leader of the local union at 'Bluestar' airlines.
7. Other films, also in 1987, which stress the values of family, individualism, and work, include *Moonstruck*, *Fatal Attraction*, *Broadcast News*, *The Untouchables*, *Lethal Weapon*, *Stakeout*, *The Secret of My Success*, *Tin Men*; in 1988, *The Accidental Tourist*, *Everybody's All American*, *The Boost*, *Dominick and Eugene*, *Running On Empty*; in 1989, *Field of Dreams*, *Rainman*, *Beaches*, *Shirley Valentine*, *When Harry Met Sally*, *Indiana Jones and the Last Crusade*, *Driving Miss Daisy*, *sex, lies and videotape*, *Crimes and Misdemeanors*, and (problematically) *Do the Right Thing*. These themes are continued in the summer of 1990 with films like *Back to the Future: Part III*, *Bird on a Wire*, *Pretty Woman*, *Cadillac*

Man, and challenged with *The Cook, the Thief, His Wife and Her Lover*.

8. 'Fly me to the moon. Let me play among the stars. Let me see what spring is like on Jupiter and Mars.'

9. A crash a year earlier was caused by manufacturer's error. The ruling will allow the company to go for new airline routes. Bud asks, 'You sure about this announcement?' Carl, 'You got that mischievous look in your eye.'

10. He then gives him the information he had earlier gained from his father about the forthcoming FAA decision.

11. In the next scene Bud and Gordon are in a restaurant. Gordon gives him a check for one million dollars, 'That should cover that "Bluestar" buy. Put a coupla 100 thou on those bow wow stocks you mentioned . . . and buy a decent suit. Put the rest of the money in a tax-free fund. I wanta see how you do before I invest in ya.'

12. Gordon offers his theory of how the market works in the following lines. 'The public's out there throwin' darts at boards sport. I bet on sure things . . . It's trench warfare out there pal.'

13. Several scenes later, in a move which aligns Bud's father with Gordon's father, Carl has a heart attack.

14. Gordon's view of love is given in the following lines. He and Darien are walking along Wall Street. 'You and I are the same, Darien. We are smart enough not to buy into the oldest myth runnin', love. A fiction created by people to keep 'em from jumpin' out of windows.' As he rejects this myth Gordon fails to escape the even longer-running myth of Oedipus, which is simply shored up by love. He confuses the symptom with the cause.

15. Looking out at Manhattan, from his balcony, after having just left Darien in his mammoth bed, he asks, 'Who am I?'

16. He begins his speech with the following lines, which reflect the film's attempts to be historical, radical, and chic at the same time: 'Ladies and gentlemen. We are not out here to indulge in fantasy, but in political and economic reality.'

17. In a speech to a group of business students in 1985 Boesky stated, 'Greed is right, by the way. I think greed is healthy. You can be greedy and still feel good about yourself' (Glaberson, 1987: 20).

18. Moved by this speech, and now working day and night, Bud announces to Darien, who has just complained that she is going psychotic, from a lack of REM sleep, that 'You think I'm gonna broker for the rest of my life? . . . I'm gonna be an entrepreneur in the Italian 16th century sense of the word.' Darien, as if in an attempt to top Bud, later describes her goals in these words, 'I'd like to do for interiors what Laura Ashley did for interior fabric. Produce a line of high quality antiques at a low price.' Despite its glossy, surface representations of successful women, the film really takes a traditional, anti-feminist stance on women, work, and their relations with men. Darien, after all, is Gekko's mistress, and achieved everything she has through his material wealth and her sexuality. James W. Carey underscored this point for me.

19. 'You've got a loss of 20 million dollars, dividends cut to zero, and you're bein' squeezed dead by the majors.'

20. In his rejection he also repudiates the new voice Bud has acquired; the voice of Gekko.

21. As this occurs Carl has his heart attack. Bud makes up with him in the hospital room and in the process relinquishes Gekko's voice and takes back Carl's.

22. In a degradation ceremony he is led in handcuffs out of the office, through a long gauntlet-like corridor of onlooking co-workers.

23. In this penultimate scene, he wears a 'wire.' Afterwards he is told by federal agents that, 'You did the right thing, Bud.'

24. Stone's father, a retail stockbroker and conservative Goldwater Republican, who left his son with the following dictates, 'Love justice, Do Mercy, Walk humbly with thy God' (*Vogue*, 1987: 172).

25. 'Pick me up and turn me around, guess I must be havin' fun . . . Hi ho, we drift in and out. I'm just an animal looking for a home.'

26. He had won Academy Awards in 1987 for writing and directing *Platoon*, and in 1985 he had received critical acclaim for *Salvador* (*Vogue*, 1987: 166). Even before the film was released it was common knowledge that Stone was going for realism. He employed stockbrokers as advisors (Cowan, 1987: 16), privately screened the film for Wall Street luminaries (Fabrikant, 1987), consulted with brokers over the lines he wrote, had Charlie Sheen spend two days with David Brown, a former Goldman Sachs trader who pleaded guilty to insider trading in 1986 (*Time*, 1987a: 76–7), trotted out 'real' Manhattan characters like James Rosenquist, and Richard Feigen (Canby, 1987), and consulted with novelists Joseph Heller and Kurt Vonnegut on his characters and the words they spoke (Cowan, 1987).

27. This same reviewer, in discussing Stone's morality play, invoked the earlier Hollywood production, *Sweet Smell of Success* (1957), which also exposed the evils of power and the seduction of the pure.

28. Even though the narrative was perceived as flawed, reviewers praised the performances of Douglas and the two Sheens.

29. In addition, Rattner, managing director at Morgan Stanley & Co., compared the film to Tom Wolfe's *Bonfire of the Vanities* (also made into a 1990 film, directed by Brian De Palma), which 'in a single phrase – Masters of the Universe – defined the investment mentality as aptly as all 125 minutes of "Wall Street"' (Rattner, 1987: 80), and Sprinkler (1988: 367) suggested that the viewer interested in the psychology of Wall Street read Matthew Josephson's 'unparalleled classic about nineteenth century capitalism. *The Robber Barons* (1934). One will quickly see that nothing much has changed on the street from that day to this.'

30. I thank Katherine Ryan-Denzin for pointing this out to me. There is little that indicates why Bud would suddenly capitulate to his father's value system.

31. Human experience gets lost in the endless swirl of signifiers, which signify nothing but themselves. Bud had to leave that world in order to be saved. Gekko remained inside it and was (presumably) destroyed by it.

32. As Baudrillard (1983a: 22) observes (quoted p. 83) 'Reality no longer has the time to take on the appearance of reality.' The same time, the historical markers of 'reality's' transformations, have been disconnected from the world of the living, turned into instantaneous memories without a past (Baudrillard, 1988a: 22). The media's signified representations of the past (e.g. cold war clips from the Berlin Wall) lack referentiality in contemporary lives. Nostalgia, which reenacts a purified past, established that sense of presence which has no presence (see the discussion in Ch. 8 of the forms of nostalgia that circulate in the postmodern moment).

33. The animal theme is prominent throughout the film's text, including the Darwinian, evolutionary theory of greed, the elephant metaphor, and Gekko's recurrent use of the word dog to characterize certain kinds of stock. Gekko's profane excretory phrases are closely connected to the animalistic metaphors. They contribute to the general impression that Gekko, a profane, dirty being, is outside society. In bringing Bud home the film retains its conservative commitment to family as the ultimate site of pure subjectivity, identity, and meaning.

34. Lawrence Grossberg, in conversation, 2 August 1989.

35. Compare here the recent HUD (Housing and Urban Development) scandal, where a new group of 'immoral' capitalists succeeded in manipulating the housing market in a way that excluded real people from real homes (see Gerth, 1989).

7

Crimes and Misdemeanors in Manhattan

Moral precepts from *Crimes and Misdemeanors*:

'You have to confess your wrongs and seek forgiveness. Life is a moral structure, there is a higher power.' (Ben the Rabbi)

'The Eyes of God see all.' (Old Rabbi)

'If he can do it [murder] and chooses not to be bothered by the ethics, he's home free.' (Judah's aunt)

'In one way or another he will be punished.' (Judah's father)

'One sin leads to another.' (Judah)

'When we fall in love we are seeking to find the people we were attached to in childhood.' (Professor Levy)

'We define ourselves by the choices we make. We have within us the ability to give love [and] that gives meaning to the indifferent universe.' (Professor Levy)

Crimes and Misdemeanors (1989) is a story of love, death, sin, guilt, and betrayal in upper-middle-class America.[1] A counterpart to *Wall Street*, it takes a wholly different approach to crime and its punishment in contemporary America. In unraveling its text, I intend to show how Woody Allen offers a moralistic tale which challenges, while it complements, the world view of Gordon Gekko, and the crass morality which operates as one of the cultural logics of late capitalism. Allen's main character (Judah Rosenthal) murders his mistress (Dolores), gets away with it, suffers a small amount of guilt (the banality of evil), and in the end finds pleasure and love with his wife (Miriam). His crime becomes a misdemeanor requiring only a small punishment.

Woody Allen is postmodern America's cinematic moralist.[2] His comedic, yet serious texts are directed to a literate, upper-middle-class audience who take pleasure in hearing and seeing the names and phrases of Marshall McLuhan, Humphrey Bogart, Donald Trump, Freud, Sartre, and Nietszche bandied around by Allen or one of his characters. His men and women suffer failed careers, are blacklisted, wrestle with life after divorce, attempt to integrate family with work, worry about the meaning of the universe, are haunted by mother (and father) figures, have affairs, make huge amounts of money, confront corrupt political regimes, live through the depression, rob banks, attempt to make sense of modern science, medicine, psychiatry, and psychoanalysis and live in a version of New York City that only the rich can ever experience.

The above themes, always filtered through the existential problems of sexuality, love, death wishes (and anxieties) are the recurring issues Allen has explored in recent (and not so recent) films.[3] These topics are inevitably treated within a cinematic system which reflexively calls attention to the place of movies in American life. Allen's films are marked by the use of scenes (also music and soundtracks) from old news clips, documentaries, and neglected (and classic) Hollywood films. These scenes, clips, and songs are typically viewed and heard by Allen's character as he sits in a movie theater, with a girlfriend, ex-lover, or a child. They are used as framing devices to underscore a point Allen is attempting to make in the larger narrative that drives the story (being seen, being guilty in the eyes of another and so on). Casting himself as the cinematic voyeur of his own films (and life), often paired with his current love (Mia Farrow, Diane Keaton), Allen frequently plays the part of a film-maker, a screenwriter, or a film editor. A lover of old movies, he can only read his life through the texts Hollywood has produced. In making himself the moral center of his films, Allen the voyeur invites the viewer to look over his shoulder, share his gaze (and moral vision) and with him, engage contemporary life through the cinematic eye, memories, clips, songs, and music of a time gone by. A positive nostalgia drives Allen's films. The present can only be understood by seeing it through the eyes (and films) of the past.

Underneath it all a single complex theme is constantly explored. Played over and over again, it is Oedipus and his many myths who move Allen. The weak, neurotic, Jewish male intellectual (every literate male) and his sexual plight are examined within an existential framework which places the burden of decisions on man himself (seldom woman). These questions turn on moral choices, the meaning of life, the presence of a God, the power of mother and father figures and the inability of contemporary man to find a woman who will be an ideal sexual object, who satisfies mother and serves as her replacement.

Judah's Crime [and] Punishment

Crimes and Misdemeanors is a story of the eye (I), of vision, the gaze, the look, of seeing and being seen. Like Stone (who perhaps borrowed from him, but unlike Lynch, who used the ear as his opening into the postmodern), Allen's protagonist(s) (Judah Rosenthal, Cliff Stern) see their fate before they hear it. Each works in a visual field. Cliff is an unsuccessful film-maker. Judah is an ophthalmologist. Each makes his livelihood looking, either into other people's eyes, or using the camera as an eye into the lives of others. The narrative is complex, involving two interrelated but seldom connecting stories. The first, the one which allows Allen to make 'Crime' part of his title, involves Judah Rosenthal, a rich, famous, highly successful Manhattan ophthalmologist. Judah is married to strikingly beautiful Miriam, but has been involved, for the past two years, in an affair with Dolores Paley, a hysterical, ex-airline stewardess, who, as the film begins, announces that she wants to tell Miriam about their affair. Feeling neglected, sensing that Judah is about to end their relationship, Dolores sends letters to Judah's home, calls him at all hours, demands to see him, and threatens to tell Miriam, not only about their affair, but also about his management of large philanthropic funds intended for the establishment of a new 'eye' wing at his hospital. Unable to sleep, driven near crazy by Dolores, Judah confides in his friend Ben, a rabbi who is going blind, that he has been having an affair with another woman. Ben urges him to confess all to Miriam, to seek her forgiveness, and to bring his life in line with the moral structures of the universe which is guided by a higher power. Judah cannot accept Ben's advice and turns to his brother Jack, a questionable character with mob contacts. Jack assures him that the problem can be easily taken care of, telling Judah that he must confront reality: 'You have a problem, take care of it.' Judah finally agrees, and Jack has Dolores killed in her apartment.

The crime committed, Judah now begins to feel guilt. He rushes to Dolores's apartment and stares at her dead body. Her open eyes gaze up at him. Drinking heavily, close to confessing, fighting constantly with Miriam, who tells him that 'the eyes are the window to the soul,' he returns to blind Ben and tells him the problem has gone away. Still unsettled, Judah visits the family home and relives a scene with his father, aunt, and mother, where his father tells him that murderers will be punished. A detective comes to see him. Near hysteria, he turns to Jack who tells him to forget the event and go back to his happy, successful life. Within days Judah begins to feel fine again, and, at the end of the film joyfully embraces Miriam, after having told Cliff a fictional version of his story. Judah's conflicts over the murder, and his sense that God has witnessed his crime is underscored by several cinematic devices, including film clips from Hitchcock's *Mr and Mrs Smith* (1941), *The Last Gangster* (1937), *This Gun for Hire* (1942), *Frances The Talking Mule* (1950), shots from Mussolini's filmed speeches, and songs that focus upon seeing and knowing: 'I'll Be Seeing You,' 'I'll See You Again,' 'Star Eyes,' 'I Know That You Know.'

The second storyline involves Cliff and the misdemeanors of the people (including Cliff's) who surround him. Cliff is unhappily married to Wendy, who teaches Emily Dickinson 'to a bunch of upper-middle class crack addicts' (Cliff: 'We haven't had sex in a year, I remember the date clearly, April 23, Hitler's birthday!') He is unsuccessful in his career as a documentary film-maker. His film on leukemia won a prize (a bottle of champagne) at a French film festival. He is currently busily involved recording the words and life of Professor Louis Levy, a Jewish philosopher who commits suicide at the end of the film ('I see a loving God who cares and demands that you behave morally,' 'We need love to stay in life,' 'the universe is a cold place,' 'I've gone out the window.'). At a cocktail party given for Lester (Ben and Wendy's brother), a wildly successful, mindless, manic, pompous producer of situation comedies ('If it bends it's comedy, if it breaks it isn't comedy;' 'Oedipus is funny. Who did this horrible thing to our city? Oh my God, it's me!'), Cliff meets and falls in love with Halley. She has a law degree from Columbia. A fledgling producer herself, she is recently divorced. Her weakness is 'Going to the movies in the day time.' She watches part of his documentary on Professor Levy and promises to get him a spot on public TV. Lester hires Cliff to do a documentary on his life, for a TV series on 'The Creative Mind.' Cliff despises Lester and all he stands for and is soon fired. (Halley: 'He is a phenomenon of our time.' Cliff: 'So is acid rain.') Lester steals Halley away from Cliff (she returns his love letters which he had plagiarized from James Joyce), leaving him estranged from Wendy ('Once sex goes, it all goes,' 'The last time I was inside a woman, it was the Statue of Liberty') and having to deal with the suicide of Professor Levy ('A major intellectual is gone.').

The film's final sequence of scenes joins Cliff and Judah. They have attended a Jewish wedding. Cliff, sitting by himself on a piano bench, drinking and mourning the loss of Halley, looks up to see Judah: 'Off by your self.' Cliff: 'I was planning the perfect murder' [Lester]. Judah:

> 'I have a great murder story, a great plot. There's this man, has everything, and after the awful deed is done, he is plagued by guilt. A spark of his religious background which he'd rejected comes back. He imagines that God is watching him, that this is a just and moral universe and he's violated it. He's an inch away from confessing. But one morning he awakens, the sun is shining, his family is around him. Mysteriously his crisis is lifted. He takes his family on a vacation to Europe and finds he is not punished. He prospers. The killing is attributed to a drifter. Now he is scot free. He goes back to his protected world of wealth and privilege.'

Cliff: 'Can he go back, really?' Judah: 'People carry sins around. Once in a while he has a bad moment, in time it all fades.' Cliff: 'Tough to live with that.' Judah: 'People carry terrible things around with them. This is reality. In reality we rationalize, we deny, or we couldn't go on living.' Cliff: 'Here's what I'd have him do. Turn himself in. Then the story has tragic proportions, because in the absence of a god he is forced to assume that responsibility himself, then you have tragedy.' Judah: 'But that's fiction. That's movies. I'm talking about reality. If you want a happy ending go see a Hollywood movie.'

The film ends with this dialogue. A voice-over from Professor Levy is heard ('We are all facing our lives, making moral choices, some are on a grand scale, others on a lesser scale. We are the sum total of the choices we make. Most human beings find joy from simple things, like their family, their work'), as blind rabbi Ben dances with his daughter, the new bride. A series of flashbacks repeats the significant encounters between each of the main characters and are connected to Levy's words (Lester and Halley, Judah and Dolores, Jack and Judah and so on). Dixieland jazz music (another Allen signifier) plays over the credits.

The Visual Logic of *Crimes and Misdemeanors*

The film was praised by critics as a memorable companion piece to *Hannah and Her Sisters* (Canby, 1989). While Allen was called the most rigorous and ambitious cinematic moralist of his time (Maslin, 1989), and compared to Ingmar Bergman (Sterritt, 1989a) in his treatment of philosophical issues, Howe (1989) labeled the film 'a soap-operatic dramedy [with] an undigested chunk of *Crime and Punishment* stuck in its gut . . . you may not care to sit through 90 minutes . . . to get to Allen's handwringing, midlife-crisis message that life in this modern world is meaningless without a Moral Center' (for views similar to Howe's see Hinson, 1989, and Salamon, 1989a). Maslin (1989) saw the film as indicative of a recent moral turn in Hollywood and read it in conjunction with *Sea of Love, sex, lies and videotape*, and *Do the Right Thing*. A symposium on the film in the *New York Times* (1989d) offered views which ranged from, 'Standard modernist fare . . . . What Woody Allen gives us . . . is the perspective of a man who wants to believe but cannot bring himself to do so – seemingly the plight among contemporary intellectuals,' to: 'Allen's response to post-liberal disillusionment is at least positive [and his] footage displays the truth of faith,' and the claim that the ambiguous ending avoids the key moral issues, 'by using love to disguise ethical analysis.'

Crimes and Misdemeanors is a moral parable for the postmodern age. It keeps alive the classic Jewish taboos of adultery, murder, and idolatry of self. It relives the Holocaust, and even has one character (Judah's aunt) argue that there is no morality: 'Morality is a ritual, a habit.' In this version the crimes of the Nazis can be read as either misdemeanors, or as events that were misunderstood. The film's versions of God, guilt, and moral choice move between three extremes: an all-seeing, punishing God (Judah's father); the all-seeing, forgiving God (Ben); and existential man who has no God (Professor Levy: 'We make our own choices'). Its crimes are big (murder) and its misdemeanors small (vanity, pride). Both are registered, felt, and judged by moral and amoral men and women, even as Judah's crime is transformed, at the end, into a minor irritation, a misdemeanor, a mistake which causes fleeting guilt. Indeed those who commit the big crimes are rewarded, and unpunished. Judah experiences a restoration of marital happiness. Dolores is not even a bad memory. Those who do the misdemeanors or have misfortune fall on them are punished. Ben goes blind and Cliff suffers innumerable sexual professional, and marital humiliations. Lester gets the beautiful woman.

In these gestures Allen appears to be arguing that the world is indifferent to our actions. His film, while addressing the key question of how one lives with dignity in such a world, deconstructs and denies the very answers it appears to endorse. There is no justice, no distinction between the wicked and the righteous. There is no all-seeing God who sees to it that justice is done. Nor is there a God who forgives men and women for their sins. Those men and women (the existentialists) who forge their own morality and seek love and meaning in their everyday affairs are manipulated, destroyed, and humiliated by the self-righteous moralists in the world (the Lesters and the Judahs).

Two versions of the postmodern person and self thus emerge . . . there are those, like Judah, who can argue that 'I want what's best for everyone' and mean quite the opposite (Maslin, 1989: 25). Such persons can contemplate murder while wailing about the injustices done to them. Judah, as postmodern amoral moralist, can, at the same time, deal with the news of a murder and discuss the virtues of France versus Switzerland and Italy as vacation sites. In a single breath he can say he believes in God, argue that one sin leads to another, and tell Cliff that he feels no regret about a murder. Judah, 'like the lovestruck philanderer played by Michael Caine in *Hannah and Her Sisters*, guides himself by several different moral codes simultaneously. [He] can lie as smoothly to himself as he does to others, and never register any real problem' (Maslin, 1989: 25).

Not unique, of course, to the postmodern period, this type of individual is not completely unlike the Gordon Gekkos of the world; those immoral capitalists who have not fallen for the longest-running myth called love and family. Judah may think he believes in love, but he only believes in himself. In his self-righteousness he justifies anything that brings pleasure. Lester is his twin, a self-centered egotist, who differs only in that his head is not filled with moral abstractions concerning God, guilt, and justice. In Allen's world these are the people who get ahead. (Even minor characters, like the stockbroker doing time for stock fraud, is held up as a marriage partner to an attractive woman in the film.)

Allen's other postmodern figure is given, of course, in the characters of Cliff Stern, Ben, and Professor Levy. These people worry about justice, tragedy, meaning, and truth. They ponder the universe's mysteries, seek love, and commit misdemeanors (proposed adultery) and crimes (against God – suicide), and pay the ultimate penalty for being feeling, thinking, moral individuals who either go blind, take their own lives, or sit alone, punished by those who do not hold to their moral code.

In Allen's existential world, where moral issues matter, the sufferers are the good people. Evil is a guise for banality, not the monstrous, and love is the answer to life's perplexing questions. God is in the eye of the beholder, and, as Judah's aunt notes, 'if the Nazis had won, a different version of history would have been written.' 'Reality' is the world-out-there where 'God is a luxury,' and people like Judah, according to Jack, 'own four acres of land, have rich friends, belong to the country club, and the kingdom of God is simply a way to avoid the real world.'

The film fails to answer its big questions: 'Is there a moral order? Does God exist? Is the universe meaningful?' Since the bad men (Judah and Lester) and at least one of the good men (Ben) are happy, moral judgements are rendered irrelevant at the end. The viewer is left with competing visual pictures: morose, bewildered, betrayed Cliff, on the one hand, and the fulfilled, blind Ben dancing with his daughter, on the other. This ambiguous conclusion suggests that love and sentimentality are all that matter. More deeply, Allen seems to be saying that even asking the big questions is pointless, 'for they have no answers' (*New York Times*, 1989c).

But is this his message? Clearly Allen is bedeviled with moral questions and he sees in the characters of Lester and Judah archetypes of hedonistic, postmodern (and modern) individuals who have no inner moral center, or compass. He wants to argue, it appears, that the real moralists are the little people, the Cliff Sterns (and Professor Levys) the people who can sternly meet life's failures and keep their heads up. These are the people who nostalgically and wistfully believe in the values of the past, in the longest-running myths, and their cinematic reincarnations in Hollywood movies. Cynicism, self-doubt, angst, anxiety, rejection, and fear are the emotional attitudes that structure the lives of these people. Unhappy lovers, matched always with aggressive or fickle women, his men experience sexual failure as a symptom of a larger impotence; the inability to find pleasure in and establish a place for oneself in an immoral world. As Lyman (1990: 3) observes, Allen's men (and women) suffer from 'anhedonia,' the technical psychoanalytic term which refers to a 'pathological condition wherein an individual is unable to experience pleasure.' Allen had considered entitling his film *Annie Hall* (1977), anhedonia: 'by that he meant to indicate not a pathology, but rather [post] modern, urban humankind's helplessness in the face of unsatisfied love, unstoppable aging, and the undeniability of death' (Lyman, 1990: 3). Cliff Stern endures 'anhedonia.'

This condition makes him a voyeur. Impotent in his own life, he vicariously finds pleasures in the fulfillment of the scopophilic (pleasure from seeing) impulse. Allen's heroes are anhedonic scopophilics. Cinematic, and everyday, voyeurs, like Narcissus, gaze at themselves through the eyes of others. Never fulfilled in love, unable to understand sexuality (Cliff: 'Human sexuality is so mysterious, which is good, you know, in a way') haunted by Oedipal figures, attracted more to children (who understand), than to adults, the Allen male suffers his fate wistfully, like a child lost in the postmodern forest. This romantic misfit, who has the admirable qualities of professional integrity and personal sincerity *is* postmodern man. He has bought into the culture's myths, believes and values them, and over and over again finds that they are unattainable in today's world.

Woody Allen and C. Wright Mills

Here is Allen's postmodern message, and here is where he differs from Oliver Stone, David Lynch, Jean Baudrillard, Jean Lyotard, and Fredric Jameson. Like C. Wright Mills he wants to write (film) and read (gaze at) the postmodern epoch. He wants to examine the kinds of men, women, and children this cultural moment has produced. He wants to examine how the modernist (and ancient) cultural myths concerning family, love, honor, sexuality, guilt, morality, greed, God, and meaning have worked their ways into contemporary life. For him there are no simplistic answers. The wayward son (Stone's Bud) cannot simply return to family, for its codes are not clear cut. His world is more complex than Stones's black-and-white universe where they are either greedy, immoral people (Gordon, Darien), or rock-solid, conservative moralists (Carl). Furthermore, his moralists who fall and sin feel no, or only minimal guilt, unlike Stone's Bud, who is brought back into line in part because of the punishment he has received for his crime. Stone's immoral capitalists scarcely define their crimes as misdemeanors, for in their mind everybody is doing the same thing, so it isn't a crime to cheat others, and so on.

Allen's characters know Baudrillard's hyperreality. They produce it, live in it, value it, know the world through it. It is more real than reality, and it contains the truths they value. Understanding that the world of the 'real' does not match up with the hyperreal cinematic world, Allen's male voyeurs find solace in cinema's comforting, nostalgic images of the past where men were men, women were women, and codes of honor really existed. Cultural romantics, historical-nostalgic conservatives, their cynicism leads to a nihilistic fatalism always tempered with a sense of comedy and the absurd. Their good projects always fail. Anhedonia triumphs. But this does not produce a helplessness that leads to inaction. Allen's men rise up, again and again. Inspired, always by those old movies, they take on the world once more, believing that this time the myths will work.

Lyotard's incredulity toward metanarratives does not define the postmodern for these men and women. Psychoanalysis, Marxism, existentialism, and humanism are all alive, not doing well, but alive nonetheless. As these myths work their ways into the lives of ordinary people, (Ben, Halley, Cliff Stern) they become connected to epiphanal moments of experience. A depth of emotionality, which Jameson claims is missing from the current scene, is thereby produced. Even Allen's shallow characters (Judah, Lester) feel pain and joy. No depthlessness of emotionality, or waning of affect here. Contrary to Jameson (1984b: 63), alienation and anxiety are everywhere present. Allen's postmodern individual does have a self present to do the feeling. His or her intensities are not free-floating and impersonal, as Jameson (1984b: 64) argues. There are no 'really' wildly erotic women out there for Allen's men, like there are for Lynch's Jeffrey, or Stone's Bud, to find sexual pleasures with. The women Allen's men find aren't sure they want to go to bed; and the really wild ones exist only in the imagination anyway. Nor do Allen's characters live in squalid urban environments which are impossible to map. His urban space is not the one Jameson (1984b: 76) sees. However utopian, Allen's Manhattan is a world that some people

(Gordon, Bud, Cliff, Lester, Judah) do inhabit, if only in their fantasies.

Allen's people, like Mills's little people, are caught up in the problems of making sense of families which are collapsing, marriages which do not work, jobs which are unfulfilling, and careers which won't permit a merger of work with family life. They are fearful of robots displacing them in the workplace, often suffer from an interminable psychoanalysis which never seems to work, and have friends and relatives who are drug addicts and alcoholics. They see corrupt political regimes and wonder how to change them. They understand deceit and fraud, fakes and forgeries, but seek the truth. These characters are baffled by the cultural logics of late capitalism. They can't understand meaning systems that reward the greedy and punish the faithful.

Allen's Cinematic Solution to the Postmodern Condition
Here Allen turns back on Stone and Lynch. His cinematic impulse cuts in two directions at the same time. It exposes, without mocking or flaunting, the myths of psychoanalysis (it never works) and capitalism (it rewards greed). At the same time it takes a deadly serious view of family. He sees in family structures unresolved conflicts between fathers and sons (Judah and his father), mothers and daughters (*Hannah and Her Sisters*), mothers and sons (*Oedipus Wrecks*) sisters and sisters (Hannah again), brothers and brothers (Jack and Judah), brothers and sisters (Lester and Wendy). Family, Allen's (and society's) most primordial of social structures, is a site of inevitable conflict, tension, and dispute. It is not a safe harbor from society's ills for the wayward son or daughter.

The moral visions of right and wrong that a son or daughter acquires in the family always come in conflict, for Allen, with the cultural logics that work in the 'real' world. Here corruption and fraud, mindless, successful idiots, fickle women, and knowing little children abound. The world outside family is as sick as the world inside the family, only in a different way. This is why Allen's males are always seeking a new family or woman. The one they've just left didn't work and the one they were born into doesn't work either. Hence they have only one recourse, the one embodied in the cultural myths kept alive in Hollywood's fictions. This dream factory is all we have left. It must not be mocked. It is society's most sacred of social institutions. Inside its fairy tales the myths always work out. (This is why Halley and Cliff are addicted to going to the movies in the daytime. Some people need help to make it through the day.) And, in the working out of the myths, in a cinematic way, these old movies tell us that deep down we are good, for only good people would be watching these old movies.

Here, inside these movies we are safe. We are protected voyeurs. Our natural place in postmodern society is in the theater, lights out, popcorn in hand, lover at our side. No one will mock or challenge us, or dispute our interpretations. Here we can look to our heart's desire. It doesn't matter if these looks won't carry over into the real world. We know they never will. They can't because real people are imperfect. Knowing this, we can escape, at a moment's notice, back into the fantasies the movies give us. Here is where truth resides. Allen's solution to the postmodern situation is purely cinematic. Like the unconscious of a psychoanalytic dream, my real world is dreamlike. This is how it should be. The real world is too much to take, for long stretches of time, anyway.

Wit and fantasy are Allen's vehicles for survival in a chaotic, hostile world. His characters mourn the loss of meaning in their own lives. They experience anhedonia; always ready with a joke, they turn back on their circumstances with laughter. In puns and jokes they mock themselves, the insane world that surrounds them, and their own seriousness. In wit they deconstruct, as they reaffirm, the myths they believe in (sexuality, Oedipus). Always confronting Oedipus and the riddle of the Sphinx, and never solving it, Allen's men and women enter the real, symbolic, and imaginary realms of experience, not through mourning and loss, but with comedy, Allen's preferred form of discourse (see Ulmer, 1989: 52 on the joke as the prototype of a new genre of academic discourse). In Allen's version of Oedipus, every story involves, as Barthes (1975: 10) argued of all narratives, 'a staging of the . . . absent, hidden, or hypostatized father.' Add Allen's Jewish mother to the missing and absent father and you have his picture of Oedipus. Trapped in circumstances outside their control (some even go blind like Oedipus), finding that no answer to life's mysteries ever holds, for meaning is always contradictory and illusive, they blame themselves (or God) for their own failures.

Crimes and Misdemeanors (like other Allen films), is, to borrow from de Lauretis's (1984: 157) description of the most recent exciting work in cinema and feminism today not 'anti-narrative or anti-Oedipal; quite the opposite. It is . . . Oedipal . . . with a vengeance, for it seeks to stress the duplicity of that scenario and the specific contradictions of the female [and male] subject in it, the contradiction by which historical women [and men] must work with and against Oedipus.' The Oedipal vengeance that Allen deploys in *Crime and Misdemeanors* turns wives into versions of bitchy mothers (Wendy), and fathers into weak moral authority figures who convey contradictory messages to their sons. Mothers, as in *Oedipus Wrecks*, become screaming shrews who are only happy when they make their sons miserable. Their sons, in turn, are only happy when their mothers appear to have died, or at least have disappeard from sight. As Allen and his men (and women) write their own histories (*mystories*: Ulmer, 1989: 82) out of the Oedipal myth they reaffirm the need for a dream-world in order to discover and make sense of the real world they inhabit (Ulmer, 1989: 29). In this imaginary, cinematic world they make their mothers disappear, contradict their fathers, and find father figures who fail, just like they do. Unlike Oedipus these men never go into permanent exile from life. Yet they are haunted always by the knowledge that the guilty man is none other than themself. Their identities are built up, like collages, out of the bits and pieces of the familied, sexual meanings that litter the oral, literate and electronic discourses of daily life and popular culture.

Drawing upon Ulmer's (1989: 43) description of Freud's enterprise, it can be argued that Allen's project consists of the telling and generalization of his peculiar, personal, ethnic, familial, sexual, fantasy stories into a series of popular culture texts which offer a radical, humorous, deconstructive interpretation of the postmodern condition. This interpretation refuses the melancholia and mourning of Mills, Lyotard, Baudrillard, and Jameson. It approaches the current moment with jubilation, laughter, and hope. In so doing it rejects a mournful nostalgia attached to a romanticized picture of the past. It counters sadness with humor. It activates a modernist and postmodernist cultural memory which critiques the present and the past in terms of a thoroughly radical aesthetics and morality of experience. It celebrates the voyeur as a cultural figure who, in his (and her) looking, becomes a tourist of the contemporary scene. Like a scavenger, this voyeur searches for meaningful items in the cultural refuse of the past and the present that litter everyday life.[4] For Allen the personal is always political, and the political is always personal. Like Erasmus, his works praise human folly, while they take dead seriously this postmodern moment and all its moral contradictions.

Notes

1. *Crimes and Misdemeanors*, written and directed by Woody Allen; director of photography, Sven Nykvst; produced by Robert Greenhut; released by Orion pictures. Cast: Judah Rosenthal (Martin Landau), Dolores Paley (Angelica Huston), Cliff Stern (Woody Allen), Wendy Stern (Joanna Gleason), Lester (Alan Alda), Halley Reed (Mia Farrow), Jack Rosenthal (Jerry Orbach), Miriam Rosenthal (Claire Bloom), Ben (Sam Waterston), Professor Louis Levy (Martin Bergmann). Currently a top twenty video rental.

2. In the *American Film* 'Critics Poll' of the 1980s, Woody Allen's *Hannah and Her Sisters* was voted one of the top ten films of the decade. Allen was voted best screenwriter of the decade and the number two director, after Martin Scorsese.

3. His list of films includes *What's Up, Tiger Lily?* (1966) *Take the Money and Run* (1969), *Play it Again, Sam* (1972), *Sleeper* (1973), *The Front* (1976), *Annie Hall* (1977), *Interiors* (1978), *Manhattan* (1979), *Stardust Memories* (1980), *A Midsummer Night's Sex Comedy* (1982), *Zelig* (1983), *Broadway Danny Rose* (1984), *The Purple Rose of Cairo* (1985), *Hannah and Her Sisters* (1986), *Radio Days* (1987), *September* (1987), *Another Woman* (1988), and *Oedipus Wrecks* (1989).

4. In this context Allen's character Leonard Zelig, in the film of the same name *Zelig* (1983), emerges as a prototypical postmodern hero. Leonard, a once-famous American, suffered from a most curious disease: he was a human chameleon. Always eager to please, loath to give offense, so willing to blend in, he would take on the social, intellectual, and even physical characteristics of the people he interacted with. Put him with a psychiatrist and he would discuss complexes; next to a Chinese man, he began to look Oriental, and so on. This ability to fit in propelled Leonard to the heights of fame. He hobnobbed with presidents, was honored by ticker-tape parades and his case was debated by learned societies. Allen tells his story through the use of documentary footage, making it impossible to separate the real from the fictional. Allen seems to be arguing that the postmodern condition

stems, in part, from this 'chameleon-like' disease to fit in, to merge the real with the fictional, and never to know, deep down, who one is, for the representations of the real have now become the real.

8

The Postmodern Sexual Order: sex, lies, and Yuppie Love

Moral precepts from:

sex, lies and videotape
   'Sex is overrated.' (Ann to Graham)

   'Lying is like alcoholism. You are always recovering.' (Graham to Ann)

When Harry Met Sally . . .
   'No man can be friends with a woman he finds attractive. He always wants
   to have sex with her. Sex is always out there. Friendship is ultimately
   doomed and that is the end of the story.' (Harry to Sally)

   'You are a human affront to all women . . . Most women at one time or
   another have faked it [orgasm] . . . All men are sure it never happened to
   them, you do the math.' (Sally to Harry)

Michel Foucault (1980a: 155), 'The Eye of Power':
   Just a gaze. An inspecting gaze, a gaze which each individual under its
   weight will end by interiorising to the point that he is his own overseer, each
   individual thus exercising this surveillance over, and against, him[her]self.

In Katz's Delicatessen just moments after Harry (*When Harry Met Sally
. . .*),[1] has told her that he makes love to women, and then leaves,
knowing that he has given them an orgasm, Sally Albright speaks the
above lines. She then proceeds to fake an orgasm, proving that,
unbeknown to men, women fake their sexual pleasures (see Cohen, 1989a,
1989b). She begins to moan, exclaims, 'Oh God, Oh God, Oh, Ah,' rubs
her face and neck, 'Oh God, Yeah, Right there, Oh God, Oh God, Oh
God, Yes, Yes, Yes, Yes,' pounding the table, her body is moving up and
down, people in the deli are staring at her, 'Yes, Yes, Yes, Yes, Oh, Oh
– Oh God!' and then she starts to eat her salad.

Mid-way through *sex, lies and videotape*,[2] Cynthia takes off her
clothes and masturbates in front of Graham's video camera, after telling
him about the first time she saw and touched a penis: 'I didn't think it
would have ridges and veins. I thought it would be like a test tube, an
organ, a separate thing. When he pulled it out I forgot it was attached.
He said my hand felt good.'

These two award-winning 1989 films take the topics of sex, love, friendship, marriage, and the postmodern voyeur into new, but also familiar
regions. In exploring the sexual politics of the 1980s ('Is the sexual revolution over?': see Champlin, 1989),[3] these romantic comedies complement
Blue Velvet, Wall Street, and *Crimes and Misdemeanors*. While violent,
degraded, and high-priced sexuality are absent in these texts,[4] their

surfaces write and inscribe a superficially quiescent sexual order that spans the Reagan years. The films address romantic commitment and sexual permissiveness, without, in Reagan-like fashion, ever examining the consequences of permissiveness in the age of AIDS.[5] They speak, accordingly, to the sexual 'crimes,' mistakes, and misdemeanors of the ordinary middle-class, college-educated, young professional men and women who came of age and found their places in the American class and gender structures in the 1980s (see Garrett, 1989; Sterritt, 1989b). They are, to steal the title of one review (Garrett, 1989), sexual 'field guides to yuppies . . . illustrated yuppie handbooks,' a composite picture of the characteristics and values of the baby-boomers who have traded in the political idealism of the 1960s for the materialism of the eighties and nineties.

The troubles the people in these films encounter are of their own emotional making. Their problems are personal, involving love, intimacy, and a fulfilling relationship with a member of the opposite sex. They commit no murders, or stock frauds. They don't have college loans to pay off. They live comfortable lives in fashionable Manhattan apartments, or well-appointed homes in Baton Rouge, Louisiana. They grasp after possessions and tell (or could tell) jokes like: 'What do you call a car crash between two yuppies?' Answer: 'A Saab story' (Garrett, 1989: 93). They are coming-of-age childlike adults.[6] They wear designer jeans, Reebok and Nike tennis shoes, expensive sweaters, navy-blue power suits and Ferragamo pumps, bow ties and suspenders, have yuppie toys (VCRs, Saabs, BMWs), carry real leather briefcases, drink Evian bottled water and fine wines, have Mexican ceramic tile floors, shop at the Sharper Image, workout, play squash, eat power food snacks, are self-centered (John to Ann: 'I don't know what your problem is. I make a good living. We have a nice house. A lot of women think that's OK. They'd love lying down next to a good-looking guy every night'), and believe that 'having it all' is 'a thumbnail bill of rights' for their generation (Garrett, 1989: 93).

The central characters in each film are postmodern simulacra for whom sex 'has become a free-standing item, related to nothing else' (Champlin, 1989: 1). They interact with one another as images and objects. Harry and John see all women as sex objects. Sally, Marie, and Ann see men as husbands who will take them out of the dating game. Cynthia sees every male as a sex object.

The video camera and the old Hollywood film are the perfect metaphors for these individuals. Harry and Sally read their lives through *Casablanca*; significant moments in their relationship are interpreted by lines spoken by Ingrid Bergman, Humphrey Bogart, and Claude Rains, as the images of these screen idols flicker on their TV screens. (Harry thinks Bergman should have stayed with Bogart because she had the greatest sex of her life and Sally says she wouldn't want to spend the rest of her life with a man who ran a bar, besides she thinks it might be wise to leave and become the first lady of Czechoslovakia.) Graham, the video-cam voyeur in *sex, lies and videotape*, mediates his world of sexuality through the camera's eye and its soundtrack which captures women talking about their sexuality, including masturbation.

Sally Albright's faked orgasm, like Graham's tapes, laughs at, while it ridicules all men who think they can control a woman's sexuality. Sally, the beautiful, compulsive, controlling woman whom Harry finally marries, emerges as an icon for the yuppie, post-ERA 'cockeyed feminist' (Kempley, 1989: B 11) women/fighters of the 1980s who have learned that their bodies and sexuality are their own to control. Harry, the man who claims to make women 'meow' in his bed, is the iconic male chauvinist, pushy sexist of the 1980s. John could be Harry's brother, for he knows only passionate sexuality without love. Cynthia, the extroverted, sexually hungry, lustful sister symbolizes the repressed sexual side of her sister Ann. Her exclusion, at the film's end, from any stable relationship reflects society's traditional taboo on the wild, sexual woman. Graham, the video voyeur, carries to the outer extreme Woody Allen's hero who sees the world through the camera's eye. (Of course Graham, like Woody, makes his own pictures, but his pictures, contained in his cardboard-boxed video library, are about a taboo topic – women's auto-eroticism – that seldom finds its way to the film screen.)

These two films transgress the sexually personal terrains of the postmodern woman (and man). They reproduce the sexual stereotypes of the gender order by manipulating the cinematic and ideological apparatuses that bring these worlds into play. In so doing they further explode the boundaries which have hitherto kept certain unpresentables from the public's eye.[7] However, each narrative operates within the traditional melodramatic Oedipal framework. Graham has withdrawn from the world, because of his past sins (his lies). Harry finally finds love and sexuality after learning that he is the guilty party in the relationship with Sally. John, Ann's unfaithful husband, is punished. He loses his job and his wife. In the end each woman's sexuality is contained within the real or implied marital system. Harry marries Sally, and Ann cures Graham's neuroses and sexual impotence. Each male is tamed (and treated) by a patient, loving woman who has waited for him to come around to her position (see Lyman, 1990).

Video Voyeurs: *sex, lies and videotape*[8]

In a collage of opening scenes Soderbergh cuts back and forth between guileless beauty (James, 1989a) and Ann Millaney who sits cross-legged on the couch in her psychiatrist's office, describing her fear of the week ('What will we do with all the garbage in the world?'), to an image of Graham (with video camera) splashing water in his armpits in the men's room of Ray's Bait Shop, before he drives into Baton Rouge to Ann's house. Meanwhile John is spinning his wedding ring on the desk of his law office, talking about how easy it is to get women now that he is married, as he heads off to Cynthia's for a sexual interlude. The camera cuts back to Ann, 'I'm kinda goin' through this thing where I don't want him to touch me,' and then to Cynthia and John making love. Cynthia expresses her desire to make love on her sister's bed. Next Graham is asking Ann about her marriage and if she has ever been on television. Over dinner he expresses the belief that liars are the second lowest form of human beings; lawyers being the lowest. At lunch the next day with Ann he reveals that he is punishing himself for having lied to and deceived an old girlfriend. Sexually impotent ('I can't get an erection in the presence of another person'), he is now only aroused when he tapes women discussing their sexuality (Cynthia: 'He gets it off watching women talk about sex'). Ann tells him that she thinks 'Sex is overrated. That women want it as much as men is a bunch of crap. I mean I think they want it, but not for the same reasons that men think they do.' Graham tells her that 'you shouldn't take advice from a person who doesn't know you intimately,' and 'that men come to love the person they're attracted to and women become more and more attracted to the person that they love' (meaning sexually). Within minutes the film has established its territory: lies, deceptions, truth, self-denial, and sexual infidelities.

The story's climax builds quickly. Discovering John's affair with Cynthia, who has called John a liar ('You're fucking your wife's sister') Ann returns to Graham, exclaiming, 'My life is shit. Nothing is what I thought it was. Let's make a video together.' Ann returns home and tells John, 'I want out of this marriage.' Learning that she was at Graham's ('Mr Apostle of Truth. I know he didn't fuck you') John races to his apartment, beats him up and watches Ann's tape. Ann is shown answering Graham's questions: 'Do you have sex?' 'Not very often.' 'Do you have orgasms?' 'I don't think so. Never had one.' 'Have you had sex with anyone other than your husband or imagined sex with someone other than your husband?' Ann's face fills the screen as she says 'Yes.'

Video Therapy
The tape from the video camera now turns black as Soderbergh cuts from 'filmed' reality to the real interactions that occurred between Ann and Graham. She tells him that she has thought of having sex with him. He tells her that he is thinking about what she would look like 'having an orgasm.' She replies, 'I'd like to know what I'd look like. Can you and that [camera] give a woman an orgasm?' Graham, 'Yes.' Suddenly Ann turns the camera on him. He tells her 'I was the problem. I was a pathological liar – was – I am,' and then speaks the lines quoted earlier concerning recovery, alcoholism, and lying. She asks, 'You lied, what else?' He answers, 'I used to express my feelings non-verbally, I often scared people close to me.' Ann asks, 'You still do that?' He answers 'No.' Rejecting Ann's offer to make love ('I'm not in love with you. Forget about the sex. I'm not the same person I was'), Graham then

brings his ex-girlfriend into the situation, 'This was never possible before, she and I.'

> *Ann:* Who's she? Elizabeth?
> *Graham:* Yes.
> *Ann:* So you're still in contact with her? Have you told her about these video tapes since you don't lie anymore?
> *Graham:* I moved here to get a sense of closure. I wanted somebody very important to me to understand.
> *Ann:* That's pathetic! You can't just walk up to her. Look what you've changed into. Nine years. Look at you! Are you going to do this for the rest of your life?!

Now in control of the situation, Ann pushes:

> *Ann:* Why do you tape women?
> *Graham:* Why should I tell you why. You don't know who I am. I can't just recount all the points in my life up to this moment. I have no idea who I am. Why explain myself to you?
> *Ann:* Your problems.
> *Graham:* Problems. I look around this town and I feel and see John and Cynthia and I feel comparatively healthy.
> *Ann:* You've got a problem.
> *Graham:* Right. I've got a lot of problems. They belong to me.
> *Ann* [*holding the camera on Graham*]: You think they're yours. They're not. Everybody who walks into your life is affected. I'm leaving my husband because of you. You've had an effect on my life.

Arguing that this isn't supposed to be happening, Graham states, 'I've spent nine years structuring my life so this didn't happen.'

The crisis passed through, Ann puts the camera down, and they become intimate. The film then cuts back to John, as he leaves Graham's, who, in a fit of rage, destroys his remaining tapes. The film's final scene has Graham and Ann sitting together in the rain (which was also present when Graham drove into town) on the front porch. John has lost his job and his wife.

This is video therapy. Underscoring its position that voyeurs (therapist, video artists, and married ladies: Salamon, 1989b) aren't really living, Soderbergh has Ann unmask Graham, forcing him to reveal why he likes to make and watch his tapes (Salamon, 1989b). This is pure catharsis.

> In the end, Soderbergh's film boils down to one of the most questionable dramatic clichés of our times: that there is no emotional problem so thorny or difficult that it can't be cured by confession. Ann talks and Graham talks, and magically the wrong couples are sorted out and the right couples come together (Kehr, 1989a).

As Kehr observes, this is less a conclusion to a complex narrative, than the 'fantasy outcome of the perfect therapy session, which is what *sex, lies and videotape* ultimately wants to be.'

Asking viewers to see his characters, less as our doubles or inferiors, and more as our clients (Kehr, 1989a), Soderbergh has reproduced the clinical-therapeutic setting in the yuppie living-room. The illness is sexuality, which is connected in this case to Graham's impotence; Graham also believes that sex is something worth dying for. (His black dress, and withdrawal from the world signify death.) He has died a social death because of his past sexual sins. These forms of sexual illness are cured through talking. The film reproduces the ideal therapy session (See Foucault, 1980a: 191 on sexuality, illness, and confessions). Graham's cure, carried by a woman, involves, in the classic-psychoanalytic sense, a confession.

But more is involved. The cure requires 'talk-on-camera.' As Baudrillard (1983a: 12–13) observes, this attempt to capture lived experience is typical of the age of the hyperreal, where an obscene ecstasy (and economy) of communication surround sexuality and its representations. Nothing is any longer hidden. Graham's tapes capture everything. The camera has become the 'eye of power' and its gaze, now interiorized, is turned inward on our most sacred sexual secrets. These secrets, once revealed, unlock the key to our being, for they tell us who we are. As Foucault (1980b: 155–6) observes,

> It is through sex . . . an imaginary point determined by the deployment of sexuality – that each individual has to pass in order to have access to his own intelligibility (seeing that it is both the hidden aspect and the generative principle of meaning), to the whole of his body . . . [and] to his history.

Through a reversal of his video technology Graham comes to discover who he is. His guilt exposed, his secrets visible (I hurt people), his sexuality restored through the technology of video, he is now free to re-enter the world and be one with Ann, a woman he was first attracted to and now clearly loves.

The Gendered Video Text

This film is about video sexual voyeurs, men watching women on videotape, women watching themselves on tape, and women taping men. It is a study in looking. Superficially close to pornography (John is afraid Cynthia's tape will be sold as porn), Graham's tapes never record sexual intercourse (excluding masturbation), only sexual discourse, including when women want to do it, where, with whom, the most unusual places they've done it (a plane), what they've done, what they've never done, what they'd like to do but were never asked, when they had their first sexual experience, what their orgasms were like and if they've had one, when they first saw a penis and so on.

These seemingly private and personal texts, only seen by Graham, are meant to show that what women think about sexuality is not what men think they think. Yet by having the male cameraman elicit the sexual discourse, the film monopolizes the male gaze and makes the woman the subject of a masculine, sexual text. Soderbergh attempts to escape this charge in two ways. First, he has Ann turn the camera on Graham, making him the subject of her gaze. Yet when the camera turns on

Graham, and the screen dissolves into real time and real life, the gaze captures the two of them interacting; it does not single out Graham as a sexual subject. Secondly, by going beneath voyeurism to the lies and deceptions that people tell one another when they are in love, married, or having affairs, Soderbergh seems to be saying that his camera is an eye to truth which knows no gender. In this move, the film implies that the camera reveals only the truth (Graham never asks his women if they are lying). More importantly it is suggested that by withdrawing from the world with the camera one can stop lying and hurting people. These are its benign effects.

In unmasking the sexual desires of women, and in telling the story of the adulterous John, *sex, lies and videotape* charts a multifaceted contemporary sexual world. Multiple meanings are brought to sexuality. It is all of the following: intimacy, lying and being lied to, adultery, wild, free, auto-erotic, dirty-as-in-pornography, akin to being touched, fucking, intercourse, looks at the penis, satisfying, unsatisfying, sickness, illness, overrated, different for men than for women, on tape and impersonal. Sexuality in this film is a gendered production which when enacted reveals the truth of being. Men come to love the women they are sexually attracted to, while women place love before sexual attraction.

After surrounding sexuality with these meanings, the film comes to its basic point. There are two kinds of sex: that which is truthful and that which is false, or based on lies. For Graham, adultery, which violates the marriage bed, debases and falsifies sex, which is intimacy, beauty, and truth. The videotape, Graham's form of retreat from the world, yielded for him truth-about-sex, the truth about himself. In his tapings he was not lying to his women, nor was he harming them. Ann's sincere sexuality, which turned to frigidity when John started the affair with Cynthia, becomes another form of Graham's impotence. Both withdrew from sexuality when they were harmed (lied to), or harmed others by lying. They re-enter sexuality and intimacy when Ann clears away the lies that have surrounded John's project ('You affect people!'), and shows him how he can take advice from her now that they have been intimate. At the same time they can now fall in love. They are attracted to one another out of the same pure project, which is to be truthful.

Soderbergh argues that his film 'was an "expulsion" of his observations about three things dominating American life – the selling of sex, the telling of lies, and the inundation of video' (Mathews, 1989).[9] Unfortunately it becomes little more than a morality tale which reproduces a patriarchal view of feminine sexuality, the punishment the adulterous male must receive from a post-ERA culture, and the outsider fate that has always fallen to the sexually promiscuous female. In reproducing one of the therapeutic clichés of the 1980s concerning confession and recovery, the film aligns itself with those other social texts which code pleasure with unmasked (erotic) sexuality. It does so at the expense of a more 'general economy of pleasure that is not based on sexual norms' (Foucault, 1980a: 191).

Unfaithful to the form of his title, Soderbergh should have capitalized SEX, for this is what his film is all about; sex and its pleasures. In its Puritanical tone, *sex, lies and videotape* reinforces a conservative economy of sexuality which is completely at home in the post-Reagan, George Bush era. It shows, that is, how the new video technology can be used to shore up a shaking, fragile, sexual moral order which still rests on the chauvinistic sexisms of the 1980s. This technology, like Foucault's panoptic gaze (1977: 200–1), keeps the 'new' camera steadily turned inward on the bodies, selves, and sexual lives of the 'thirtysomething' generation, making its members the instruments of the gaze that determines their collective fate.

When Harry Met Sally

Harry and Sally are narcissistic neurotics. Woody Allen[10] and Neil Simon look-alikes (Carr, 1989b; James, 1989b), they inhabit the transitional relational and emotional landscapes of the late 1980s, trying 'to make their way from the strenuous demands of the anything-goes years [the late sixties and seventies] to the heart's continuing demand for a singular, knock-out-take-all-of-me love' (Champlin, 1989: 7). They attempt, that is, to achieve 'love in a time when permissibility embraces everything except commitment' (Champlin, 1989: 1). Harry and Sally are proof that opposites attract, and that when a couple is destined by the gods to come together, sooner or later they will (Kehr, 1989b: 3). This is an old-fashioned love story for yuppies; even the music and the films (*Casablanca*, Gershwin, Arlen, Porter, Carmichael, Ellington) are from the 1940s and 1950s).[11] Reminiscent of romantic couples from the past (Cary Grant and Irene Dunne, Tracy and Hepburn), *When Harry Met Sally . . .* is arch 1940s screwball comedy, part relationship comedy *à la Annie Hall* (set in Woody Allen's neurotic metropolis), and part a comedy of recognition, built on a weak sitcom model (Kehr, 1989b: 3) with shallow characters (James, 1989b), who live a sanitized existence where politics and mundane reality never intrude (Garrett, 1989: 93), and truthful statements are only expressed in witty epigrammatic jokes (James, 1989b).

The text unfolds in predictable Allen-like phases. It starts with a satiric-sentimental, comedic treatment of contemporary courtship rituals: (Harry on how long you stay with a woman after you have sex: 'How long do I have to lie there and hold her before I can get up and go home? Is thirty seconds enough?'; Marie to Sally: 'I sent flowers to myself so he would think I had a man in my life.') It then introduces melodramatic complexity. Both are victims of failed relationships and are dealing with loneliness and being 'single again.' (Harry: 'if you are over love, why haven't you slept with somebody?' Sally: 'Proof I'm over Joe? Fuck somebody. You make love like you're out for revenge. I'll make love when it's making love, not when it's out for revenge!') The couple is then brought together in a happy, warmly traditional, un-Allen-like conclusion where romantic fulfillment (marriage) is achieved.

Along the way, Reiner manipulates his audience by reproducing a number of contemporary courtship scenes which are humorous and immediately recognizable. These include Sally's lunch with her Manhattan women friends where they discuss dates and available men, Harry sharing his pain of divorce with Jess at a football game ('I got married so I could stop dating. There's no incentive in dating your wife'), Harry, Sally, Jess, and Marie doing a painful double date, Harry meeting his ex-wife for the first time after the divorce (he is with Sally), and the first kiss between Harry and Sally. Harry and Sally are types, not people, and their experiences, while familiar, are shallow, lacking in specific observations which reveal a depth of character (see Kehr, 1989b: 3).

He is a political consultant and she a journalist. Recognizable yuppie types, in their early thirties, they have jobs appropriate to the contemporary world where images and their manipulations constitute reality. Harry expresses every extreme thought he thinks (Harry to Sally: 'You're not a deep person. You've never thought about death – a fleeting thought drifts in and out of the transom of your mind. I spend days thinking about death'). He is insecure, suspicious, and pessimistic. He always believes in the worst, reading the last pages of books first for fear of dying before he gets to the end. Sally is a repressed, lovable WASP, who never has a self-revelation, regards herself as a cheerful, happy, well-adjusted person, but attempts to control every situation (to a waitress: 'I'll have the Chef Salad, oil on the side, and apple pie *à la mode*. I'd like the pie heated and don't put the ice cream on top, but on the side, and I'd like strawberry, not vanilla, if you have it, if not, whip cream, but only if it is real, not out of a can, if not nothing, just the pie, not heated'). She is, in Harry's typology, a high-maintenance woman.

> *Harry*: There are two kinds of women: low and high maintenance. You're the worst kind. You're high maintenance, but you think you are low maintenance. You don't see that. 'Waiter, I'll begin with the house salad, but I don't want the regular dressing. I want the mustard dressing, but on the side.' On the side is very big with you.
> *Sally*: I just want it the way I want it.
> *Harry*: I know. High maintenance.

They met three times. The first time, in 1977, at the University of Chicago, they hated each other, or at least Sally hated Harry. (She could not accept his theory that men and women can never remain close friends without ever making love; that is men always want sex.)[12] The second time they met, in an airport in 1982, Harry didn't remember who Sally was, but she remembered him and his theory of sex and love, which he has now revised:

> Men and women can't be friends unless they're both involved with other people, then they can. This is the amendment to the earlier rule. If two people are in a relationship the pressure of other involvement is lifted. That doesn't

work either, because then the person you're involved with can't understand why
you're friends with a person you're just friends with. Something is missing in
the relationship. They think you're involved secretly, which brings you back to
the earlier rule, before the amendment: men and women can't be friends.

The third time they met, in 1987, Harry was going through a divorce and
Sally had just broken up with her longtime boyfriend. This time they
became friends. (Harry: 'We're friends now. Great. A woman friend.
You're the first attractive woman I didn't want to have sex with.' Harry
to Jess: 'I've never had a relationship without sex. This is a growth
experience'.) Then they made love (and Harry left immediately after), and
weren't friends anymore. Then they came together again on New Year's
Eve, 1989 and fell in love. Twelve years and three months after they first
met they were married. This film is the story of what happened between
Harry and Sally after they became friends.[13]

Every time Harry met Sally she saw him first. A more accurate title for
the film would be *When Sally Saw Harry and Harry Met Her*. Harry is
always the object of Sally's gaze. When they leave for New York in 1977
she honks her car horn to get his attention. When they meet five years
later she sees him before he sees her. Five years later she sees him first,
in the Personal Growth Section of the bookstore. Her gaze, always
perplexed, slightly troubled, bemused and superior, defines Harry's standing in every situation. Intense, self-involved, deep in his own thought,
certain that he is the only person who thinks dark thoughts, Harry is a
sexual predator, a believer in a friendship code which perpetuates the
gendered sexual order. Sally's gaze defuses Harry's certainty and
authority, yet inevitably elicits a thought or aphorism that simultaneously
outrages and intrigues (for example Sally [Harry has just proposed to
her]: 'That is just like you Harry. You say things like that and you make
it impossible for me to hate you and I hate you Harry. I really hate
you!'). For Harry friendship between men and women is doomed because
sex is always out there. Men are friends with men, women are friends with
women, and women are the sexual objects of men's desires. Even
marriage is doomed, because now sex becomes routinized (or as Sally
says, 'The kids take sex out of the marriage') and there is nothing to talk
about. Husbands and wives can't be friends, or lovers. Sally, on the other
hand, has male friends with whom sex is not an issue and believes that
friends can also be lovers. This film is the test of the above propositions
(such as 'Can men and women remain close friends without making
love?'). Put simply, as the lines to the song go, 'Can lovers become
friends?' or, as another song argues, should they just 'call the whole thing
off?' In refuting Harry's theory, the text affirms the lines from yet
another song: 'It had to be you.'

Postmodern Sexuality in the Yuppie Wilderness

The movie, as argued earlier, is a 'Field Guide for Single Yuppies' who are attempting to find their way through the sexual wilderness of the late 1980s. As such it takes a stand on and defines the following problematic terms: being single versus being married; sexuality and women's orgasms; love, sexuality, and friendship; life after divorce, or after breaking up with a lover. These terms are presented as obstacles that must be overcome if men and women are to find happiness. The solutions are gender specific. Women must not be single, must learn how to fake orgasms, so that males think they have sexual power, must learn how to be friends with men, and must be patient, if a man is to be caught. Men, on the other hand, must have a woman who lets them think they can make them sexually happy. They need male friends to talk to, because women don't understand male sexuality. In this battle between the sexes, sex must be overcome, before love and friendship can be achieved.

Each of the main characters (Harry and his best friend Jess, Sally and her best friend Marie) enact gendered variations on these sexual themes. Harry, a mix of a self-defined Don Juan and a Woody Allen Alvy Singer, wants a woman to lay. Jess wants the same, although he is woman-shy: he wants her to respect his work. Marie is 'tired of being out there fighting for a man' and is happy to be married. She keeps a file of eligible men who can be dated ('Who wants to be alone on National Holidays?') Sally's biological clock is ticking (she's thirty-two) and she wants to have children before it's too late ('I'll be forty in eight years – it's sitting there – like a dead end – not like that for men. Charlie Chaplin had babies when he was seventy-three'). She and Marie divide the world of males into three categories: lovers, transitional dates (when you are between lovers), and the man you love and marry. 'Being-not-single' is the most important accomplishment for Marie and Sally. Harry and Jess have a slightly different typology (which is subsumed by Harry's high- and low-maintenance classification system): women you date, women you lay, and the one you marry (who will eventually divorce you). (Since Harry has never had an attractive woman friend, this kind does fit into his typology.)

Friendship, Sex, Lies, and Love
Sex is a game for Harry and Sally. Only it is different game for each. For Harry it is a contest. To Jess: 'I made her meow last night.' Harry to Sally: 'I had my dream again. I was making love in the Olympics. I had received 9.5s from all the judges for my mount and dismount. My mother was watching and she gave me a 5.6.' For Sally sex is a game to be faked, along the way to making a man think he's made you happy. (If you are happy along the way that is fine, but it's not a necessity.) Since all women fake orgasms, and 'all men are sure it never happened to them,' women are successful players in the game of lying about sexuality. For Sally sex

blends with love ('I'll make love when it's making love'); like Ann she is sexually attracted to the man she loves. She codes love with making love (sex). Harry, on the other hand, has no conception of love; there is only sex and pleasure.

Like *sex, lies and videotape*, *When Harry Met Sally* . . . is about the lies men and women tell one another; only the lies here are different. John and Graham's lies are about infidelity. Sally's lies are gendered productions; part of being a woman is learning how to fake an orgasm. Like Cynthia and Ann, she has learned how to fake these things that lie at the core of male–female sexuality. While masturbation does not appear to be an option for her, it is clear that she has learned how to be a satisfying sexual partner for men, and this is all that counts.

Here is where Harry's lies enter the picture. Since he doesn't believe in any connection between love and sex, all he seeks is sexual pleasure. Duped by the women he makes meow, he is the victim of a double lie. His chauvinistic sexuality is an affront to all women who have to put up with his self-defined sexual prowess; hence they fake their orgasms in order to get rid of him. But he feels guilt about leaving early ('How long should I hold her?') and this guilt undercuts any sexual pleasure he might feel. A victim of his own sexual standards, he must fake his pleasures in order to get away safely. Unable to give, or show affection, he is trapped in a masculine sexual world that is devoid of feeling. He suffers anhedonia.

This is why his relationship with Sally, prior to their sleeping together, is so paradoxical. For the first time he has found a member of the opposite sex with whom he can share the most intimate of thoughts. By putting sex out of the situation, he opens himself to a cross-sex relationship, one that he calls, echoing the lines from *Casablanca*, 'The beginning of a beautiful friendship.' Sexuality destroys the friendship. Harry, the pure chauvinist, has not learned how to combine love with intimacy and sexuality. This is why, the day after they make love, he must tell Sally that 'it was a mistake.' Sally refuses to forgive him, (Harry: 'Can't we get past this! It happened three weeks ago'). She accuses him of calling her a dog (Harry: 'You know a year for a person is seven years for a dog'). He argues, 'I didn't go to make love!' She retorts, 'You took pity on me. Fuck you!'

The Taming of Harry Who Gets Love
When Harry comes back to Sally, he begs again for her forgiveness. He begins by telling her 'I'm sorry,' and then: 'I've done a lot of thinking. I love you.' She rejects his offer, 'How do you expect me to respond to that? I know it's New Year's Eve. I know you're lonely. But you can't show up here and expect that to make everything alright. It doesn't work that way.' Harry tries again:

'How about this way. I love it that you get cold when it's 71 degrees out. I love it that it takes you an hour and a half to order a sandwich. I love it that you get that little wrinkle above your nose when you're looking at me like I'm nuts.

I love it that when I spend the day with you I still smell your perfume on my clothes and I love that you are the last person I want to talk to before I go to sleep. It's not because I'm lonely. It's not because it is New Year's Eve ('Auld Lang Syne' begins playing). I came here tonight because when you realize you want to spend the rest of your life with somebody, you want the rest of your life to start as soon as possible.'

At this point Sally speaks the lines quoted above concerning hating Harry when he says things like this. They then kiss,[14] and the film closes with each of them recounting the history of the three times they met, including their wedding and how Sally insisted on having the rich chocolate sauce served on the side of their enormous wedding cake.

Sally wins. Friends can be lovers, and lovers can be friends. How did Harry get love? How did he overcome his particular case of anhedonia? It's not clear that he did. What he got were memories of Sally's friendship, memories of her eccentricities, the wrinkles in her brow, her compulsive high-maintenance traits, memories of their shared conversations before they go to sleep at night. Harry got a friend who happened to be a woman, who is now his wife, and presumably his lover. No longer young, around the divorce circuit once, and the singles route twice, Harry wants out of the sexual wilderness. In order to get out he must buy into the ideology of love, and this he does, repeating over and over again, 'I love you.' Refusing to address his earlier theory, and its deficiencies, Harry now accepts Sally's original position that you can be friends without being lovers, but that lovers who are friends have the best possible world, especially when they are married and plan to have kids. Like Graham, Harry ends up loving the person he is attracted to.

Caught in Sally's web, Harry, punished for his sexual misdemeanors, surrenders his freedom, promiscuity, and independence to the demands of marriage, family, and home. Attracted to the woman who refuses his attentions, trapped in her version of playing coy, Harry becomes a victim of that ancient myth called love that Gordon Gekko long ago saw through. Harry and Sally's love story which comes out right reenacts the classic comic romantic love stories of Hollywood's past (Haskell, 1987) and in so doing offers promise and hope to those yuppies who are still 'out there' wandering in the wilderness, looking for a good man or woman who will marry them.

Anhedonia Undone
In these ideological moves *When Harry Met Sally . . .* refuses Woody Allen's argument (as elaborated in the last chapter) that anhedonia is a basic feature of the contemporary condition. Every character in this film, including the six documentary couples, finds happiness in marriage. As if taking a line from the pro-family, pro-Oedipus activists, Reiner, like Soderbergh is arguing that each individual must anchor his or her sexuality in marriage and then, and only then, will love and full personhood come. Woody Allen's anhedonia is cured by love and marriage.

But Reiner's characters never really experience this inability to receive or give pleasure. They never feel deep pain; even Sally, when she learns that her ex-boyfriend is getting married, can only utter 'He didn't want to marry me! He didn't love me! I'm too structured. Too closed off. I drove him away.' Two minutes later she's making love to Harry, and later offering to watch an old movie with him. Shallow to the core, these people offer easy answers to the problems of love and marriage in the last decade of this century.

The Songs

Conservative and pro-family from the start, chauvinistic through and through, Reiner's film, like Soderbergh's, is a perfect text for the contemporary moment. It is a 'retro' postmodern, modernist movie which uses the songs, lyrics of the pre- and postwar years to interpret the current baby-boomer generation's desire to have love, sex, and family all at the same time. The voices and sounds of Frank Sinatra, Louis Armstrong, Tony Bennett, Ella Fitzgerald, and Steve Lawrence croon Gershwin, Arlen, and Porter love songs ('It Had to be You', 'Our Love is Here to Stay', 'Right Time of the Night', 'Let's Call the Whole Thing Off', 'I Could Write a Book', 'But Not For Me', 'Winter Wonderland', 'Stompin' at the Savoy', 'Say It Isn't So', 'Surrey with the Fringe on Top', 'Call Me', 'Don't Get Around Much Anymore', 'Have a Merry Christmas'). These singers (and their songs) are icons from the past; stars of the 1950s, who reproduced imaginary solutions to the problems of love, romance, and marriage in an age when families and careers were falling apart.

That these singers and songs should be used in a contemporary film at first appears surprising, but remember this is a film for the coming-of-age-thirtysomething-person; the second postwar teenager cohort to reach maturity. They are materialists, not idealists. They are the new traditional men and women discussed in Chapter One. The ideals of the women and men center (in part at least) on marriage and family. This cohort is self-centered. 'They believe that everything in history is happening to them for the first time' (Garrett, 1989: 93). They have no sense of the past, no sense of politics, even though they may be, like Sally and Harry, journalists and political consultants. No wonder, then, that Reiner used the great love songs of the forties and fifties to define the experiences of Harry and Sally. These are mid-century people locked in the twilight years of the twentieth century. Unable to invent new solutions to the problems of love and sex, they fall back on the old clichés, and like Reagan and Bush, they meet the future by turning their heads (and their hearts) towards the past.

The New Traditional Man and Woman

Patriarchy is alive and well in these two films. It is disturbing that they have received so much popular attention and acclaim. Paradoxically in their seemingly radical, provocative, yet blatantly conservative postures (videotapes, overt sex and sexism), they parody themselves. These are not laughing matters. They bring the worst features of a patriarchal order to the surface. They refuse to consider the possibility of new social formations of pleasure and discourse, including men and women being friends without having sex. They reproduce the myth that appropriately fulfilled sexual desires (making love with the one you love) unlock the key to the self. They offer simplistic ideological and traditional solutions to the problems of this system. In so doing they expose the impoverished nature of their respective interpretive systems which turn on sex and its deployment in the traditional marriage and family system.

The Cultural Logic of Postmodern Love

Romantic love is the key to this yuppie social order, with its new traditional man and woman. Love neutralizes, contains, and defines sexuality. Love outlaws promiscuity, and punishes the wild male. Love rewards the faithful mate. Love is the cement of this new social order, and in order for love to work, it needs all the help it can get. More imaginary than real, it requires love songs for its realization. These songs contain the new traditional man and woman in a romantic, marital bond which stands outside sexual politics and economics. Pure fantasy, this romantic love recreates the traditional American family where identity is rooted in home, children, work, commitment, material objects, family vacations, and watching old movies together (*New York Times*, 1989b). The 'neo-traditionalist' yuppies of the 1990s (Ann, Graham, John, Harry, Sally) are materialists and realists (Dougherty, 1988). They have bought into the 'retro' version of the American dream that their parents and grandparents fought to achieve.

Reading the present through the myths (the songs, movies) of the past, they hunger for a love that lasts, a love that sweeps you off your feet, a love that weds sexuality with feeling, intimacy and commitment. This is love with a purpose, and that purpose is straightforward, yet complex. It tames, as it always has (Lyman, 1990: 17), the wayward male. It locks him into a marriage and family system that reproduces the economic logics of a cultural system that values material possessions and makes the family the central purchasing and consumptive system in the economy.

The yuppie couple, with its combined income which can approach six figures, is a powerful economic unit. This system can buy expensive homes, prestige automobiles, trendy electronic toys, take exotic vacations, and make investments in condos and junk bonds which prop up a faltering multinational, US debtor economic system. Yuppie couples are cultural consumers, cultural connoisseurs of the latest fads and fashions (see Featherstone, 1988: 211). They are 'post-tourists' who travel through and make expensive purchases in the postmodern museum culture (Featherstone, 1988: 211). This new middle class works in and furnishes the economic resources that reproduce the cultural and economic needs of late multinational capitalism. At the same time, this relational, monogamous system, with its women and their ticking biological clocks, ensures a birthrate which reproduces this social stratum, without putting strains on the general economy. Yuppie children get expensive educations.

Underneath this system of romantic love and its renewal of the traditional meanings of family and marriage lurks the hyperreal, the lie, the simulation, the faked orgasm, and the sexual truths about male and female sexuality. Cohen (1989a) puts it this way, in his discussion of Sally's faked orgasm.

> Men fake it too. Not orgasms . . . We pretend to listen. Mostly we pretend to listen to women . . . A man is called upon to fake [it] several times a day, dozens of times a week, hundreds of times a month . . . . As a result of the women's movement, out of this awesome fear of not being thought sensitive, many men now spend most of their time faking it . . . . They pretend to see women colleagues as persons . . . . They pretend not to notice other women. They pretend to be interested in parenting, in housework, in relationships.

Older men, those who came of age before 1973, Cohen contends, place no such demands upon themselves: 'You see them all the time. They will come into a restaurant with their wife, order a drink, and say nothing for the rest of the meal. The new, sensitive, contemporary male does not do this. All during the meal he pretends to listen. But it is fake. His mind is elsewhere.'

Consider the implications of this argument. The new sexual order is based on lies. It is a marriage of convenience. It reflects not what is real, or truthfully felt, but what is pretended, what is thought to be appropriate, not what is. Baudrillard's hyperreal has become the real; the lie has become the truth. Truthful communication is whatever an audience will accept (Manning, 1988: 266). The postmodern simulational technologies of communication (the videotape) now dissolve any distinction between the real and the fake; if it looks and feels real, it is real.

This is what *sex, lies and videotape* and *When Harry Met Sally* . . . are all about: the fraudulent foundations of the postmodern sexual order. Each offers a superficial remedy to the fraud. This remedy is love and the emotions of love, including deeply felt feelings about the self, the other, the self's sins, its feelings of guilt, and its desires to be truthfully loved by another. Each of these movies presumes that the fraud can be exposed; that the faked orgasm can be replaced by the real orgasm, and that faked listening can be replaced by sincere listening and sincere commitment to the other; this woman who is the love and sex idol of all contemporary, sensitive men.

Here is where the deeper fraud is exposed. By failing to critique the underlying ideological foundations of their own cultural logics, Reiner and Soderbergh (like Stone, but not Allen) reproduce the very systems that led to the original challenges to capitalism (the idealism of the 1960s) and its formations that their films seek to correct. These are dangerous, hedonistic, apolitical texts, with important political consequences. They endorse a conservative economy of sexual pleasures masquerading behind a simulacrum of truth which offers emotional, romantic solutions to 'real' gender, economic, class (and racial) problems which will not go away with the singing of a song from the 1950s. Thinking they are doing the right thing, Graham, Ann, Harry, and Sally are in fact doing the wrong thing, and this is neither funny, nor farcical. It is closer to tragedy, for these texts are repeating errors which have been made before. What is sad is that they could have been different (on such repetitions in history see Marx, 1983: 287). I turn next to another version of doing the right thing, in this case Spike Lee's 1989 film.

Notes

1. Nominated for the Golden Globe Award from the Hollywood Foreign Press Association. Screenwriter Nora Ephron won the British Academy Award for best original screenplay, and was also nominated for an Oscar. Meg Ryan and Billy Crystal each received American Comedy Awards for their starring roles. Directed by Rob Reiner; screenplay by Nora Ephron; produced by Rob Reiner and Andrew Scheinman; released by Castlerock Entertainment. Cast: Harry Burns (Billy Crystal), Sally Albright (Meg Ryan), Marie (Carrie Fisher), Jess (Bruno Kirby), Joe (Steven Ford), Alice (Lisa Jane Persky), Amanda (Michelle Nicastro).

2. Winner of the Grand Prize at the 1989 Cannes Film Festival, beating Spike Lee's *Do the Right Thing*, which will be discussed in the next chapter. James Spader also received the 'Best Actor' Award at the Cannes Festival. Soderbergh was nominated for the Golden Globe Award for his screenplay. Written and directed by Steven Soderbergh; produced by Robert Newmyer and John Hardy; released by Miramex Films. Cast: Graham (James Spader), Ann (Andie MacDowell), John (Peter Gallagher), Cynthia (Laura San Giacomo), therapist (Ron Vawter). A top video rental, like *When Harry Met Sally . . .* in 1990.

3. Of her screenplay Ephron said, 'It struck me that the movies had spent more than half a century saying "They lived happily ever after" and the following quarter-century warning that they'll be lucky to make it through the weekend. Possibly now we are entering a third era in which the movies will be sounding a note of cautious optimism: You know it just might work' (Champlin, 1989).

4. Except for Sally's sexual dream (fantasy), which started when she was twelve years old, that a faceless man rips her clothes off.

5. For example, Sally to Harry: 'You will have to move to New Jersey because you've made love with every woman in New York City.' Safe sex is not a topic of these films.

6. The original yuppie film was *The Return of the Secaucus Seven* (1980), which was ripped off in *The Big Chill* (1983), turned into a yuppie horror film in *Fatal Attraction* (1987), and given softer touches in *Legal Eagles* (1986), *The Money Pit* (1986), and *Baby Boom* (1987). Yuppies lust after real estate and status properties, as seen in *Wall Street*, have conservative politics, feel that being single is the worst thing that can happen to a woman, confront trendy issues (garbage, the families of airline fatalities, starving children in Africa), and engage in a form of material nostalgia which eclectically consumes anything the popular culture currently values, including collecting Roy Roger's wagon-wheel coffee-tables and speaking lines like, 'Restaurants are to the 80s what theater was to the 60s.'

7. Compare and contrast, in this regard, the auto-erotic acts of Dorothy in *Blue Velvet* with those of Sally, Ann, and Cynthia. Dorothy's and Sally's are seen, while Ann's and Cynthia's are recorded on tape, but never shown.

8. In using the lower-case title, what Kehr (1989a) calls 'one of the film's less happy idiosyncrasies,' Soderbergh places each of his terms (sex, lies, videotape) on an ordinary, equal footing, drawing attention to his text by highlighting its refusal to be self-important. The word low, when applied to clothing, as in low-cut, exposes the neck and the bosom. Cynthia wears low-cut dresses. Ann does not. The lower-case title for this film also points

to a low-keyed, quiet, laconic, rhythmic text with dialogue that trails off into silences. Low further implies base, lowness, the mean and the vulgar (e.g. the liar and the adulterer).

9. He also argued (Siskel, 1989: 6) that 'this culture is obsessed with sex . . . . I wanted to deal with the real responsibilities and implications and repercussions of sex' which, he claims 'the movies don't deal with.' He was influenced by three films (Siskel, 1989: 7): *The Last Picture Show* (1971), *Five Easy Pieces* (1970), and *Carnal Knowledge* (1971).

10. The opening credits, white type on a black background, with a piano rendition of a pop standard ('It Had to be You') invoke Allen's style. Nearly every reviewer read the film as a pale reflection of Allen's work. Sterritt (1989b) is representative, 'Reiner borrows a lot of his style from Mr Allen, including a sunny view of New York City and a bouncy jazz-and-pop score. What he forgot to ask Woody for, regrettably, is the keen understanding of middle-class folkways that the best Allen comedies have.'

11. Harry Connick Jr's soundtrack made the pop Top 40 charts in 1989 and in 1990 it has sold more than 500,000 copies (Holden, 1990).

12. This is Rob Reiner's theory as well: 'I've discovered over the years that people – more women than men, but men as well – initially believe that men and women can be friends, but when you dig a little deeper, you find out in fact that it is not true: they may be friends, but it's because there is going to be sex, or neither of them is involved with anybody else and the minute one of them finds a lover, they can no longer maintain that relationship. Young women especially like to entertain the fantasy, but as they grow older they realize that an intimate, deep friendship with a man just isn't possible. There'll always be the sexual component that'll keep infringing on it' (Yakir, 1989).

13. Interspersed through the film are clips (in a manner reminiscent of *Reds*, 1981) from six elderly documentary couples (Jewish, Chinese, Caucasian), who discuss the first time they met, when they first dated, when they were engaged, when they were married, and how happy they are now. Each couple sits on the same love seat and tells its story. At the end of the film Harry and Sally sit on this seat and tell the story of the three times they met.

14. Harry then asks her what the lines to the song 'Auld Lang Syne' mean: 'My whole life, I don't know what this song means. Does it mean we should forget old acquaintances. Does it mean if we happen to forget them then we should remember them, which is not possible, because we already forgot.' Sally answers, 'Maybe it means that we should remember that we forget them, or something, anyway, it's about old friends.'

9

Do the Right Thing: Race in the USA[1]

Moral precepts from *Do the Right Thing*:

'Violence as a way of achieving racial justice is both impractical and immoral.'
(Martin Luther King, Jr)

'I am not against using violence in self-defense. I don't even call it violence
when it is self-defense. I call it intelligence.' (Malcolm X)

'I think there are plenty of good people in America, but there are plenty of bad
people and the bad ones are the ones who seem to have all the power.'
(Malcolm X)

'Fight the Power that be. Fight the Power.' (Theme song)

'Do the right thing.' (Da Mayor)

Spike Lee's highly controversial[2] 1989 film *Do the Right Thing*[3] turns on
the economic, visual, and political meanings brought to a small class of
social objects, namely the radio (ghetto-blaster), beer (Miller High Life,
versus Miller Lite), the T-shirt, and its several codes, the photograph, and
the photographic display of pictures of prominent Italian Americans
(Rocky Marciano, Sylvester Stallone, Robert De Niro, Frankie Vallie,
Frank Sinatra) in the 'Hall of Fame' at Sal's Famous Pizzeria ('The Best
Pizzeria in the World') which is located in the black ghetto in Brooklyn
(Bed-Stey). The site, at film's (and day's) end, of a vicious racial incident,
Sal's Pizzeria symbolizes, for the militant blacks in the film, the
oppressive presence of white power in the black world. Sal's refusal to
place the photographs of iconic black men and women (Martin Luther
King, Malcolm X, and Michael Jordan) on the walls of his restaurant
provokes the racial outburst in the film, which leads to the destruction of
Sal's Place.

In a symbolic ending, Lee has the mumbling, stuttering, retarded black
male Smiley, who sells the photos of King and Malcolm on the street,
place their burning pictures on the wall that has been destroyed by the
fire; the black face replaces the white man's picture. Significantly, this
black man wears a plain white T-shirt (as an undergarment), in contrast
to the other symbolic T-shirts worn in the film, which carry the names of
Bird (Larry of the Boston Celtics), Robinson (Jackie of the Dodgers)[4]
'Bed-Stey Or Die,' black for Vito (Sal's son who gets along with blacks),
and white for Pino (Sal's older, racist son).[5]

Lee's world is everywhere present; noticeable in every medium-sized
American city with their black ghettos, somewhat invisible on American
college campuses, and a real presence in grade, high schools, and prisons
where race is an issue that cannot be ignored. Yet it remains hidden from

the postmodern scene, seldom a topic taken seriously, in either film, or social analysis (see West, 1988a; Hall, 1988: 75–9). Race is America's invisible problem; everywhere present, it is never seen. When it does erupt, as in a ghetto riot, or in a film like Lee's, it is not taken seriously. Pushed aside, its importance is denied, or its solutions, as given in Lee's film, to the racial problem are rejected.

Lee's film elaborates the multiple political codes (Uncle Tom, honkie, violent, non-violent) and symbolic meanings that surround race, the racial self, popular culture heroes, and the T-shirt in contemporary American culture.[6] It offers the outlines of a political semiotics, a political economy of the sign, to use Baudrillard's phrase (1981), that stresses the politics as well as the sign functions of the semiotic object and its racial meanings.

Do the Right Thing provides an apt contrast to the films thus far considered. It takes its problems seriously, critiques its own solutions, and offers no easy answers to the conditions that it sees. It forces the viewer (black and white) to confront hard, moral choices concerning the racial order in America today (see Maslin, 1989). Its treatment of violence is political, not personal, although it understands that the personal is always political; as such it transcends Lynch's (*Blue Velvet*) pathological, sado-masochistic violence which is directed solely to personal, sexual ends. Lee's people (Sal, Vito, Pino, Mother Sister, Buggin' Out, Mookie, Tina, Jane, Sweet Dick Willie, Coconut Sid, Radio Raheem, Senior Love Daddy, ML, Da Mayor, Smiley, the children and teenagers) understand nihilism, hope, self-doubt, broken dreams, suicide, and walking insanity (West, 1988a). They live on the raw edges of hard reality, close to the heat of the street, the sound of the police siren, and the ever-present white man, the honkie, and the Koreans who threaten to control their lives, take away their means of livelihood and deprive them of their favorite beer.

This is a non-yuppie film. It is not surprising it lost out to *sex, lies and videotape* at the 1989 Cannes Film Festival. It is too disturbing for contemporary taste. Its politics of racial experience has no place in a world preoccupied with sex, confessions, material possessions, and warped theories of male–female friendship.

Race and Prejudice, Love and Violence in Bed-Stey

Do the Right Thing is an ethnography of the lived experiences of ordinary, everyday black and white, Italian, Korean, Puerto Rican, and Spanish-American men, women, and children in Brooklyn. Its focus is the racially divided urban world and the levels and layers of violence, hate, non-violence, and love that structure this world. Superficially nostalgic in its use of the writings and pictures of Martin Luther King Jr and Malcolm X, the film in fact argues that these two historical figures define the paradoxical situation of contemporary blacks (and whites). Doing the right thing involves resolving the conflicts between love and hate, non-violence and violence, self-defense and fighting the power that be. While violence is neither practical, nor moral, for an 'eye for an eye' can leave everybody blind (King), creating 'bitterness in the survivors and brutality in the destroyers' (King), it may be the intelligent thing to do, when self-defense is involved (Malcolm X).

The text maintains a necessary distinction between racial prejudice and institutional racism, while showing that these two phenomena are inter-dependent. Lee's characters talk in racial slurs (white honkie mother-fucker, nigger, monkey, ape, Puerto Rican, cocksucker and so on), which reproduce the institutions of racism. Lee attacks institutional racism at the levels of the legal system (the police), the economy (Sal's Place), and the everyday interactional order on the street, showing how these structures reinforce racial prejudices, and reproduce a racial and ethnic group's subordinate standing in the social, moral, economic, and political orders of 'Bed-Stey.' Here he connects talk and interaction with social structure. This is made explicit when Buggin' Out attempts to organize a boycott of Sal's Place, and finds little support among the residents of the community. Arguing, in the end, that the solution to the racial crisis in America lies with whites (see Ebert, 1989b: 893), the film suggests that it is not fair to put the burden of doing the right thing on black shoulders.[7]

The love in this film is not the love of *sex, lies and videotape*, nor the love of Sally for Harry. It is a love which engages the entirety of a group's humanity. It is a love for fellow human beings; a love which is more than sex, or sexual intimacy. It is a Christian love which says that hate destroys, and love creates. It is the love of a father (Sal) for his sons. The love of brother for brother (Vito and Pino), the love of Mookie for his child, and for his child's mother (Tina), and his sister (Jane). It is the love of Da Mayor and Mother Sister for all their people on the street. It is the love of Senior Love Daddy for all his people who live in Bed-Stey.

In the words of Radio Raheem, who puts on his 'love and hate' knuckles for Mookie,

> Love, hate, each hand, the tale of good and evil, the right hand, the left hand. Love, these five fingers go straight to the soul of man, the right hand, the hand of love. The left hand, the hand that Cain used to kill his brother. The story of life is this. Static: one hand always fighting the other hand, the left hand kickin' ass, the right hand comin' back, got the left hand on the ropes, K.O.'d by love. I love you, I love you. Love and hate and peace. Fight the power that be.'

This is a political love, a love embedded in violence, hate, self-interest, racial slurs, and ethnic pride. A love that mobilizes peace and non-violence, and a love which justifies violence and hate. A love that cuts through the fabrics of family, group, and work identity, to the heart of the racially defined self; a self divided against itself, a self which loves and hates itself at the same time. How, Lee asks, can people like Mookie love themselves when they are constantly confronted by racial hatred? How can they do the right thing, when hate becomes a form of self-protection against an institutional system that constantly represses, denigrates, slurs, and slanders the contours of one's sacred, loving, moral self?

But Lee doesn't stop with white–black love and hatred. After all he has Sal question Pino's hatred of blacks, even though he puts it in economic terms: 'Why you got so much anger in you? Do your friends put money in your pocket? I never had no trouble with these people. I watch their little kids get older and the old people get older. They grew up on my food. I'm very proud of that. Sal's Pizzeria's here to stay.' He also shows that within the black community denigration occurs. Both Jane and Tina tell Mookie that he is a bad father, that he doesn't know how to take responsibility, get a real job, or be a father.

Love becomes entangled with the very racial order that exploits the blacks in the film. If Sal is proud of all the little kids who grew up eating his pizza, these same kids, now teenagers and adults, love his pizza and see no reason to boycott his place. Buggin' Out has just asked a teenage girl to sign his boycott. Girl: 'Boycott Sal's? Shit, I born and raised on Sal's pizza. Ya crazy man? Black Panther eat pizza, we eat pizza.'

Race, Names, and Popular Culture

Do the Right Thing is a study in racism and American popular culture; an in-depth analysis of the symbolic meanings brought to the heroes of young and old Americans, in particular Italian Americans and African Americans. It is an examination of how cultural heroes are appropriated by racial and ethnic groups, and in the process used, by dominant groups, as signifiers of repression and control. At the same time it is a treatment of how oppressed racial groups attempt to reclaim symbolic heroes for their own purposes. The film is a litany of names, which signifies the clash, at the level of the popular, between white and black America in the late 1980s.

Consider the following conversation between Mookie and Vito.

Mookie: The best pitcher in the game is Dwight Gooden.
Vito: Why bring that up? Roger Clements is better.
Mookie: Clements sucks. He can't carry Dwight's jock strap. Who's your favorite basketball player?
Vito: Magic Johnson.
Mookie: Who's your favorite movie star?
Vito: Eddie Murphy.
Mookie: Who's your favorite Rock Star? Prince?
Vito: No! Bruce. Magic, Eddie, Prince – They're not niggers. They're not really black. They're more than black. I've been readin' about your leaders. Reverend Al, Mr. Sharp-Do-Do, Jesse, 'keep an open eye.'
Mookie: That's fucked up! Don't talk about Jesse.
Vito: The other guy, Farr-a-khan.
Mookie: Minister Farrakhan.
Vito: Mr. F. talks about the day the black man will rise up.
Mookie: We started civilization. Fuck you, fuck your fuckin' pizza and fuck Frank Sinatra.
Vito: Fuck Michael Jackson.[8]

This is more than verbal bantering over names. It is racial, cultural politics, with Vito stripping the heroes of black culture of their blackness, while he mocks their political doings. It is no accident that the debate surrounds the names Michael Jordan, Eddie Murphy, Magic Johnson, and Michael Jackson; for the decade of the 1980s, these were the heroes of young Americans. But clearly they function as different heroes for white and black Americans. For whites they cease to be black. They are entertainers. For blacks they represent cultural leaders whose heritage extends back to the beginning of civilization.

Now African American musicians. Senior Love Daddy, the ever-present DJ, reads off the 'We Love Roll Call: Ray Charles, Anita Baker, Salt and Pepper, Sugar Bear, Coltrane, James Brown, Public Enemy, Tracy Chapman, Duke Ellington, Count Basie, Stevie Wonder, Sarah Vaughn, Bob Marley, Steel Punks, Cannon Ball, Ottis Redding, Miles Davis.' This impressive encyclopedia of black musicians covers jazz, blues, popular, rhythm and blues, rock-'n-roll, soul, Rap, reggae, folk, and classical music. It encompasses what is African American music in America today.

Naming is a political act, and names are economic signifiers. To change a picture which carries a name is to engage in a political and economic act. Here is Sal responding to Buggin' Out who demands that a black man's picture be mounted in Sal's Hall of Fame 'No brothers up on the wall. Hey, Sal, how come no brothers up on the wall?' Sal: 'You want brothers up on the wall, get your own place. Your uncle, your step-father, your nieces, whoever you want. But this is my pizzeria. American Italians on the wall.' Buggin' Out: 'Fine Sal, but do I see any American Italians eating in here? All I see is black folks. We spend much money in here. We do have a say.' Sal picks up a baseball bat and threatens Buggin' Out, who responds: 'Get some brothers on the wall – Nelson Mandela, Malcolm X, Michael Jordan!'

Tennis shoes. The white man with the Bird T-shirt rides his bicycle over Buggin' Out's Air Jordans. Buggin' Out: 'My new Air Jordans! Get out of my neighborhood. What you doin' in a black neighborhood? I should make you buy me another pair. I'm a righteous black man.'

There is, as noted earlier, a sense of racial positioning in Lee's world; each racial or ethnic group is known by a handful of stereotypes. These labels keep the members at a safe distance from one another, while prejudice is defined by a collective sense of group position in the racial hierarchy of the neighborhood (see Blumer, 1958). In a pivotal moment, as the heat rises on the street, Lee has members of each racial group hurl vicious words at one another. *Mookie to Sal (and his sons)*: 'Dago, Wop, guinea, garlic breath, pizza slingin', spaghetti bender, Vic Damone, Perry Como, Pavarotti.' *Pino to Mookie (and the blacks)*: 'Gold chain wearin' fried chicken and biscuit eatin' monkey, ape, baboon, fast runnin', high jumpin', spear chuckin', basketball dunkin' titso spade, take your fuckin' pizza and go back to Africa.' A *Puerto Rican man to the Korean grocer*: 'Little slanty eyed, me-no speakie American, own every fruit and vegetable stand in New York, Bull Shit, Reverend Sun Young Moon, Summer 88 Olympic kick-ass boxer, sonofabitch.' The *white policeman*: 'You goya bean eatin' 15 in the car, 30 in the apartment, pointy red shoes wearin' Puerto Ricans, cocksuckers.' The *Korean grocer*: 'I got good price for you, how am I doing? Chocolate, egg cream, drinking, bagel and lochs, Jew ass-hole.' This racial hatred is turned inward. Here is Sweet Dick Willie on the Korean grocers: 'Korean motherfuckers. Either those Koreans are geniuses or that dude was brought up that way before he got off the boat. He opened up that store that was boarded up for years, while you didn't do a goddamn thing except sit on your monkey ass here on this corner and do nothin.'

Sex is not a luxury for these people; it is an act of procreation that carries consequences, including children and unwanted pregnancies (Tina to Mookie: 'The last time we did nasty we got a baby'). When it occurs (as with Mookie and Tina), it is on the run, time stolen from work, although Lee treats its presence with a gentle, loving eroticism that connects love with sexuality. For the old men, it is a memory and a part of manhood. Sweet Dick Willie: 'It's never too hot or too cold to fuck,' while Coconut Sid reminds him 'You Negroes always talkin' about your dick,' and Buggin' Out describes himself as 'a strugglin' black tryin' to keep my dick hard in a cruel, harsh world.' Nor is therapy or self-analysis an option for these people. No yuppie problems in Bed-Stey.

Here the electronic toy is not the TV, the VCR, or the video camera. It is the jambox, the ghetto-blaster, the radio that plays the radical tapes, the reggae, the Rap sounds, and the black music that preaches revolution, hope, and love. The jambox, which is violently destroyed at the end of the film, is symbolic of the contemporary urban black situation. Having no real private place to live, the streets and their corners become home. The ghetto-blaster blasts its listener out of this space into a symbolic realm where dreams can be dreamt, hopes heard, if not lived. Its presence in public places defies the white racial order. The music it plays is privately coded; it carries racial and ethnic meanings special to the black listener. Lee, however, is not content to leave the conflict over music at the white/black level. At one point the Puerto Ricans tell Radio Raheem to turn his music down, and he refuses. In a scene reminiscent of an old western, the Puerto Ricans turn their radio up and point it at Radio Raheem, while he does the same to them. The music from the two ethnic and racial worlds collide, meet in mid-air and create a violent cacophony that nobody can understand.

Dressing the Racial Self

It is the fate of black Americans to embody their cultural stigma on their skins and to wear their positive identities on their backs and their chests. As if this were not enough, the heroes they claim as their own are the very same people that white America values, buys and owns. For example, wearing a T-shirt with the name of the LA Lakers (as one of the teenagers in the film does) attaches the wearer to a near all-black championship basketball team that is coached and owned by white men. The same observation holds for the shirt Mookie wears, with 'Robinson' on the back and 'Dodgers' on the front. White men allowed Jackie Robinson to integrate an all-white team and sport. Hence the cultural identity claimed by the shirt is undercut by the economic realities that bring the name to the shirt in the first place.

The T-shirt is *the* garment in Lee's text. It is an everyday, political text. Its multiple forms speak to the heterogeneity of voices and positions within Sal's and Mookie's worlds. The signs it bears locate its wearer in the political economy of this version of the ghetto which is divided into two camps, symbolized by the photographs and words of Martin Luther King and Malcolm X which open and end the film. King's abhorrence of violence is contrasted to Malcolm's position that violence can be a form of education and self-protection. The text joins these two voices in a single photograph, suggesting that doing the right thing may not always be easy. Non-violence and violence are thus coded into Lee's text, emblazoned on the T-shirts worn by the key players in the story.

Sal's name on a shirt identifies the wearer with a position of power that must be overturned. Bird's name reflects another version of white, racist, honkie America, as given in two other icons: Elvis and John Wayne, both of whom are ridiculed at the beginning and end of the film. Robinson's name signifies non-violence and complicity with the power structure. The plain white shirt worn by the seller of Malcolm and Martin's photo suggests a neutrality; a refusal to endorse violence or non-violence. The 'Bed-Stey Or Die' shirt worn by Radio Raheem suggests rebellion and violence, even as his silver knuckles spell out love and hate. The 'We FM Love' sign outside the radio station symbolizes conciliation between the two communities, and an alignment with Martin; even the names Malcolm and Martin take on iconic status in the text, as their faces become signs of the violence that lurks just below the surface in this racial community.

The T-shirt comes in many forms: plain white, colored, printed with slogans, the names of professional basketball players (Bird), personal names (Mookie), and the name of Sal's establishment. It is worn to work, to dinner, is taken off when love-making occurs, put on first thing in the morning. It is an undergarment for the old men on the street and the policemen. It is a badge of honor for the Bird-man, a statement of defiance for Radio Raheem, and a declaration of personal ambiguity and doubt for Mookie.

The T-shirt, as such, is a multiple thing: an utilitarian, mass-produced, outer- and undergarment; a simulacrum of the hyperreal, prideful racial identities of the black male which are attached to sporting idols and teams (Robinson, LA Lakers, Mets and so on); a fluid, expressive, problematic, visual icon ('Bed-Stey Or Die') which challenges the viewer. The T-shirt is the racial symbol of 'Bed-Stey.' Its wearing embodies the attempt to capture a piece of the 'real' as a part of the persona of the person wearing the garment. The T-shirt stands for the racial self.

As a conveyer of meaning, it is no longer a direct index of experience, for the signs it bears reference experiences the person hasn't had, but symbolically identifies with (such as the Lakers). These signs embody dreams and fantasies, and their wearing attaches the wearer to cultural idols. Those shirts which advertise commodities ('Coca-Cola,' 'Nike' or 'Wilson,' 'Sal's Famous Pizzeria') connect the wearer to a product and a status community; they express a personal choice, although the person may not drink Coca-Cola, own a pair of Nike tennis shoes, or eat at Sal's. However those who advertise these products for profit may then be connected to the worlds of experiences of those who do wear or consume these objects. For example Spike Lee has been criticized for his tennis shoe commercials with Michael Jordan. African·American urban males now appear to rob and kill one another for these shoes. Mookie was connected to Sal's in part by his shirt, the place he hated to work at, and a place he ordered his sister to stay away from, even though he wore a shirt advertising its products.

In the dressing of the racial self, the people in Lee's film take a stand on contemporary popular culture; alternatively mocking it through shirts which push its boundaries and flaunt its moral codes ('Bed-Stey Or Die'), while redefining its public identities (Mookie's name on a shirt advertising 'Sal's Pizzeria' compromises, confuses, and conflates the signifiers of whiteness and blackness). These contemporary sign functions of the T-shirt point to the evocative, elusive, floating, adrift racial signifiers which define the age of the simulacrum. A sign no longer refers to a thing, but to another sign. In the shadows and the echoes of these signs, the sights and sounds of the postmodern moment and its racial orders can be heard. As Manning (1990) suggests, these T-shirts allude to the loss of meaning and permanency in the current age. Their presence everywhere announces this desire to control what is no longer controllable. In Lee's film they announce the desire to seize the day, and return lost identities to the black self.

The T-shirt transforms the person into the object of the other's gaze; in this move a scopophilic need is met. The postmodern, racial self is a voyeur. The camera and its eye are our windows into the world (even Smiley wears a camera around his neck). The photographs in *Do the Right Thing* become the vehicles and the metaphors of a looking, gazing culture, which is tired of being put outside the gaze of white, Italian Americans. The photographs symbolize and instantiate a black culture that knows itself only through the self-reflective projections of lived experiences (and its representations) which are controlled by white economic interests. On two occasions Lee draws the viewer's attention to these representations (the poster that states, 'Brooklyn's own – Mike Tyson,' showing a picture of Tyson in a boxing pose, and the painting on the wall that states, 'Twana told the truth'). These·signs appear on the walls of the public spaces that define and constrain the neighborhood. His black people gaze out on this world of free-floating signs as bemused, perplexed lookers, seeing not persons, but the signs they bear on their bodies, understanding now that these signs stand for and are the person. The T-shirt presumes that voyeurs everywhere will read the signs of the racial self that are announced by the shirt that is worn on the person's body. The sign has replaced the person.

Spike Lee's Racial World: Radios, Music, and Murder

Staking out the political positions of his people through their dress, Lee then collapses this entire signifying structure in the violent scene that brings the film to its climax. Here is how it happens.

The hottest day of the year is nearly over. It is closing time at Sal's. Radio Raheem walks in with his radio blasting, 'Fight the Power. Fight the Power that be' and tells Sal, 'Black people on that motherfuckin' wall now!' Sal, angrily, 'Turn that jungle music off. Fuck you!' Radio Raheem puts his radio on the bar. Sal picks up his baseball bat and begins shouting, 'Cocksucker, nigger ass' as he pounds the radio. Mookie tells him to put the bat down. Sal continues to smash the radio, 'I killed your fuckin' radio!' Radio Raheem dives over the bar at Sal and grabs him by the throat (the screen cuts to a shot of two boxers fighting). A crowd appears outside the door. Sal and Radio Raheem are in the street fighting. Da Mayor and Mother Sister run to the scene, and try to break up the fight. The police come. Radio Raheem is choked with a nightstick, pulled off the ground, feet dangling above the pavement, as a shot of Air Jordans flying over the ground flashes on screen. Radio Raheem dies, falls to the ground and is kicked by the police. A shot of his love knuckle fills part of the screen. The police take Radio Raheem and a handcuffed Buggin' Out to the police car. The crowd attacks the car. The Korean grocer pounds the trunk. Smiley puts his hands over his ears and moans, 'No, No.' Mookie screams, 'Why did you kill him. You murdered him! Never anymore, never anymore will this be!' Coconut Sid comments, 'Plain as day. They didn't have to kill that boy.' Sal, to the crowd, 'You do what you gotta do.' Da Mayor to the crowd, 'Go home. Don't do somethin' we regret for the rest of our lives. He had a radio. All he wanted were pictures on the wall and he died.'

Mookie crosses the street, gets a garbage can and throws it into Sal's front window. A crowd rushes in, destroying everything. Smiley lights a match and drops it. Fire breaks out and leaps around Frank Sinatra's cracked photograph. The crowd moves to the Korean grocery store and threatens the Korean man and his wife. The man says, 'We black,' and the crowd moves away. The police and firemen return. The crowd disperses. A shot of the broken radio is shown, as the words, 'Fight the Power, Fight the Power' are heard. Smiley enters Sal's and puts the picture of Malcolm and Martin up on the wall, near where the Sinatra picture hung.

The screen turns black, then fills with scenes from early the next day.
Da Mayor wakes up in Mother Sister's bed. Kids are playing basketball
on the street. Senior Love Daddy speaks, 'My people, my people, What
can I say? Say what I can. I don't believe what I saw. Are we gonna live?
Together we live.' Mookie gets up and Tina tells him to get a 'fuckin'
life.' The rhythm of the street returns; it's as if the murder and the riot
had never occurred.

Sal drives up to his Pizzeria, kicks the garbage can, looks up and sees
Mookie. 'What you want?' Mookie: 'Money.' Sal: 'You don't work
here.' Mookie: 'Radio Raheem is dead.' Sal: 'Cocksucker caused this.'
Sal pays Mookie. They throw 50-dollar bills back and forth at one
another. Sal: 'I don't believe this. You're sick. What you gonna do
today?' Mookie: 'Make that money up, get paid, see my son, alright with
you?' Senior Love Daddy croons, 'Hey, Mookie, Mookie man, go home
to your son.' The screen fills with the words from Martin and Malcolm.

Reading the Riot

Mookie (the man between the two camps, the man who works for Sal)
throws the garbage can that starts the fire. A murder and a riot caused
by a radio, a song, and a picture. When Sal kills Radio Raheem's radio,
he kills the music. This violent, political act is a response to Radio
Raheem's equally political act of demanding that a picture of a black man
go up on the wall. As he makes this demand his radio blasts, 'Fight the
Power, Fight the Power that be!' Killing the radio annihilates Raheem's
attack on Sal's power. Raheem's murder is a symbolic extension of this
political act; he died when his radio and his music were murdered. As the
radio is smashed, Sal screams, 'Jungle music!', thereby connecting racial
prejudice with the institution of racism, as embodied in his Pizzeria.

As Sal's place blazes, the pictures of Malcolm and Martin suddenly
appear, indicating that the two sides of Lee's film coexist, even in the
moment of destruction. Yet Smiley, the film's mediator, like Radio
Raheem, and Da Mayor, between violence and non-violence, starts the
fire. Lee is making a deeper point here, aligning himself with Malcolm,
by suggesting that violence (destruction) may be the only way to get the
white establishment to accept the black's voice and presence. The next
day, Mookie, in his T-shirt again, reconciles with Sal who is wearing a
plain white shirt without his name, suggesting a stripping of identity as
a result of the fire. The two men meet again, as employee and employer.
An uneasy status quo is in place.

In this moment of violence and its aftermath, Lee projects a political
economy of signs which make a difference; for now the signs of the self
are connected to real political action. The personal becomes political, and
the political is personal. In a single motion Lee politicizes semiotics, and
suddenly gives a real force to the blurred, evocative, floating signifiers
that, in another world -- the postmodern -- drift by, are gazed at for a

moment, and then read as fleeting markers of the self. For Lee what you wear is who you are. Who you are is marked by your politics and whether or not you will take a stand against the 'power' that rules, the 'power' that is, that 'power' who is the white man.

Here then, in urban, ghetto America, where race counts and makes a difference, signs on T-shirts function as things which have real consequences. In moving from the semiotic to the real, from the sign and its signifiers, to the realm of the signified, Lee has accomplished something other postmodern theorists have been unable to do. He has shown how signs connect to and shape real lived experience. In so doing he has produced one of the most disturbing films of the 1980s. It speaks today, where on American college campuses racism is becoming a real issue, and the positions marked out by Malcolm and Martin are more relevant than they were twenty years ago. It speaks too, to the freeing of Nelson Mandela,[9] the continued existence of racism in South Africa (Derrida, 1985), and the rise to power of White Supremacist groups in the United States, who claim to be expressing the values of mainstream Americans when they call for the murdering of niggers.

In asking us to do the right thing, Spike Lee asks that we reconsider the meanings we have thus far brought, unthinkingly, to the ordinary signifiers that we wear on our backs. In opening our eyes in this way Lee has created a way to see past semiotics to a political economy of signs that does more than set the postmodern world adrift in a sea of unattached signifiers without meaning. Race is the unraveled sign of the contemporary age.

Notes

1. An earlier version of this chapter, a comment on Peter K. Manning's manuscript, 'The new T-shirt: codes, chronotypes and everyday objects,' was presented (as was Manning's manuscript) to the 12th International Summer Institute for Semiotic and Structural Studies, University of Toronto, 23 June 1990, in a colloquium entitled, 'The socio-semiotics of objects: the role of artifacts in social symbolic processes.'

2. It generated immediate controversy, much of which turned on the belief that Lee was advocating violence as a solution to racism in America (see for example *New York Times*, 1989e). From July to November of 1989 over 60 articles, editorials, and reviews of the film appeared in such major national newspapers as *The New York Times*, the *Washington Post*, the *Christian Science Monitor*, the *Wall Street Journal*, the *Los Angeles Times*, the *Chicago Tribune*, the *Boston Globe*, and the *Atlanta Constitution*. Spike Lee became a national celebrity, as professors, politicians, psychiatrists, social workers, movie reviewers, and the residents of Brooklyn discussed the racial implications of his film, which was the most talked-about film at the 1989 Cannes Film Festival. The documentary, *Roger and Me*, not discussed because of space limitations, is another major 1989 film. Its topics are labor, class, and the multinational corporation. It has been compared to *Do the Right Thing*: 'Twenty years from now when they look back at the Reagan era, two films will stand out as the statement of our times – *Do the Right Thing*, and *Roger and Me*' (Siskell, in Moore, 1990: 12).

3. Directed, produced, and written by Spike Lee. Forty Acres and A Mule Filmworks Production, A Spike Lee Joint. Cast: Sal (Danny Aiello), Da Mayor (Ossie Davis), Mother Sister (Ruby Dee), Mookie (Spike Lee), Radio Raheem (Bill Nunn), Buggin' Out (Giancarlo

Exposito), Pino (John Turturro), Vito (Richard Edison), ML (Paul Benjamin), Coconut Sid (Franki Faison), Sweet Dick Willie (Robin Harris). Nominated for the 1989 Golden Palm Award at the 1989 Cannes Film Festival, losing, as noted in the last chapter, to *sex, lies, and videotape*.

4. Presumably the Jackie Robinson who integrated Major League American Baseball in 1947.

5. A white man, born in Brooklyn, wears the Bird T-shirt and a black man, Mookie, wears Robinson's T-shirt.

6. I reference here not only the codes of the T-shirt (e.g. utilitarian, manufactured item, outer garment, expressive sign, problematic icon, walking pun, copies and real copies, see Manning, 1990), but also the codes that pun, mock, and denigrate race, black heroes, black music, and black culture (e.g. ape, baboon, monkey-ass, jungle music, niggers, etc.).

7. In an interview with Roger Ebert (Ebert, 1989b: 893) Lee stated, 'Racism is when you have laws set up, systematically put in a way to keep people from advancing, to stop the advancement of a people. Black people have never had the power to enforce racism, and so this is something that white America is going to have to work out themselves. If they decide they want to stop it, or curtail it, or do the right thing . . . then it will be done, but not until then.'

8. Lee expands this list of names to include Don Corleone (Radio Raheem's name for Sal), and Kunte Kinte (from the famous made-for-television film, *Roots*, 1977), when Mookie tells Jane, 'I ain't no slave, I ain't Kunte Kinte.'

9. Recently T-shirts have begun to appear in northern US cities like Detroit carrying the names of Martin/Malcolm and Mandela, fitted around a map of Africa.

10

Paris, Texas: Mills and Baudrillard in *America*

> What is new in America is the clash of the first level (primitive and wild) and
> the 'third kind' (the absolute simulacrum). There is no second level . . . . Let
> us grant this country the admiration it deserves and open our eyes to the absur-
> dity of our own customs. (Baudrillard, 1988b: 104)

The name Paris, Texas appears to be an oxymoron, a forging together of
contradictory terms. But it is an actual town in East Texas and it provides
the name for Wim Wenders's film, *Paris, Texas* (1984), which won the
prestigious Golden Palm Award at the 1984 Cannes Film Festival
(Studlar, 1985: 359). Paris, Texas is also an oxymoron for Baudrillard
(1988b) in *America*, for his book is about the reflections of a man who
lives in Paris, writes about the American way of life, and more than once
has traveled through Texas on his way to America. Seeing this country in
its cinema and on its TV screens, Baudrillard uses the metaphor of the
movie to map his understanding of what this country is all about.

The Texas side of Paris carries another meaning for this chapter. C.
Wright Mills was born and raised in Texas, the land of the wild west and
the cowboy. Although he appeared to have lost his Texas roots once he
traveled North, Mills's sociological imagination, and his preoccupations
with the lives of ordinary people, were grounded, in part, in his Texas
experiences. He is fantasized by one reader in the following way:

> Imagine a burly cowpuncher on the long, slow ride from the Panhandle of
> Texas to Columbia University, carrying in his saddle-bag some books which he
> reads with absorption while his horse trots along . . . Imagine the style and
> imagery that would result from the interaction of the cowboy student and his
> studies . . . The end result of such an imaginary grand tour would be a work
> like *The Sociological Imagination*. (Shils, 1960: 77)

Mills, the cowboy from Texas, Baudrillard, the man from Paris in
Texas, *Paris, Texas*, the name of a film; I shall work back and forth
between these oxymoronic meanings of Paris, Texas in my interpretation
of Baudrillard's book, as I contrast his image of America with Mills's. In
so doing I will examine Baudrillard's central thesis, quoted above, concerning what is new about America; that is the absence of a self-reflexive,
self-mirroring level of the simulacrum. Wenders's film first, and then the
assertion that the cinema and TV are America's reality. I will not quarrel
with Mills's failure to see this side of America, but I will bring his
postmodern predictions up against Baudrillard's reading of this country.

Paris, Texas

A leader in the New German Cinema movement, Wenders's film drew its inspiration from Sam Shepard's *Motel Chronicles* (1982). The film is a road movie, a modern version of the saddle-tramp story which combines the American car-centered culture as a symbol of freedom, with the concept of the traveler as living on the edge of society.[1] Building on the myth that the desert is America's last frontier, The Wenders–Shepard story (Wenders and Shepard collaborated on *Paris, Texas*) involves a father, Travis, who has abandoned his wife (Jane) and son (Hunter) to wander through the desert in search of himself. Discovered one day by a German physician in a sleepwalking, near-dead state, he is rescued by his brother Walt, but escapes to continue his wanderings in the desert. Initially refusing to talk, Travis pulls a crumpled photo from his pocket which shows an empty lot where he hoped to build a house for his family. He reveals that he has been walking towards Paris, Texas where he believes his parents conceived him in love. He then recalls a story his father told many times about his wife being born in Paris, France (not Texas, which was the case). The story was told so many times that the father came to believe its truth. This myth destroyed the family. Travis seeks to resurrect the myth and start his life over again. Walt takes him to Los Angeles, where he lives with Hunter and Walt and his wife Anne. After a period of recuperation, Travis and Hunter set off in a pick-up truck for Houston, in search of Jane. Crossing the desert again they find Jane working in a brothel. In a penultimate scene, where Travis confronts Jane and their faces merge into one, he reveals why he left her and Hunter. The next day he returns Hunter to Jane and returns to the desert, driving off into the Houston night, the luminous lights of the city in the background.

Wenders presents Travis's travels as a phenomenological experience in which the senses are heightened and awarenesses are intensified. The film's cinematography (Robby Muller) beautifully captures the desert sunsets and sunrises, the skylines of Los Angeles and Houston, the billboards, junk cars, and junkyards which litter the landscape, and the freeways that never end. The film is filled with nostalgia for the past and for the family. It is self-reflexive in tone, yet framed by a conventional sense of narrative cinema (the biographical form, ambiguous closure, and so on). Panned by critics (Studlar, 1985; Kauffmann, 1984; Lennett, 1985; Hoberman, 1984; Denby, 1984; but see Reed, 1984 and Canby, 1984), *Paris, Texas* 'reverberates with the mythic resonance of the view that America is the last frontier, even as it focuses on the problematic of the American archetype of the wandering male, the outsider familiar in legend, literature and film' (Studlar, 1985: 360).

Baudrillard's *America*

Baudrillard's *America* is a child of *Cool Memories* (Baudrillard, 1987b) a French diary of Baudrillard's musings about his travels in the United States. Rejected by many American publishers because of its apparent negative, condescending images, the work was subsequently published by the British house, Verso. This 1988 English translation is selling well on both sides of the Atlantic, although it has been roundly criticized by American academics and intellectuals. He describes what he was after in his journey:

> I went in search of astral America,[2] not social and cultural America, but the America of the empty, absolute freedom of the freeways, not the deep America of mores and mentalities, but the America of desert speed, of motels and mineral surfaces. I looked . . . in the marvellously affectless succession of signs, faces, and ritual acts on the road . . . [I] looked for . . . a universe which is virtually our own, right down to its European cottages. (Baudrillard, 1988b: 5)

Baudrillard's *America*, like Wenders's *Paris, Texas*, is about Europe and its transformations on the American frontier. Baudrillard *in* America is about his search to find what he had already found, before he went to America, for what he found was an Americanized version of home. Disillusioned, cynical, road-weary from his travels, he went, as any European tourist must, from East to West: New York, Chicago, Minneapolis, Texas, the great deserts, Los Angeles, Disneyland, the Hollywood studios, the California coast.

Here is what he saw. Cinematic pictures in his head, he found that

> It is not the least of America's charms that even outside the movie theatres the whole country is cinematic. The desert you pass through is like the set of a Western, the city a screen of signs and formulas . . . . The American city seems to have stepped right out of the movies. (1988b: 56)

What's surprising about this? What else could the cities look like? After all, at some point the real does provide the foundations for its simulation. He's told us this before (Baudrillard, 1983a: 150); just as he has observed that the real and the imaginary are now forever confused, and 'reality no longer has the time to take on the appearance of reality' (1983a: 152). What's new is the application of his theory of the simulacrum to this particular setting, that is the United States.

What he finds, of course, is what he has told us earlier: that the advanced industrialized societies, those called postmodern, have skipped a level of reflexivity in their relationship to the real and its representations. What does this mean? Several answers are suggested. At the level of perception, where a political economy of signs circulates in preformatted forms, the surface is the deep. Second-order reflection on the reality of a sign is called out only when the sign (image) departs from preformatted representations, or when the event is so horrendous that it requires multiple reflexive representations (for example the holocaust:

Krug, 1989a, 1990a, 1990b). At the level of surface, glossed, everyday experience, the real is the representation. A cinematic society, a society of the spectacle, a society which constantly views itself reflected back to itself on the glare of the TV screen is only what is seen. What is seen is a 'realistic' cinematic version of what the 'real-should-be.' This is a worldwide phenomenon, not something unique to America.

As a traveler, the Frenchman no longer an outsider to American culture (he has been here too many times before), Baudrillard alternated between being the masculine outsider who makes the familiar strange ('Santa Barbara villas are all like funeral homes,' 1988b: 30), while making the strange familiar ('the Bonaventure Hotel [is like] a self-contained miniature city,' p. 60).[3] He distanced himself from the ordinary tourist, yet adopted a writing style that exploits a metaphysics of presence and stresses the immediacy of perception (p. 9). The text, that is, has the feel of a work written in haste, on the run, jotted-down impressions at the day's end. Velocity is the issue, instant reflections, like the rush of air through the car window as the driver–writer hurls through space at a high speed. The effect of the text is to distance Baudrillard from the surrounding surface images of the popular American culture which he wishes to describe. At the same time the text is written in such a way that it makes him an insider to what Americans can't see because it is too familiar to them. He thus becomes the cultural critic who writes both a politics of culture and a politics of criticism (see Morris, 1988b: 14; Grossberg, 1988c: 378), which turns the American into a foreign and strange 'other' who has become a victim of an out of control third-order simulacrum.

Like a nomad wandering through this strange cultural landscape, he studies our billboards, our junkyards and our sea-coast cities, finding all of them equally familiar in their strangeness, united by a single thread of meaning: '"What are you doing after the orgy?" What do you do when everything is available – sex, flowers, the stereotypes of life and death?' (p. 30). Seeing everything as a signifier (billboard) of this way of life, he pauses for a moment, and renders the following judgement: 'This is America's problem, and, through America, it has become the whole world's problem' (p. 30). How America caused all of this is not made clear, but it is evident that he excludes no one from America's cultural condition.

Another view of the billboard. Billboards are, as Morris (1988b) and Grossberg (1988c: 383) note, neither authentic nor inauthentic in themselves; they just are, and what they are is many different things, following only the 'logic of the next' (Morris, 1988b: 42), as they articulate specific vocabularies of the person, meaning, emotionality, beauty, and gender in everyday life. Seeing a common meaning in all of them, the one privileged by his insight into the third order of the simulacrum, Baudrillard's book speeds along, glossing all images into a single repeated frame, as if the VCR had permanently stopped in the 'pause-hold' position, the record needle had fallen into a single groove, and the compact disk was playing the same tune, over and over again. Repetition is the message here, organized only by this 'logic of the next.' Unlike Grossberg's (1988c: 384) nomadic cultural critic who rejects the idea of a single, unified, cultural subject, Baudrillard finds sameness everywhere.

A Slow *Night Train* South

The logic of his travels of course is what is at issue. He sought, like Wenders, astral reflections in the desert. Suppose he had taken another route. He could have easily taken a slow train south from Minneapolis and followed the Mississippi river to New Orleans. Another version of the country would have revealed itself: the erotic rhythm of the rails, faded Amtrak coaches filled with boozy blacks, microwave dinners, Japanese tourists with Walkmans, conductors calling out Memphis in the early morning and pointing to Graceland, urban and rural landscapes painted in Edward Hopper colors, all-night diners, country and western music, New Orleans jazz, the bayou country with the cajuns, bridges which extend forever over waterways that run to the Gulf of Mexico where oil rigs stand like skeletons in the morning fog, shanty towns, giant oaks with moss that falls like a shroud to the sidewalks where vendors sell fake-antique captains' sea trunks, and artists render realistic pictures of you and your lover for five dollars in charcoal, while hookers, addicts, street musicians, and tourists from Iowa wander the streets, looking for action, and the next meal. But American trains aren't for European travelers, and Baudrillard wasn't in search of this version of America. No *Mystery Train*[4] for him, no night reverie with ears and eyes tuned to the sounds of Elvis, while the liquor stores close before you've had your last drink, as a baby is born in the next room of the motel, and mad couples shoot at one another in the dark because their love has gotten out of hand.

But he didn't take this route, for his 'America' is in the desert, not in the frontier that the Mississippi River and other waterways mark in American literary culture.[5] No, his 'America' is in the wasteland of the desert, 'there amidst the heat, shifting multicolored sands, and bleak contours of rock back-lit by stark horizons, he discovered the essence of "America": an empty desert' (Manning, 1990: 1).[6] A wasteland of sand, and drifting signs, Baudrillard's astral America is given in the images which come at a glance, those which are already familiar before they are seen, because they have been seen before. His astral America is the world of free-floating signifiers. Unlike early European intellectuals (de Tocqueville, Weber, Adorno) who attempted interpretive readings of the American character through extensive contact with the ordinary and out of the ordinary person, Baudrillard shuns depth, finding a profound sense of peace and nostalgia in the plastic world his eyes gaze upon. Indeed he prefers the glitter of the cities to the purple sunsets of the desert; his is an urban reading of Europeanized America.

Wenders and Baudrillard

Roundly condemned by nearly all who have read it,[7] read as an indictment of the American character by a European snob, his book has not
been read for it is Baudrillard's version of Wim Wenders's *Paris, Texas*.
Compare, then, Baudrillard and Wenders. Both are disillusioned Europeans, each the carrier of a cultural tradition which has found, with few
prior exceptions, a welcome reception in the United States (German
Expressionist German film-makers, the French New Wave, Foucault,
deconstructionism and so on). Each is in quest of an identity. Wenders's
Travis seeks to find himself in his past. Each acknowledges, however
grudgingly, the influence of past masters and contemporaries on their
work. Wenders seeks to fashion a filmic identity out of an earlier
Hollywood tradition (Ray, Hawks, Hitchcock, Ford). Baudrillard
distances himself from Marx, semiotics, and Foucault while he looks for
the simulated American who is the universal subject of the hyperreal new
world. Both men are taken in by the myth of America as the last frontier.

Both seek to shatter prior cinematic conventions concerning how reality
is represented. Each produced a masculine version of a 'road movie,'
which cannibalized earlier genre representations (Wenders on John Ford,
Baudrillard on de Tocqueville). Erasing the differences between men and
women, they produce a timeless subject who laments a past that is long
gone, while racing into a future where the only thing that is certain is a
new novelty or gadget, or body conditioning fad. Drawn to the flicker of
lights, sunsets, shadows, sunrises, each sees in lightness a purity that
escapes contamination and notice by ordinary people. Each went for the
'big sky' and the open spaces, but was drawn by magnets to the cities,
and the urban landscape. Each offers up a postmodernist picture show,
museum pieces which turn the West into a giant theater of the absurd.
Denby (1984: 52 observes) of Wenders's film:

> Yes, there it is, the West: huge open spaces, scraggly, inadequate little buildings
> under vast skies; the comic surrealism of plastic and neon out in the great
> Nowhere. For Wenders the landscape of the West is instant myth – it's a myth
> that has passed through the media and become self-conscious. He and Robby
> Muller love red-orange skies that look like postcards; they photograph a neon
> stagecoach galloping endlessly in front of a motel; they produce frame after
> frame with the superhard outlines and deep saturated color of photo-realist
> paintings. They turn the West into an ironic art landscape.

He could have been writing about Baudrillard's book which contains
photographs of cowboys on horses, in front of empty cars parked before
screens at outdoor movie theaters, and highways that run forever into the
desert mountains.

In these desert and cityscapes Baudrillard and Wenders see alienation,
loneliness, lonely crowds, desperate people on the move, driven by
unseen, unreachable desires. Each uses the metaphor of the automobile
(Travis refuses to fly, Baudrillard appears to enjoy flying), as the means

of exploring this country; finding in this self-contained, auto-erotic object the selfsame pleasures they impute to those that they speed past in search of a motel for the night ('driving is a spectacular form of amnesia' [p. 9]; 'The point is to drive . . . . All you need to know about American society can be gleaned from an anthropology of its driving behaviour' [p. 54]). Each, like a nomad, wanders the country, criticizing what he sees. Nostalgic for a past that is gone, both critics are comedians, who find laughable sights in things Americans take to be sacred. But underneath their comedy lurks melodrama and tragedy; they too lament the passing of the American frontier. Finally, and ironically, each uses a realist text (the photographs, and photo-realist paintings) to make a postmodern point.

In Search of Cinematic America

America, as the film critic Vincent Canby notes (1984: 17), is not an easy concept to comprehend. Discovered by a Genoese sailor in the service of the Spanish crown, it has been the site of multiple discoveries ever since. From the original travelers, who were looking for somewhere else, it has traditionally been viewed as a place to be gotten through, or around in order to get somewhere else. Surrounded by water, its west coast has always been the last frontier. Significantly it was Europeans who first undertook the task of representing this frontier back to America. The movies and Hollywood became the project of a small group of European capitalists at the turn of the twentieth century (Gabler, 1988; Schatz, 1988), and these men set in motion a century of film production that has become what America is to its members. No wonder Wenders and Baudrillard are drawn to Hollywood and California. If you are seeking to tell an 'origin' myth, go to the place where the story was first told. Of course neither man took this challenge seriously, choosing to mock, rather than make sense of this cinematic impulse which has, for the last hundred years, defined the American character (Denzin, 1991; forthcoming a).

What then of this deeply intertwined relationship of American culture and its representations, which started first with the newspapers, then the telegraph, radio, photography, then film, TV, and now the VCR? Already there, before film was invented, in the popular culture itself, were the dominant and marginalized voices of the American novelist, dramatist, poet, musician, and painter. These voices (and hands) produced the images of America that came back home in Hollywood. These simulated reproductions of life in America told Americans who they were and how they got the way they were. But in order to tell itself, these Americans had to look to Europe, and there they found the myths, the melodramas, the rituals, and the stories that they would learn to write and read and show to one another. From the beginning America has been described through European eyes. More than one history of the American novel (Chase, 1957; Fiedler, 1966), traces its roots to Europe (that is, to the English novel – Scott, Dickens – Christian art, the myth of the tragic individual redeemed through pain, suffering, and catharsis, the Victorian melodrama and so on).

Hollywood narrative cinema drew its roots, its stories, and its morality from these European origins which had worked their way into the books of the great American novelists, including Hawthorne, Melville, James, Twain, Fitzgerald, Faulkner, and Hemingway (Denzin, 1991: Ch. 10). The great early Hollywood film-makers from the 1920s through to the mid-century and later . . ., like their employers, were Europeans (Lang, Chaplin, von Stroheim, Renoir, Wilder, Rossellini, De Sica, Hitchcock); so too were many of the original (and contemporary) Hollywood stars, in both the silent and the sound eras (Chaplin, Garbo, Oliver, Karloff, Lugosi, Burton, Jackson, Kingsley and so on).

Not surprisingly, many contend that America was born with an inferiority complex (Canby, 1984: 17). American stories came from Europe, American myths weren't unique. It took Europeans to tell Americans who they were. The American form of government was borrowed from Europe. Until the great capitalists took their stand, Americans had no kings and queens and castles. No amount of wealth and power have erased this sense of inferiority (Canby, 1984: 17), hence the millions of Americans who must travel to Europe each summer to catch and taste a touch of class. (Perversely the obverse is true, for millions of Europeans travel here each summer to see our last frontier and see what we have done with the heritage they gave us.) America is a mirror that Americans and Europeans continually look into, hoping to find 'that which, for whatever reasons, they have been conditioned to see' (Canby, 1984: 17).

Consider, then, the evolution and transformations of the cinematic society, and Baudrillard's hypothesis that Americans lack a level of self-reflexivity about the images that are reflected back to them. From the Hollywood movies of the Great Depression, to the social realist, *film noir*, and women's films of the postwar years, to the New Wave French cinema of the 1960s, the Vietnam War (pro and anti) films of the 1970s and 1980s, and the return to realism in the eighties, American cinema has been constantly pulled by the competing tendencies to present the horrible (racism, sexism, war, rape, violence, alcoholism, incest, murder) inside a melodramatic structure which represses while it valorizes and contains that which it presents. This certain tendency (Ray, 1985) in Hollywood film contains the unpresentable within a narrative format that resolves itself either through a happy ending, or through ambiguous closures which permit viewers to complete the story to their own satisfaction. A level of reflexivity exists within these narratives, which informs the viewer that this is a story, after all, and it may not be real life, and if it is like real life, what is seen here doesn't happen to everybody.[8]

At the same time there exists another genre of films, especially science fiction and the 'journalist-newspaper' movie, which explicitly examine in a self-reflexive fashion how a society knows itself, how its representations are simulated 'mis'-representations, which distort the truth.[9] Such films self-consciously critique society's simulated representations of itself (for example *Blade Runner*, *Soylent Green*, *Mad Max*, *Citizen Kane*, *Front Page*, *All the President's Men*, *Manchurian Candidate*, *Parallax View*, *Broadcast News*, *The Killing Fields*, *Salvador*). In the process they expose the third-order simulacrum for what it is: a hyperreal representation which clashes with the first-order, primitive, and wild level of everyday experience and its representations. These texts challenge the viewer to criticize the distorted versions of their cinematic society that the various dream factories in America offer up to them on a regular basis. These texts reflexively critique the absolute simulacrum of the third kind. So alongside the unreflective third-order representations of the world out there, exists a counter-body of subversive texts which suggests that things aren't the way they appear to be. These texts are myths in their own right (Barthes, 1972) and must be subversively read. But their existence serves to counter Baudrillard's hegemonic reading of American culture and its cinematic representations.

Of course on one level Baudrillard is correct. Many Americans long for the days when things are really 'real' again, where the old myths work and are true. This is why they look to the astral reflections of themselves that come from the Hollywood stars. But at least some understand that these representations from the stars only indirectly signify the America that is lived at the level of the everyday. These reflections of reflections become distortions of the real, wherever that is, and we remember the names of these stars long after we have forgotten their fictional names (Williamson, 1987: 23).

An inspection of these reflections from the stars suggests that many Americans may have become reflections of the reflections that have been brought to them by the media-oriented, postmodern cinematic society. Some can only grasp the real when it is contained within an image which has already been captured in a prior image. To the extent that this occurs, the boundaries between the public and the private have been erased in American life. But underneath this level of the hyperreal lurks the world of the ordinary individual who turns away from these representations, or finds that they don't square with her or his life. Some of these persons dream other kinds of dreams, and find the sources of the images of their dreams in a cinematic world that is only in their head. Many travel other paths and find their metaphors, not in the cinema of the desert, but in the subversive movies that critique the standard Hollywood version of what life is really like out there in the hinterlands of America. These viewers turn away from Baudrillard's film library, and construct their own list of films that do what he says postmodern cinema cannot do.

Easy Rider Baudrillard

His reading, then, is too narrow, too restricted for current interpretive practices. Illuminating in its own right, it goes too far, by not going far enough. Consider another 'road movie.' In the late 1960s, when opposition to the Vietnam War was becoming a major political issue, Dennis Hopper's now 'classic', *Easy Rider*, was released. This film was a huge success, both in the US and in Europe. The images of Jack Nicholson, Peter Fonda, and Dennis Hopper in search of the 'real' America on motorcycles crossing the western deserts still resonates with the counterculture themes in American life. It is easy to imagine Baudrillard as Dennis Hopper, or Jack Nicholson, on board his motorcycle, in search of the essence of this country. The ad line for this film read 'They went out looking for America – and found nothing there' (Canby, 1984: 17). This is exactly what Baudrillard found: an endless chain of signifiers, signifying nothing.

Did Baudrillard ride alongside these travelers, these archetypical American males on the modern motorized steed, chasing their version of the frontier's sunset as it wound its way to the end of the rainbow in New Orleans? As an easy rider Baudrillard found nothing in America. He didn't go the wrong way. He just didn't look down. He never got to Paris, Texas. Had he stopped off at that barren patch of imagined ground, he would have found a site of 'healing spiritual and emotional return, a place captured in a battered photo . . . which attains a higher reality in the mind' (Studlar, 1985: 359). Paris, Texas signifies the earth and a return to beginnings, to new hope and growth, a turn away from the barren desert where only lonely males wander in search of themselves. *America* overlooks the 'little people searching valiantly for a center to their lives' (Reed, 1984: 19), little people that Wenders found, in that imaginary, but real place that Baudrillard couldn't see called Paris, Texas. And of course he couldn't find this place or these people because they weren't on the roadmap that he followed, nor did they smile back from the billboards that he sped by.

Mills's America

Mills died of a heart attack while riding his motorcycle, or so the myth goes. It is not clear he would have joined Baudrillard, or even Jack Nicholson, on a trip west, or south to the heart of America, although it is clear, that he saw himself as an easy rider. His was an America seen from New York City, through the lens of European social theory. Like other Americans who took others' pictures of his society as his own, Mills was in search of an identity. A disillusioned American, he turned to Europe and Marx and Weber and Freud for his theory. Seeking to give a voice to the little people, he exposed the power elite and the power structures hidden in the military establishment. He pitied the new white-collar workers, feared for their fate, and imagined a sociological imagination that would make a difference.

Like Baudrillard he was always above the people he wrote about. Trapped in his own narrow images, he seldom went below the realm of his theory into the real world where ordinary people experienced the troubles he gave them. He never lived to see the cheerful robots, the yuppies, and the repressive racial order that would raise its ugly head again in the 1980s. He failed to imagine how ordinary people would attempt to take their lives back, through protest and recovery groups. But the sickness and the indifference that he saw is still here, and it is here with a vengeance. A narcissism he could not have imagined has taken hold, as has a preoccupation with material possessions, love, and intimacy.

America has paid a great price for the postmodern era Mills saw coming. Perhaps the cold war is over, but the costs in America have been considerable, including a massive underclass, major neglects in domestic reforms, the development of secret police organizations, the massive erosion of civil liberties, a near end to political debate, the concentration of decision-making in the executive branch, the emergence of lying as an American way of life, a weakening in public culture, and a loss of faith in government (See Lasch, 1990). The nostalgic undercurrents of postmodernism have accompanied two decades of conservative politics. This conservative political order continues to annihilate the social in the name of patriotism, individualism, love, honor, and the American flag.

The Texan in Paris

At the end, in the meeting of Mills and Baudrillard we have produced a deadlock. A Texan and a Frenchman bring us to the outer edges of the postmodern, but they don't show us how to move forward. Mills wanted to stop history, to stop the moral drift of the new postmodern society. Baudrillard celebrates this drift and explodes its insanities. Cynical beyond belief, he no longer sees a place for reason, freedom, and rationality in the postmodern society. Mills's commitment to the classical theorists leaves him contained within the metanarratives of the Enlightenment where science can still make a positive difference. The future of the postmodern cannot be done by a Texan in Paris, or a Parisian in Texas.

Notes

Paris, Texas. Directed by Wim Wenders, produced by Don Guest for Road Movies and Argos Films, released by TLC films, screenplay by Sam Shepard and L.M. Kit Carson. Cast: Harry Dean Stanton, Dean Stockwell, Nastassja Kinski, Hunter Carson. Released 1984.

1. Lynch's *Wild at Heart* embodies this tradition.

2. 'L'Amérique sidéralé': this term and its variant forms have been rendered throughout by 'astral' or the less familiar 'sidereal', according to context [tr.] (Baudrillard, 1988b: 5). *Sidereal*: 'of, like, or relative to the stars, sent from the stars, a mirror for reflecting the

rays of a star' (*Chambers 20th Century Dictionary*, 1983: 1204).

3. On these forms of the tourist see Morris (1988b), Grossberg (1988c), and Bruner (1989).

4. An 1989 Orion Classic release, written and directed by Jim Jarusch, produced by Jim Stark. This film takes you to a version of America that you feel you 'ought to be able to find by yourself, if you only knew where to look' (Ebert, 1989c).

5. Fiedler (1966: 357) observes, 'Everywhere in our fiction, the masculine paradise is laved by great rivers or the vast ocean.'

6. The metaphor of the desert suggests, of course, a barren place, where only the hearty male, sometimes half-dead survives, alone with his tumbleweeds, rusted car, and faded memory of woman. Baudrillard's America is devoid of women.

7. See Vidich (1991) and the reviews in the *Journal of Aesthetic and Art Criticism*, 47, (Spring 1989): 199, the *London Review of Books*, 19 (26 March 1989): 3, *New York Review of Books*, 36 (1 June 1989): 29, *Times Literary Supplement*, 16 Dec. 1988: 1391.

8. For example the 'alcoholism film' (Denzin, 1991) nearly always has a character who dies from his or her alcoholic condition, while another person, usually the protagonist, is saved (but see *Under the Volcano*, 1984).

9. Explicitly feminist cinema represents another reflexive category of film.

11

In Conclusion: The Eye of the Postmodern

History may indeed be made – but by narrow elite circles without effective responsibility to those who must try to suffer the consequences of their decisions and of their defaults. (Mills, 1959: 176)

This has been a journey into the postmodern; into the cultural logics of late capitalism and the dramaturgical structures which define this period of history. Our topics again: the postmodern self and its representations in social theory and contemporary Hollywood cinema. A single question has guided the discussion throughout: '*How are the crucial cultural identities grounded in class, gender, and race defined in the postmodern moment?*'

Recent social theory, in its postmodern forms has been examined. Late 1980, mainstream Hollywood films which, in one way or another, identify the main contours of the cultural logics of late capitalism have been interpreted. These logics, as reflected in the films that were studied, turn on money (capitalism), sex, and sexuality, love and intimacy, crimes of violence, passion and greed, race and its repression.

The postmodern culture, in its many contradictory forms, is a masculinized culture of Eros, love, desire, femininity, youth, and beauty. The myth of Oedipus is alive and well, and continues to argue that the path to happiness and fulfillment is sexual and lies in the marital, family bond. This myth, in its many forms, structures scholarly and popular writings about the postmodern subject. Without it there would be no contemporary films of social theory about love, desire, and intimacy. This myth serves to repress the most problematic term in contemporary culture, which is race. It does this by making sexuality the term that defines the essence of the human being. Race then becomes a secondary human characteristic which is subordinated to sexuality, and the realization of subjectivity in the bonded, sexual relationship.

The cultural logics of the postmodern are conservative to the core. The ideological legacies of the postmodern are not attractive. Capitalism has apparently won the war with communism. In the process it has given up on its commitment to the Enlightenment ideals of a democratic social order. Gone are the highest ideals of humanity, including freedom, self-respect, open dialogue, and honesty. The oppressive structures of racism and sexism are still firmly in place. State structures continue to erode the divisions between public and private lives.

Postmodern theory is a product of the postmodern decades. The political conservatism of the 1980s (Hall, 1988: 39–56), with its emphasis on a romantic nostalgia and sentimental longing for past times, attempted to undo the liberal political developments of the 1960s. The New Right constructed conceptions of who its ideal subjects were, and how they personify the sacred values of religion, hard work, health, and self-reliance. This new ideology, central to the cultural logic of postmodernism, redefines the meaning of an 'ordinary, normal, commonplace' individual. It is everywhere present in popular culture texts, including the films studied in this book.

Postmodern social theory is a reaction to these contradictory, conflictual, historical movements. It resists the temptation to reproduce and apply the 'classical sociology-is-a-science-of-the-empirical-world' model to the current moment. It argues that the grand sociological masters (Marx, Weber, Durkheim, Simmel, Mead), and their contemporaries (Blumer, Goffman, Parsons, Merton, Homans, Habermas, Giddens) can be read as producers of works which mapped and map a social world that, if it ever was, is no the longer the world that is experienced today. It seeks, as I have attempted to do throughout this book, to offer interpretive analyses which illuminate the social, and its cultural and ideological workings through the close-up readings of selected social texts. It endeavors to reveal how words, texts and their meanings play a pivotal role in the central performances of race, class, and gender relations as these experiences define what is called the postmodern. In so doing it attempts to connect the worlds of lived experience to the larger textual–cultural systems which create and impose their meanings on everyday life.

The major theories of postmodernism fail to live up to their promise. They still linger in the presence of the sociological classics, as they yearn to write a totalizing theory of this historical epoch. While concerned with the problems of representation, and commodification in everyday life, they fail to develop a politics of resistance which would have global implications for the postmodern self who must confront the repressive features of postmodern culture.

Cinematic representations of postmodernism also fail to offer anything more than superficial solutions to the present conditions. When Hollywood deals with the class struggle, racism, or sexism it perpetuates the myth that these obdurate realities can be overcome through luck or hard work. Contemporary cinema does not deal responsibly with these life situations. Consider *Wall Street*. With hard work, luck, and a willingness to bend the rules, Bud escapes, if only for a few moments, the blue-collar world of his father. Social class does not really exist. The yuppies in *When Harry Met Sally* . . . and *sex, lies and videotape* glide through a classless social structure where gender becomes eroticism, and love something one finally discovers. The crimes of the 1980s become misdemeanors, crimes of the heart, not the soul. Only Spike Lee's *Do the Right Thing* takes a hard look at racism and love, a look that the critics and American film audiences had trouble accepting.

Postmodernism and its Cultural Logics

The troublesome oxymoron postmodernism overflows with meaning. It simultaneously refers to a series of historical markers, to the new information technologies in the age of the simulacrum, to the cultural styles and aesthetics which dominate this moment, to the cultural logics that organize work, family, sexuality, race, and class, and most importantly, it references the lived experiences, the personal troubles and the public issues that define life in the late twentieth century. At the level of lived experience postmodernism refers to the attempt by contemporary men, women, and children to get a grip on this doubly modern and postmodern world and make themselves at home in it.

The postmodern is everywhere and nowhere. It has no zero point, no fixed essence. It contains all the traces of everything that has come before. Its dominating logic is that of a hybrid, never pure, always compromising, not 'either–or', but 'both–and'. The postmodern impulse is playful and paradoxical. It mocks and absorbs historical forms, always having it both ways, always modern and postmodern, nothing escapes its attention. Its logic of use and utility can turn anything from the past into a commodity that is sold, or used to sell a commodity in the present. On the surface benignly playful, this 'both–and' posture disguises ideology as entertainment (for example the Cosby show), and, as Kroker and Cook (1986: 279) note, makes the spectacle and the newsworthy event the emblematic sign of an age where lifestyle advertising has become the accepted popular psychology. At the same time, empty seriality is now the bond which unites the audience, and the electronic image is the only sign of reality that counts.

Late capitalism's 'both–and' logic constantly expands, like a rubber band, to fit all that has come before, turning everything, including lived experience, into a commodity that is bought and sold on the contemporary marketplace. This logic requires a positive nostalgia which infuses the past with high value; for if the past were worthless, it could not be sold in the present. Old is good. New is good. Old and new together are best. This popular ideology scripts a politics which keeps ancient narratives alive. These myths are many, and include: the nuclear family; heroes with white hats on horses riding into frontiers which remain to be conquered, or into cities (and nation-states) which need to be saved; and rugged individualists who overcome enormous handicaps (for example the stigmas of the age) on the way to finding wealth, happiness, and personal fulfillment. In short, capitalism needs and uses anything and everything to perpetuate its hegemonic control over popular culture.

Capitalist Pastiche, Personal Troubles, and Emotionality
This stance produces an economic and cultural pastiche that infuses every postmodern social formation. It is a pastiche that goes beyond Jameson's postmodern films. Late capitalism is a pot-pourri of precapitalist, market,

monopoly, and multinational economic formations. From the Third World market enclaves (in America, Latin America, Africa and elsewhere), to the First World nations, the cultural logics of the simulacrum interact with the classic capitalist economic logics of utility, use, and prestige value.[1]

Personal, postmodern troubles flow from these cultural formations, and as noted in Chapter Four include homelessness, poverty, AIDS, racism, sexism, divorce, abortion, child sexual abuse, domestic violence, alcoholism, and drug addiction. These existential troubles, many of which have become public issues, cut deeply to the core of lived, emotional experiences. They are stitched into the dominant cultural themes of the postmodern era. At the same time the harsh economic and racial edges of contemporary life produce anxiety, anhedonia, and ressentiment among the dispossessed.

The Popular, the Modern, and the Postmodern

Just as the popular defines the popular ('Flintstone' vitamin pills, 'Garfield' on coffee mugs, 'Dick Tracy' T-shirts, hats, and raincoats, 'Batman' watches, and so on), so too does the modern define the postmodern (*Casablanca* clips in Woody Allen movies), and the postmodern define the modern (*Wall Street, sex, lies and videotape, When Harry Met Sally* . . . and so on). In a constant dialectic, the future informs the present, the past defines the future, and the present reasserts its force over the past and the future.

The new sexual order is built on lies, pretensions, and an obscene sexual drama which no longer makes anything private and sacred. This order reinforces the economic logics of contemporary capitalism which molds the yuppie couple into a powerful, dual-career consumer machine. The manufactured needs of this new middle class reproduce, as noted in Chapters Six and Eight, the cultural and economic needs of multinational capitalism. The morality of capitalism is crass and self-centered. It turns crimes of passion and greed into misdemeanors, and celebrates the banality of evil, even as old-fashioned Oedipal morality tales celebrate the virtues of crime and its punishment (*Wall Street*). The cold, digital, computerized world of the market signifies the unfeeling, simulated postmodern world where appearances count as reality, and money isn't made or lost, only transferred from one perception to another. The illusion has become real and reality a dream.

A Cultural Studies Which Makes a Difference

The interdisciplinary movement known as 'feminist cultural studies' speaks to this need, drawing as it does on all the human disciplines, and the theoretical formations that now gather under the interpretive, critical umbrella. A feminist cultural studies (Chapter One) examines three interrelated problems: the production of gendered, ethnic, political cultural meanings, the textual analysis of these meanings, and the study of lived cultures and lived experiences and their connections to these worlds of representation. Culture, the taken-for-granted, and problematic webs of significance and meaning that human beings produce and act on when they do things together (Becker, 1986a: 13; Geertz, 1973: 5; Carey, 1989: 56), is shaped by the larger meaning-making institutions of-society-at-large. The representations of human experience as given in the mass media, film, social science, novels, art, politics, and religion constitute a critical layer of materials to be interpreted. Such texts inevitably confuse 'nature and history' in a way that suggests 'ideological abuse' (Barthes, 1972: 11), the hidden privileges of patriarchy, and the myth of autonomous interacting individuals producing unique structures of personal experience.

Two models of interpretation currently operate in the human disciplines (Derrida, 1972: 264). The first seeks to decipher, unravel, and discover the truth, the origins, the centers, the essences, the inner structures, and the obdurate meanings that operate within and shape particular forms of experience, interactional sites, social texts, and social institutions. This view has dreamed, throughout sociology's history, of representing and capturing human beings in society, and doing so scientifically. This is the classical and neo-classical version of sociology as a science of society. It holds a firm grip on most sociologists today, and was severely criticized in Chapter Two.

The second approach to interpretation (Derrida, 1972: 264–5) is not directed to the study of origins, centers, structures, laws, or empirical regularities. It holds that human beings are never fully present to themselves, or others, except through a process of deferral and delay. It argues that language is itself only a process of deferral and delay, and hence never fixed in its representations or meanings. It contends that society, as conceptualized by conventional sociologists, is a fiction. It suggests that presence and lived experience can never be fully captured because language will not allow this to occur. Hence experience can only be given in texts (interviews, fieldnotes, life stories, films and so on) which are themselves indirect representations of what they purport to represent. It seeks instead to examine how current textual practices (including theory and research) reify structures, subjects, and social experience. It proposes to deconstruct these practices so as to reveal how they keep in place a politically repressive picture of the social that is out of touch with the world as it is lived, and experienced.

A cultural studies which makes a difference builds on this second model of interpretation. It treats the personal as political. It works to connect personal troubles to public issues within a radical and plural democracy which regards personal troubles as the site of struggle (Laclau and Mouffe, 1985; Mills, 1959). It seeks to give a voice to the voiceless, as it deconstructs those popular culture texts which reproduce stereotypes about the powerless. It studies the most popular of the popular (the award winners), arguing that these productions take to the extreme and best embody the aesthetic, political, ideological, and moral meanings of the culture. At the same time it studies the small-scale productions, the marginal films, the ones that did not win awards, assuming that these deviant, outlying cases illuminate in their own way the marginal and mainstream values of the postmodern period. Understanding that texts repress, while they create and support tyrannical political structures, this deconstructive attitude resists the reactive, commercialized versions of the postmodern. It advocates pluralism and cultural diversity, but cautiously repudiates a *laissez-faire* attitude toward diversity, seeking instead a radical, non-violent pluralism that represses no one and liberates all.

A Playful, Pedagogical Postmodernism

Nostalgia, mourning, and melancholia are the pervasive postmodern theoretical emotions. From Jameson, to Lyotard and Baudrillard the lament is the same; things are not as they used to be. A certain sadness lingers over their texts. Ulmer (1989) challenges this argument, offering in its place a playful pedagogy for the age of video and television. Ulmer's project builds on the three modes of discourse – orality, the written text, and the video text – which together constitute the stuff of postmodern discourse. The technology of postmodern culture has shifted from print to video. Orality in the video age incorporates three levels of sense-making – common sense, the popular, and the scientific. These three discursive structures, which involve science, popular culture, everyday life and private experience circulate through all levels of culture, from 'high' to 'low' and back again (Ulmer, 1989: vii).

Teletheory introduces a new genre of discourse, 'mystory' into the postmodern stream. A mystory is 'always specific to its composer . . . [it] brings into relation your experience with three levels of discourse – personal (autobiography), popular (community stories, oral history or popular culture), expert (disciplines of knowledge)' (Ulmer, 1989: vii, 209). A 'mystory' begins with a personal experience (the sting of memory). It locates items significant to the writer. Once located these items are researched in terms of their representations in the popular and scientific archives of the culture. Fragments of this information most relevant to the oral life story are then assembled in an order which displays a humorous, playful, aggressive witty relationship to the text and the events that are recorded. In Ulmer's words (1989: 211) as the writer of a 'mystory', 'I am the target of the aggressive wit that replaces the monumental melancholy associated with the pedagogy of specialized high culture.' His 'Derrida at the Little Bighorn – a Fragment' (Ulmer, 1989: 212–43) is an example of such writing.

A 'mystory' personalizes the postmodern. It connects the contradictory currents of this contemporary culture to the writer's personal biography. As a pedagogical device it allows the writer as teacher to lead the student into the production of a cultural text which blends orality, print, and video into a personal document that universalizes the singularity of the student's experiences. Ulmer's aggressive wit replaces the nostalgic, mournful longing for that day when the postmodern disappears.

The Eyes of the Postmodern

The postmodern is a cinematic age; it knows itself through the reflections that flow from the camera's eye. The voyeur is the iconic, postmodern self. Accordingly, a critical cultural studies must orient itself to the cinematic images and narratives that define this age. It respects those realist, and neo-realist narrative and cinematic forms which, like their 'social consciousness' counterparts in the 1940s and 1950s (see Ray, 1985), awaken the social structure from its slumber, and force a recognition of social problems and social issues (e.g. *Long Time Companion*). At the same time it challenges those narratives which offer simplistic, ideological answers to complex questions (for example, *sex, lies and videotape*, *Wall Street*). It negatively judges those texts which resolve their problems through recourse to the old Oedipal myths of the culture (*Blue Velvet*, *Wild at Heart*). It promotes gay, lesbian, feminist, and African American, Indian, Spanish American, and Asian American films which illuminate the repressive dimensions of the Oedipal myth and its American dream. It values attempts to experiment with the cinematic apparatus in ways which expose the postmodern condition and all its contradictions (*Do the Right Thing*, *Blade Runner*). It promotes discursive, figural, and transgressive postmodern films (*Brazil*) self-reflective cinema (*Speaking Parts*), postmodernist science fiction (*The Fly*, *Videodrome*), and the morality tales of Woody Allen.

Subversive texts which unravel the cinematic eye, showing its distortions and the ways in which the third-order of the simulacrum is constructed, are central to a critical postmodernism. Those which mock and parody the 'astral' and the cinematic apparatus (*Zelig*) are also needed, as are those films which judge and compare the real against its representations and reproductions (*Broadcast News*).

The Voyeur's Place

The voyeur's place, and the limits, dangers, and benefits of voyeurism within the postmodern cinematic culture must be addressed. Traditionally this figure (for example the photo-journalist in *Rear Window*, the London photographer in *Blow-Up*, the wire-tap expert in *The Conversation*, the production editor in *Broadcast News*), has been presented in passive, occasionally self-destructive ways. His or her actions are valued and regarded as necessary in a society where the truth too often masquerades as a fiction which covers up corrupt, illegal, or immoral activities. As the seeker of truth, the postmodern voyeur sees what others cannot, or will not, see. His or her perverse desire to look is inevitably connected to a valued end.

How is this figure created? What motivates the voyeur? How is it that only certain persons, usually males, are voyeurs? What are the costs of voyeurism? In film after film this figure experiences ridicule, shame, violence, insanity, alcoholism, failure, death. The voyeur is a feared social type, a necessary evil; yet a social type which is needed, if the postmodern is to learn the truths about itself. He or she is any man or woman or child. In its ordinariness this type passes amongst us, unseen, but always seeing, feeling, and learning secrets. These secrets unmask the truth of the simulacrum, for the 'simulacrum is never that which conceals the truth . . . The simulacrum is true' (Baudrillard, 1983a: 1). Here, at the end, we confront the truth about the postmodern: 'it is the truth which conceals that there is none' (Baudrillard, 1983a: 1).

But surely there is more? And there is, for this truth which *is* none now sets the existential conditions that we all live. Here, adrift in a phenomenology and cultural analysis of late capitalism we find ourselves, voyeurs all, products of the cinematic gaze. Our challenge is clear. Begin to write, and live our own pedagogical versions of the postmodern, making our own playful 'mystories' of this bewildering, frightening, terrifying, exhilarating historical moment. No longer taking anything for granted, doubting always the fictions that pass for truths, each of us bears the burden of this moment, and lives, in our universal singularity, a fraudulent or authentic version of a postmodern self that is true or untrue to itself.

Postmodern Stories

Theorists of postmodernism are storytellers. The storyteller's 'most powerful effects come,' Frank Lentricchia notes (1990: 335)

> when he [or she] convinces us that what is particular, integrated and different in a cultural practice (film making, ethnography, postmodern theory) is part of a cultural plot that makes coherent sense of all cultural practices as a totality; not a totality that is there, waiting for us to acknowledge its presence, but a totality fashioned when the storyteller convinces us to see it her way.

The postmodern theorists examined in this book, along with the popular Hollywood film-makers, have fashioned a particular story, with variations of course, which purports to make sense of the postmodern condition. This is a totalizing story, a story of late capitalism and its cultural logics. It is a story of a global postmodernism (Featherstone, 1990: 147), a story which forecasts cultural diversity as a new universal norm. I have been part of this story, both inside and outside it, accepting and rejecting it at the same time.

Our most powerful effects as storytellers come when we expose the cultural plot and the cultural practices that guide our writing hands. The story I have been trying to tell argues that we have all fallen victims to a cultural plot which says we can capture postmodernism within a single interpretive framework. Having captured this moment, in all its complexities, we can do better sociology, or even write a postmodern sociology of postmodernism. Perhaps this is an impossibility.

Perhaps the myth of a total cinema (Bazin, 1967) extends to sociology and anthropology. When cinema was born film-makers believed that their cameras would faithfully and realistically capture and reproduce social life. They quickly abandoned this myth and turned to a more narrow, narrative focus. Perhaps we cannot produce a sociology that realistically captures the postmodern world out there. It is simply too complex, too diverse, and too heterogeneous. Our focus must become narrower.

Like the film-maker, we can tell tiny stories about the human condition, showing how these histories we live, the freedoms we gain and lose, are constrained by larger cultural narratives that work their interpretive ways behind our backs. Mindful of the narratives that structure our tales, we can turn to a personal cinematic-ethnographic interpretive sociology which begins always with our personal experiences and works outward, attempting to discover a mode and style of representation that universalizes our experiences, while taking pleasure in the texts that we produce.

Our dilemma is this, as it always has been:

> By the time we understand the pattern we are in, the definition we are making for ourselves, it is too late to break out of the box. We can only live in terms of the definition, like the prisoner in the cage . . . Yet the definition we have made of ourselves is ourselves. To break out of it, we must make a new self. But how can the self make a new self when the selfness which it is, is the only substance from which the new self can be made? (Warren, 1959: 351)

Hopefully, the postmodern pattern is by now more clear. It is not too late to break out of the box. The self which emerges will itself be a tangled web of all that has come before. This is what the postmodern is all about; all that has come before.

Note

1. An extended example. In Mexico City four firms rent the same small room, taking turns over a 24-hour period in the tiny space they share with fellow entrepreneurs. Meanwhile each worker drives an ancient American automobile, pays dues to a union that is on strike, wears clothes designed in Paris, catches a quick lunch at McDonald's, watches an NFL football game, or reruns of *I Love Lucy* on a TV in the local bar, and takes his lover to *When Harry Met Sally* . . . at the neighborhood theater. On the bus to work his lover reads the *National Inquirer* admires Princess Diana, and moonlights at three jobs, all in an attempt to save enough money for a family vacation at a coastal resort. Precapitalist, market, monopoly, and multinational capitalist formations all impinge, on a daily basis, on this person's life. Hovering over everything are the cultural logics of postmodernism. These logics reinforce, while they define and create, the very economic conditions that determine lived experiences.

References

Adorno, Theodor W. (1973) *Negative Dialectics*. New York: Seabury Press.

Agger, Ben (1990) *The Decline of Discourse: Reading, Writing and Resistance in Postmodern Capitalism*. Bristol, PA: Falmer Press.

Alexander, Jeffrey C. (ed.) (1985) *Neofunctionalism*. Beverly Hills, CA: Sage.

Alexander, Jeffrey C. (1987a) 'Action and its environments', in J.C. Alexander *et al.* (eds), *The Micro-Macro Link*. Berkeley: University of California Press. pp. 289–318.

Alexander, Jeffrey C. (1987b) 'The centrality of the classics', in A. Giddens and J. Turner (eds), *Social Theory Today*. Stanford, CA: Stanford University Press. pp. 11–57.

Alexander, Jeffrey C. (1988a) 'The new theoretical movement', in N. Smelser (ed.), *Handbook of Sociology*. Newbury Park, CA: Sage. pp. 77–101.

Alexander, Jeffrey C. (1988b) 'Parsons's "structure" in American sociology', *Sociological Theory*, 6: 96–102.

Alexander, Jeffrey C. and Giesen, Bernhard (1987) 'From reduction to linkage: the long view of the micro-macro link', in Jeffrey C. Alexander *et al.* (eds), *The Micro-Macro Link*. Berkeley: University of California Press. pp. 1–42.

Altheide, David (1985) *Media Power*. Beverly Hills, CA: Sage.

Altheide, David L. and Robert Snow (1991) *Media Worlds in the Era of Postjournalism*. New York: Aldine de Gruyter.

Althusser, Louis (1971) *Lenin and Philosophy*. New York: Monthly Review Press.

Ansen, David (1986) 'Stranger than paradise', review of *Blue Velvet, Newsweek*, 108 (15 Sept.): 69.

Arac, Jonathan (ed.) (1986) 'Introduction', in J. Arac (ed.), *Postmodernism and Politics*. Minneapolis: University of Minnesota Press. pp. ix–xliii.

Ashmore, Malcolm (1989) *The Reflexive Thesis*. Chicago: University of Chicago Press.

Balsamo, Ann (1987) 'Unwrapping the postmodern: a feminist glance', *Journal of Communication Inquiry*, 11: 64–72.

Balsamo, Ann (1988) 'Reading cyborgs writing feminism', *Communication*, 10: 331–44.

Balsamo, Ann (1989) 'Imagining cyborgs: postmodernism and symbolic interactionism', in N.K. Denzin (ed.) *Studies in Symbolic Interaction* Vol. 10. Greenwich, CT: JAI Press. pp. 369–79.

Balsamo, Ann (1990) 'Technologies of the gendered body: a feminist cultural study'. Doctoral dissertation, Institute of Communications Research, University of Illinois at Urbana-Champaign.

Barthes, Roland (1972) *Mythologies*. New York: Hill & Wang. (Originally published 1957).

Barthes Roland (1975) *The Pleasure of the Text*. New York: Hill & Wang.

Barthes, Roland (1982) 'From *Writing Degree Zero*' in Susan Sontag (ed.), *A Barthes Reader*. New York: Hill & Wang. pp. 31–61. (Originally published in 1977).

Bataille, Georges (1982) *The Story of the Eye* (1928). New York: Berkley Books.

Baudrillard, Jean (1968) *Le système des objets*. Paris: Gallimard.

Baudrillard, Jean (1970) *La société de consummation: Ses mythes, ses structures*. Paris: Gallimard.

Baudrillard, Jean (1975) *The Mirror of Production*. St Louis, MO: Telos Press.

Baudrillard, Jean (1979) *De la séduction*. Paris: Denoel-Gonthier.

Baudrillard, Jean (1981) *For a Critique of the Political Economy of the Sign*. St Louis, MO: Telos Press.

Baudrillard, Jean (1983a) *Simulations*. New York: Semiotext (e).

Baudrillard, Jean (1983b) *In the Shadow of the Silent Majorities*. New York: Semiotext (e).

Baudrillard, Jean (1983c) 'Ecstasy of communication', in Hal Foster (ed.), *The Anti-Aesthetic*. Port Townsend, WA: Bay Press. pp. 126–34.

Baudrillard, Jean (1983d) 'What are you doing after the orgy?', *Artforum*, Oct: 42–6.

Baudrillard, Jean (1984) 'Interview: game with vestiges', *On the Beach*, 5 (Winter): 19–25.

Baudrillard, Jean (1987a) *Forget Foucault*. New York: Semiotext (e).

Baudrillard, Jean (1987b) *Cool Memories*. Paris: Editions Galilée.

Baudrillard, Jean (1988a) *The Ecstasy of Communication*. New York: Semiotext (e).

Baudrillard, Jean (1988b) *America*. London: Verso.

Bauman, Zygmunt (1988) 'Is there a postmodern sociology?', *Theory, Culture & Society*, 5: 217–37.

Bazin, André (1967) *What Is Cinema?* Berkeley: University of California Press.

Becker, Howard S. (1986a) *Doing Things Together*. Evanston: Northwestern University Press.

Becker, Howard S. (1986b) *Writing for Social Scientists*. Chicago: University of Chicago Press.

Bell, Daniel (1976) *The Cultural Contradictions of Capitalism*. New York: Basic Books.

Benhabib, Seyla (1990) 'Epistemologies of postmodernism: a rejoinder to Jean-François Lyotard', in L.J. Nicholson (ed.), *Feminism Postmodernism*. New York: Routledge. pp. 107–32. (Originally published in *New German Critique*, 33 (1984): 103–26.)

Benjamin, Walter (1968) 'The work of art in the age of mechanical reproduction', in W. Benjamin, *Illuminations*. New York: Harcourt. pp. 219–53. (Originally published in 1955).

Bennetts, Leslie (1987) 'Oliver Stone easing out of violence', *New York Times*, 13 April: C 13.

Bennington, Geoff (1988) *Lyotard: Writing the Event*. Manchester: Manchester University Press.

Benson, Sheila (1982) 'Review of *Blade Runner*', *Los Angeles Times*, 25 June (Calendar): 1.

Benson, Sheila (1986) 'Review of *Blue Velvet*', *Los Angeles Times*, 19 Sept. (Calendar): 1.

Benson, Sheila (1989) 'Review of *sex, lies and videotape*', *Los Angeles Times*, 4 Aug. (Sect. VI): 1, 17.

Bentz, Valerie Malhotra (1989) *Becoming Mature: Childhood Ghosts and Spirits in Adult Life*. New York: Aldine de Gruyter.

Berman, Marshall (1988) *All That Is Solid Melts Into Air*. Harmondsworth: Penguin.

Biga, Tracy (1987) 'Review of *Blue Velvet*', *Film Quarterly*, Fall: 44–8.

Blumer, Herbert (1958) 'Race prejudice as a sense of group position', *The Pacific Sociological Review*, 1: 3–7.

Blumer, Herbert (1969) *Symbolic Interactionism*. Englewood Cliffs, NJ: Prentice-Hall.

Blumer, Herbert (1990) *Industrialization as an Agent of Social Change: A Critical Analysis*. Edited with an introduction by David R. Maines and Thomas J. Morrione. New York: Aldine de Gruyter.

Booth, Wayne C. (1988) *The Company We Keep: An Ethics of Fiction*. Berkeley: University of California Press.

Bourdieu. P. (1984) *Distinction*. London: Routledge & Kegan Paul.

Brissett, Dennis and Edgley, Charles (eds), (1990) *Life as Theater: A Dramaturgical Sourcebook*. 2nd ed. New York: Aldine de Gruyter.

Broeske, Pat H. (1983) 'Review of *Blade Runner*', in Frank N. Magill (ed.), *Magill's Cinema Annual: 1983*. Englewood Cliffs, NJ: Salem Press. pp. 76–81.

Brown, Patricia Leigh (1989) 'A Stones set of steel and magic', *New York Times*, 5 Oct.: 15.

Broyard, Anatole (1989) 'Fiction: a user's model', review of *The Company We Keep*, by Wayne Booth, *New York Times Book Review*, 22 Jan.: 3, 27.

Bruner, Edward M. (1989) 'Tourism, creativity, and authenticity', in N.K. Denzin (ed.), *Studies in Symbolic Interaction*, Vol. 10. Greenwich, CT: JAI Press. pp. 109–14.

Burger, Peter (1984) *Theory of the Avant-Garde*. Minneapolis: University of Minnesota Press.

Canby, Vincent (1984) 'Directors evoke many Americas: review of *Paris, Texas*', *New York Times*, 11 Nov. (Sec. II): 17.

Canby, Vincent (1987) 'Review of Stone's *Wall Street*', *New York Times*, 11 Dec.: C 3.

Canby, Vincent (1989) 'Review of *Crimes and Misdemeanors*', *New York Times*, 13 Oct.: C 19.

Carey, James W. (1986) 'The dark continent of American journalism', in Robert K. Mannoff and Michael Schudson (eds), *Reading Journalism: The Pantheon Guide to Popular Culture*. New York: Pantheon. pp. 146-96.

Carey, James W. (1989) *Communication as Culture: Essays on Media and Society*. Boston: Unwin Hyman.

Carey James W. and Quirk, John J. (1989) 'The history of the future', in J.W. Carey, *Communication as Culture*. Boston: Unwin Hyman. pp. 173-200.

Carlson, Timothy (1990) 'Welcome to the weird new world of *Twin Peaks*', *TV Guide*, 28 (7 April): 20-3.

Carr, Jay (1989a) 'Review of *sex, lies and videotape*', *Boston Globe*, 11 Aug.: 41, 51.

Carr, Jay (1989b) 'Review of *When Harry Met Sally*', *Boston Globe*, 12 July: 69.

Cerone, Daniel (1989) 'Review of *sex, lies and videotape*', *Los Angeles Times*, 9 Aug. (Sect. VI): 1, 4.

Champlin, Charles (1989) 'Review of *When Harry Met Sally*', *Los Angeles Times*, 27 July (Sect. VI): 1, 7.

Chang, Briankle G. (1986) 'Mass, media, mass media-tion: Jean Baudrillard's implosive critique of modern mass-mediated culture', *Current Perspectives in Social Theory*, 7: 157-81.

Chase, Richard (1957) *The American Novel and Its Tradition*. New York: Doubleday.

Chute, David (1986) 'Out to Lynch', *Film Comment*, 22 (Sept./Oct.): 32-5.

Clark, Mike (1987) 'Stone's stock soars', review of "Wall Street"', *USA Today*, 11 Dec.: 16.

Clifford, James (1986) 'Introduction: Partial Truths', in James Clifford and George E. Marcus (eds), *Writing Culture: The Poetics and Politics of Ethnography*. Berkeley: University of California Press. pp. 1-26.

Clifford, James and Marcus, George E. (eds) (1986) *Writing Culture: The Poetics and Politics of Ethnography*. Berkeley: University of California Press.

Clough, Patricia T. (1988a) 'Feminist theory and social psychology', in N.K. Denzin (ed.), *Studies in Symbolic Interaction*, Vol. 8. Greenwich, CT: JAI Press. pp. 3-22.

Clough, Patricia T. (1988b) 'The movies and social observation: reading Blumer's *Movies and Conduct*', *Symbolic Interaction*, 11: 85-94.

Clough, Patricia T. (1989a) 'Letters from Pamela: reading Howard S. Becker's *Writing(s) for Social Scientists*', *Symbolic Interacton*, 12: 159-70.

Clough, Patricia T. (1989b) 'Women writing and the life history: a reading of Toni Morrison's *The Bluest Eye*', unpublished manuscript.

Clough, Patricia T. (1990a) 'Writing technologies of the subject: ethnography, narrativity, and sociological discourse', unpublished manuscript.

Clough, Patricia T. (1990b) 'Deconstructionism and feminism', in David Dickens and Andrea Fontana (eds), *Postmodernism and Sociology*. Chicago: University of Chicago Press.

Cohen, Richard (1989a) 'Fakin' it: review of *When Harry Met Sally*', *Washington Post (Magazine)*, 13 Aug: 4.

Cohen Richard (1989b) 'What I meant', *Washington Post (Magazine)*, 15 Oct.: 13.

Collins, Randall (1981) *Sociology Since Midcentury: Essays in Theory Cumulation*. New York: Academic Press.

Collins, Randall (1985) *Three Sociological Traditions*. New York: Oxford University Press.

Collins, Randall (1988a) *Theoretical Sociology*. San Diego: Harcourt.

Collins, Randall (1988b) 'The micro contribution to macro sociology', *Sociological Theory*, 6: 242-53.

Collins, Randall (1989) 'Sociology: proscience or antiscience?', *American Sociological Review*, 54: 124-39.

Connor, Steve (1989) *Postmodernist Culture*. Oxford: Basil Blackwell.

Corliss, Richard (1982) 'Review of *Blade Runner*', *Time*, 12 July: 68.

Corliss, Richard (1986) 'Our town: George Bailey meets 'True, Blue and Peggy Sue'. *Film Comment*, 22 (Nov./Dec.): 9-17.

Coser, Lewis A. (1975) 'Two methods in search of a substance', *American Sociological Review*, 40: 691–700.

Coser, Lewis A. (1978) 'American trends', in Tom Bottomore and Robert Nisbet (eds), *A History of Sociological Analysis*. New York: Basic Books. pp. 287–320.

Couch, Carl J. (1984) *Constructing Civilizations*. Greenwich, CT: JAI Press.

Couch, Carl J. (1986) 'Questionnaires, naturalistic observations and recordings', *Studies in Symbolic Interaction: (Supplement 2): The Iowa School, (Part A)*: 45–59.

Couch, Carl J. (1987) *Researching Social Processes in the Laboratory*. Greenwich, CT: JAI Press.

Cowan, Allison Leigh (1987) 'Making *Wall Street* Look like Wall Street', *New York Times*, 30 Dec.: C 16.

Coward, Rosalind (1985) *Feminine Desires*. New York: Grove.

Creed, Barbara (1988) 'A journey through *Blue Velvet*: film, fantasy and the female spectator', *New Formations*, 7: 95–115.

Culler, Jonathan (1981). *The Pursuit of Signs: Semiotics, Literature, Deconstruction*. Ithaca, NY: Cornell University Press.

Daly, Mary (1980) *Gyn/Ecology: The Metaethics of Radical Feminism*. Boston: Allen & Unwin.

Davis, Ed (1989) 'Making Sense of the News', Unpublished Doctorial Dissertation, Department of Geography, University of Illinois at Urbana-Champaign.

De Certeau, Michel (1984) *The Practice of Everyday Life*. Berkeley: University of California Press.

Deegan, Mary Jo and Hill, Michael (eds) (1987) *Women and Symbolic Interaction*. Boston: Allen & Unwin.

Delaney, Samuel R. (1989) *The Motion of Light in Water: Sex and Science Fiction in the East Village, 1957–1965*. New York: NAL.

De Lauretis, Teresa (1984) *Alice Doesn't: Feminism, Semiotics, Cinema*. Bloomington: Indiana University Press.

De Lauretis, Teresa (1987) *Technologies of Gender: Essays on Theory, Film, and Fiction*. Bloomington: Indiana University Press.

Deleuze, Giles and Guattari, Felix (1977) *Anti-Oedipus: Capitalism and Schizophrenia*. New York: Viking Press.

Denby, David (1984) 'Review of *Paris, Texas*', *New York Times*, 19 Nov.: 52.

Denby, David (1986) 'Review of *Blue Velvet*', *New York Times*, 29 Sept.: 85.

Denzin, Norman K. (1984) *On Understanding Emotion*. San Francisco: Jossey-Bass.

Denzin, Norman K. (1985) 'On the phenomenology of sexuality, desire, and violence', *Current Perspectives in Social Theory*, 6: 39–56.

Denzin, Norman K. (1986) 'Postmodern social theory', *Sociological Theory*, 4: 194–202.

Denzin, Norman K. (1987a) 'On semiotics and symbolic interaction', *Symbolic Interaction*, 10: 1–19.

Denzin, Norman K. (1987b) *The Alcoholic Self*. Newbury Park, CA: Sage.

Denzin, Norman K. (1987c) *The Recovering Alcoholic*. Newbury Park, CA: Sage.

Denzin, Norman K. (1987d) 'The death of sociology', *American Journal of Sociology*, 93: 175–80.

Denzin, Norman K. (1988) '*Blue Velvet*: postmodern contradictions', *Theory, Culture & Society*, 5: 461–73.

Denzin, Norman K. (1989a) *Interpretive Interactionism*. Newbury Park, CA: Sage.

Denzin, Norman K. (1989b) *Interpretive Biography*. Newbury Park, CA: Sage.

Denzin, Norman K. (1989c) *The Research Act*, 3rd ed. Englewood Cliffs, NJ: Prentice-Hall.

Denzin, Norman K. (1989d) 'Re-reading *The Sociological Imagination*', *The American Sociologist*, 20: 278–82.

Denzin, Norman K. (1989e) 'Reading *Tender Mercies*: two interpretations', *The Sociological Quarterly*, 30: 37–57.

Denzin, Norman K. (1990a) 'On understanding emotion: the interpretive-cultural agenda', in Theodore D. Kemper (ed.) *Research Agendas in the Sociology of Emotions*. Albany:

State University of New York Press. pp. 85–116.

Denzin, Norman K. (1990b) 'Presidential address on *The Sociological Imagination* revisited', *The Sociological Quarterly*, 31: 1–22.

Denzin, Norman K. (1990c) 'Reading cultural texts', *American Journal of Sociology*, 95: 1577–80.

Denzin, Norman K. (1990d) 'The spaces of postmodernism: reading Plummer on Blumer', *Symbolic Interaction*, Vol. 13: 145–54.

Denzin, Norman K. (1990e) 'Empiricist cultural studies in America: a deconstructive reading', *Current Perspectives in Social Theory*, 11: 17–39.

Denzin, Norman K. (1990f) 'Postmodernism and deconstructionism', in D. Dickens and A. Fontana (eds), *Postmodernism and Sociology*. Chicago: University of Chicago Press.

Denzin, Norman K. (1990g) 'Reading *Wall Street*: postmodern contradictions in the American social structure', in Bryan S. Turner (ed.), *Theories of Modernism and Postmodernism*. London: Sage.

Denzin, Norman K. (1990h) '*Paris, Texas* and Baudrillard in *America*', *Theory, Culture & Society*, 8: 121–33.

Denzin, Norman K. (1990i) 'Reading rational choice theory', *Rationality and Society*, 2: 172–89.

Denzin, Norman K. (1991) *Hollywood Shot by Shot: Alcoholism in American Cinema*. New York: Aldine de Gruyter.

Denzin, Norman K. (forthcoming a) *The Voyeur and the Cinematic Society*. London: Sage.

Denzin, Norman K. (forthcoming b) *Symbolic Interactionism as Cultural Studies*. London and New York: Basil Blackwell.

Derrida, Jacques (1972) 'Structure, sign, and play in the discourse of the human sciences', in R. Macksey and E. Donato (eds), *The Structuralist Controversy*. Baltimore, MD: Johns Hopkins University Press. pp. 247–64.

Derrida, Jacques (1973) *Speech and Phenomena and Other Essays on Husserl's Theory of Signs*. Evanston: Northwestern University Press.

Derrida Jacques (1976) *Of Grammatology*. Baltimore, MD: Johns Hopkins University Press. (Originally published in 1974).

Derrida, Jacques (1978) *Writing and Difference*. Chicago: University of Chicago Press.

Derrida Jacques (1981) *Positions*. Chicago: University of Chicago Press.

Derrida, Jacques (1983) 'The principle of reason: the university in the eyes of its pupils', *Diacritics*, Fall: 3–20.

Derrida, Jacques (1985) 'Racism's last word', *Critical Inquiry*, 12: 290–9.

Derrida, Jacques (1986) 'Critical response II: but beyond . . . open letter to Anne McClintock and Rob Nixon', *Critical Inquiry*, 13: 155–70.

Dickens, David and Fontana, Andrea (eds) (1990a) *Postmodernism and Sociology*. Chicago: University of Chicago Press.

Dickens, David, and Fontana, Andrea (1990b) 'Introduction: postmodernism and sociology', in D. Dickens and A. Fontana (eds), *Postmodernism and Social Inquiry*. Chicago: University of Chicago Press.

Doane, Mary Anne (1987) *The Desire to Desire: Woman's Film of the 1940s*. Bloomington: Indiana University Press.

Donougho, Martin (1989) 'Postmodern Jameson', in D. Kellner (ed.), *Postmodernism/Jameson/Critique*. Washington, DC: Maisonneuve Press. pp. 75–95.

Dougherty, Philip H. (1988) 'Social analysis from *Good Housekeeping*', *New York Times*, 11 Aug.: 49.

Douglas, Jack D. and Johnson, John M. (eds) (1977) *Existential Sociology*. New York: Cambridge University Press.

Downing, David B. (1987) 'Deconstructionism's scruples: the politics of enlightened critique', *Diacritics*, 17: 66–81.

Eagleton, Terry (1985) 'Capitalism, modernism and postmodernism', *New Left Review*: 60–73.

Eagleton, Terry (1989) *The Ideology of the Aesthetic*. Cambridge: Basil Blackwell.

Ebert, Roger (1987) '*Wall Street* takes aim at value system: review of *Wall Street*', *Chicago Sun Times*, 11 Dec.: 20–1.

Ebert, Roger (1989a) 'Review of *Blue Velvet*', in *Roger Ebert's Movie Home Companion: 1990 Edition*. New York: Andrews & McMeel. p. 85.

Ebert, Roger (1989b) 'Spike Lee interview', in *Roger Ebert's Movie Home Companion: 1990 Edition*. New York: Andrews & McMeel. pp. 889–93.

Ebert, Roger (1989c) 'Review of *Mystery Train*', *Chicago Sun Times*, 11 Dec.: 24.

Ebert, Roger (1990a) 'Review of *Wild at Heart*', *News Gazette*, 11 Oct. (Sect. F): 1–2.

Ebert, Roger (1990b) '*Wild at Heart* cop-outs make the film offensive', *Chicago Tribune*, 17 Oct.: 18.

Eco, Umberto (1984) 'A guide to the neo-television of the 1980s', *Framework*, 25: 18–25.

Elbaz, Robert (1987) *The Changing Nature of the Self: A Critical Study of the Autobiographic Discourse*. Iowa City: University of Iowa Press.

Elias, Norbert (1982) *The Civilizing Process, Vol. II: State Formation and Civilization*. Oxford: Basil Blackwell.

Elias, Norbert (1987) 'The retreat of sociologists into the present', *Theory, Culture & Society*, 4: 223–47.

Ellis, John M. (1989) *Against Deconstruction*. Princeton, NJ: Princeton University Press.

Fabrikant, Geraldine (1987) 'Wall Street reviews *Wall Street*', *New York Times*, 10 Dec.: D, 1, 5.

Farberman, Harvey (1981) 'The political economy of fantasy in everyday life', *Symbolic Interaction* 2: 1–18.

Featherstone, Mike (1983) 'The body in consumer culture', *Theory, Culture & Society*, 1: 18–33.

Featherstone, Mike (1985) 'The fate of modernity', *Theory, Culture & Society*, 2: 1–5.

Featherstone, Mike (1987) 'Lifestyle and consumer culture', *Theory, Culture & Society*, 4: 55–70.

Featherstone, Mike (1988) 'In pursuit of the postmodern', *Theory, Culture & Society*, 5: 195–215.

Featherstone, Mike (1989a) 'Towards a sociology of postmodern culture', in H. Haferkamp (ed.), *Culture and Social Structure*: Belin: de Gruyter.

Featherstone, Mike (1989b) 'Postmodernism, cultural change, and social practice', in D. Kellner (ed.), *Postmodernism/Jameson/Critique*. Washington, DC: Maisonneuve Press. pp. 117–38.

Featherstone, Mike (1990) *Consumer Culture and Postmodernism*. London: Sage.

Featherstone, Mike, and Hepworth, Mike (1989) 'Aging and old age: reflections on the postmodern life course', in B. Bytheway *et al.* (eds.), *Being and Becoming Old*. London: Sage.

Fiedler, Leslie A. (1966) *Love and Death in the American Novel*, revised edn. New York: Stein & Day.

Fiedler, Leslie A. (1975) 'Cross the border – close that gap: post-modernism', in M. Cunliffe (ed.), *American Literature since 1900*. London: Sphere. pp. 344–66.

Fields, Belden A. (1988) *Trotskyism and Maosim: Theory and Practice in France and the United States*. New York: Praeger.

Film Review Annual (1984) 'Reviews of *Blade Runner*', Englewood, NJ: Jerome S. Ozer. pp. 90–114.

Finkelstein, Joanne (1989) *Dining Out: A Sociology of Modern Manners*. Oxford: Polity Press.

Finkelstein, Joanne (1991) *The Fashioned Self*. Cambridge: Polity Press.

Foucault, Michel (1970) *The Order of Things*. New York: Vintage Books.

Foucault, Michel (1977) *Discipline and Punish*. New York: Pantheon.

Foucault, Michel (1980a) *Power/Knowledge*. New York: Pantheon.

Foucault, Michel (1980b) *The History of Sexuality: Vol. 1: An Introduction*. New York: Pantheon.

Foucault, Michel (1982) 'Afterword: the subject and power', in H. Dreyfus and P. Rabinow (eds), *Michel Foucault*. Chicago: University of Chicago Press. pp. 208–26.

Foucault, Michel (1986) *The Care of the Self: Vol. 3 of The History of Sexuality*. New York: Pantheon.

Frank, Arthur W. (1985) 'Out of ethnomethodology', in H.J. Helle and S. Eisenstadt (eds), *Micro-Sociological Theory*. Newbury Park, CA: Sage. pp. 110–16.

Frank, Arthur W. (1987) 'Review essay: *Fragments of Modernity* by D. Frisby, *The Flight from Ambiguity* by D. Levine, *Schopenhauer and Nietzsche* by G. Simmel', *Symbolic Interaction*, 10: 295–311.

Frank, Arthur W. (1989) 'Habermas's interactionism: the micro–macro link to politics', *Symbolic Interaction*, 12: 353–60.

Frank, Arthur W. (1990a) 'Bringing bodies back in: a decade of review', *Theory, Culture & Society*, 7: 131–62.

Frank, Arthur W. (1990b) 'The self at the funeral: an ethnography on the limits of postmodernism', in N.K. Denzin (ed.), *Studies in Symbolic Interaction*, Vol. 11: Greenwich, CT: JAI Press.

Frank, Arthur W. (1991) 'Postmodern sociology/postmodern review: review of N.K. Denzin, *Interpretive Interactionism*, and *Interpretive Biography*', *Symbolic Interaction*, 14: in press.

Fraser, Nancy and Nicholson Linda, (1988) 'Social criticism without philosophy: an encounter between feminism and postmodernism', *Theory, Culture & Society*, 5: 373–94.

Gabler, Neal (1988) *An Empire of their Own: How the Jews Invented Hollywood*. New York: Crown Publishers.

Games, Stephen (1987) 'Post-modern disagreements', *The Times Literary Supplement*, 413 (30 Oct.–5 Sept.): 1194.

Garfinkel, Harold (1967a) 'Passing and the managed achievement of sex status in an intersexed person', in Harold Garfinkel, *Studies in Ethnomethodology*. Englewood Cliffs, NJ: Prentice-Hall. pp. 116–85.

Garfinkel, Harold (1967b) *Studies in Ethnomethodology*. Englewood Cliffs, NJ: Prentice-Hall.

Garfinkel, Harold (1988) 'Evidence for locally produced, naturally accountable phenomena of order, logic, reason, meaning, method, etc., in and as of the essential quiddity of immortal ordinary society, (I of IV): an announcement of studies', *Sociological Theory*, 6: 103–9.

Garfinkel Harold, Lynch, M. and Livingston, E. (1981) 'The work of discovering science construed with materials from the optically discovered pulsar', *Philosophy of the Social Sciences*, 11: 131–58.

Garrett, Robert (1989) 'Field guide to yuppies: review of *When Harry Met Sally*', *Boston Globe*, 20 Aug.: 89, 93

Geertz, Clifford (1973) *The Interpretation of Cultures*. New York: Basic Books.

Geertz, Clifford (1983) *Local Knowledge*. New York: Basic Books.

Geertz, Clifford (1988) *Words and Lives*. Stanford, CA: Stanford University Press.

Gelmis, Joseph (1986) 'Review of *Blue Velvet*', *Newsday*, 19 Sept. (Part III): 3.

Gerth, Jeff (1989) 'Risks to H.U.D. rose after its shift of responsibility to private sector', *New York Times*, 31 July: 5.

Giddens, Anthony (1981) *A Contemporary Critique of Historical Materialism*. Berkeley: University of California Press.

Giddens, Anthony (1984) *The Constitution of Society*. Berkeley: University of California Press.

Giddens, Anthony (1987) 'Structuralism, post-structuralism and the production of culture', in A. Giddens and J. Turner (eds), *Social Theory Today*. Stanford, CA: Stanford University Press. pp. 195–223.

Giddens, A., and Turner, J. (eds) (1987) *Social Theory Today*. Stanford, CA.: Stanford University Press.

Gilroy, Paul (1988) *There Ain't No Black in the Union Jack: The Cultural Politics of Race and Nation*. London: Hutchinson.

Gitlin, Todd (1988) 'Hip-deep in post-modernism', *New York Times Book Review Section*, 6 Nov.: 1, 35–6.

Glaberson, William (1987) 'The plunge: a stunning blow to a gilded, impudent age', *New York Times*, 13 Dec. 1, 20.

Gledhill, Christine (1985) 'Recent developments in feminist criticism', in Gerald Mast and Marshall Cohen (eds), *Film Theory and Criticism* (3rd ed.). New York: Oxford University Press. pp. 817–45. (Originally published in 1978.)

Goffman, Erving (1959) *The Presentation of Self in Everyday Life*. New York: Doubleday.

Goldsen, Rose K. (1964) 'Mills and the profession of sociology', in Irving L. Horowitz (ed.), *The New Sociology: Essays in Social Science and Social Theory in Honor of C. Wright Mills*. New York: Oxford University Press. pp. 88–93.

Goodman, Ellen (1989) 'Kitty Dukakis shows new act to morality play', *The Champaign-Urbana News Gazette*, 14 Feb.: A–4.

Gouldner, Alvin (1970) *The Coming Crisis in Western Sociology*. New York: Basic Books.

Grossberg, Lawrence (1986) 'Reply to the critics', *Critical Studies in Mass Communication*, 3: 86–95.

Grossberg, Lawrence (1987) 'The in-difference of television', *Screen*, 28: 28–46.

Grossberg, Lawrence (1988a) *It's a Sin: Essays on Postmodernism Politics & Culture*. Sidney: Power Publications.

Grossberg, Lawrence (1988b) 'Putting the pop back into postmodernism', in A. Ross (ed.), *Universal Abandon: The Politics of Postmodernism*. Minneapolis: University of Minnesota Press. pp. 167–90.

Grossberg, Lawrence (1988c) 'Wandering audiences, nomadic critics', *Cultural Studies*, 2: 377–91.

Guattari, Felix and Negri, Antonio (1988) *Anti-Power*. New York: Semiotext(e)

Habermas, Jürgen (1983) 'Modernity – an incomplete project', in H. Foster (ed.), *The Anti-Aesthetic: Essays on Postmodern Culture*. Port Townsend, WA: Bay Press. pp. 3–15. (Originally published in 1981).

Habermas, Jürgen (1985) 'Neoconservative culture criticism in the United States and West Germany: an intellectual movement in two political cultures', in R.J. Bernstein (ed.), *Habermas and Modernity*. Cambridge, MA: MIT Press. pp. 78–94.

Habermas, Jürgen (1987) *The Philosophical Discourse of Modernity: Twelve Lectures*. Cambridge, MA: MIT Press.

Hall, Peter M. (1987) 'Presidential address: interactionism and the study of social organization', *Sociological Quarterly*, 28: 1–22.

Hall, Stuart (1980) 'Encoding/decoding', in S. Hall, D. Hobson, A. Lowe and P. Willis (eds), *Culture, Media, Language*. London: Hutchinson. pp. 128–38.

Hall, Stuart (1986a) 'On postmodernism and articulation: an interview with Stuart Hall', ed. Lawrence Grossberg, *Journal of Communication Inquiry*, 10: 45–60.

Hall, Stuart (1986b) 'History, politics and postmodernism: Stuart Hall and cultural studies', interview with Lawrence Grossberg, *Journal of Communication Inquiry*, 10 (Summer): 61–77.

Hall, Stuart (1988) *The Hard Road to Renewal*. London: Verso.

Haraway, Donna (1985) 'A manifesto for cyborgs: science, technology, and socialist feminism in the 1980s', *Socialist Review*, 80: 65–108.

Harvey, David (1989) *The Condition of Postmodernity*. Oxford: Basil Blackwell.

Harvey, Irene E. (1986) *Derrida and the Economy of Différence*. Bloomington: Indiana University Press.

Haskell, Molly (1987) *From Reverence to Rape: The Treatment of Women in the Movies*, 2nd edn. Chicago: University of Chicago Press.

Hassan, Ihab (1985) 'The culture of postmodernism', *Theory, Culture & Society*, 2: 119–32.

Hebdige, Dick (1988a) 'Postmodernism and "The Other Side"', in D. Hebdige, *Hiding in the Light: On Images and Things*. London: Routledge. pp. 181–244.

Hebdige, Dick (1988b) *Hiding in the Light: On Images and Things*. London: Routledge.

Heidegger, Martin (1962) *Being and Time*. New York: Harper & Row.

Heidegger, Martin (1977) *The Question Concerning Technology*. New York: Harper.

Hinson, Hal (1989) 'Review of *Crimes and Misdemeanors*', *Washington Post*, 13 Oct.: C 1, 7.

Hobe, Phyllis (1990) *Lovebound: Recovering from an Alcoholic Family*. New York: NAL Books.

Hoberman, J. (1984) 'Review of *Paris, Texas*', *Village Voice*, 29 Nov.: 84.

Hoberman, J. (1986) 'Review of *Blue Velvet*', *Village Voice*, 23 Sept.: 58.

Hochschild, Arlie (with Anne Machung) (1989) *Second Shift: Working Parents and the Revolution at Home*. New York: Viking.

Holden, Stephen (1990) 'The pop life', *New York Times*, 4 July: 11.

Holleran, Andrew (1989) *Ground Zero*. New York: NAL Books.

Honneth, Axel (1985) 'Averion against the universal: a commentary on Lyotard's *Postmodern Condition*', *Theory, Culture & Society*, 2: 147–57.

Horowitz, Irving Louis (1983) *C. Wright Mills: An American Utopian*. New York: Free Press.

Howe, Desson (1989) 'Review of *Crimes and Misdemeanors*', *Washington Post, Weekend Section*: 45.

Huber, Joan (1989) 'President's introduction', 1989 Program of the Annual Meetings of the American Sociological Association.

Hughes, Robert (1989) 'The patron saint of neo-pop. Review of *America* by J. Baudrillard', *New York Review of Books*, 36: 29–32.

Hutcheon, Linda (1988) *A Poetics of Postmodernism*. New York: Routledge.

Hutcheon, Linda (1989) *The Politics of Postmodernism*. New York: Routledge.

Huyssen, Andreas (1984) 'Mapping the postmodern', *New German Critique* 33: 5–52.

Huyssen, Andreas (1986) *After the Great Divide: Modernism, Mass Culture, Postmodernism*. Bloomington: Indiana University Press.

Jahiel, Edwin (1990) 'Review of David Lynch's *Wild at Heart*', *Champaign-Urbana News Gazette*, 24 Aug. (*Weekend* section): 4.

James, Caryn (1989a) 'Review of *sex, lies and videotape*', *New York Times*, 4 Aug. (Sect. C): 12.

James Caryn (1989b) 'Review of *When Harry Met Sally*', *New York Times*, 12 July (Sect. C): 15.

James, Caryn (1990) 'Critic's notebook: a new role for movies: video-age peeping Tom', *New York Times*, 21 March: B 1, 4.

Jameson, Fredric (1975–6) 'The ideology of the text', *Salmagundi*, 31–2: 204–46.

Jameson, Fredric (1981) *The Political Unconscious*. Ithaca, NY: Cornell University Press.

Jameson, Fredric (1983) 'Postmodernism and consumer society', in Hal Foster (ed.), *The Anti-Aesthetic: Essays on Postmodern Culture*. Port Townsend, WA: Bay Press. pp. 115–25.

Jameson, Fredric (1984a) 'Foreword', to Jean-François Lyotard, *The Postmodern Condition*. Minneapolis: University of Minnesota Press. pp. vii–xxi.

Jameson Fredric (1984b) 'Postmodernism, or the cultural logic of late capitalism', *New Left Review*, 146: 52–92.

Jameson, Fredric (1984c) 'Periodizing the sixties', in Sonya Sayres *et al.* (eds), *The Sixties without Apologies*. Minneapolis: University of Minnesota Press. pp. 178–209.

Jameson, Fredric (1987) 'Reading without interpretation: postmodernism and the video-text', in Derek Attridge *et al.* (eds), *The Linguistics of Writing: Arguments between Language and Literature*. Manchester: Manchester University Press. pp. 198–223.

Jameson, Fredric (1988a) 'The politics of theory: ideological positions in the postmodernism debate', in F. Jameson, *The Ideologies of Theory: Essays, 1971/1976, Vol. 2: A Syntax of History*. Minneapolis: University of Minnesota Press. pp. 103–13. (Originally published 1984).

Jameson, Fredric (1988b) 'Cognitive mapping', in C. Nelson and L. Grossberg (eds), *Marxism and the Interpretation of Culture*. Urbana: University of Illinois Press. pp. 347–57.

Jameson, Fredric (1988c) 'Discussion', in C. Nelson and L. Grossberg (eds), *Marxism and the Interpretation of Culture*. Urbana: University of Illinois Press. pp. 358–60.

Jameson, Fredric (1988d) 'The ideology of the text', in F. Jameson (ed.), *The Ideologies of Theory: Essays 1971–1986, Vol. 1: Situations of Theory*. Minneapolis: University of Minnesota Press. pp. 17–71. Originally published in *Salmagundi*, 31–2 (Fall 1975–Winter 1976): 204–46.

Jameson, Fredric (1989) 'Afterword – Marxism and postmodernism', in Douglas Kellner (ed.), *Postmodernism/Jameson/Critique*. Washington, DC: Maisonneuve Press. pp. 369–88.

Jameson, Fredric (1990) *Signatures of the Visible*. London: Routledge.

Jameson, Fredric (1991) *Postmodernism, or The Cultural Logic of Late Capitalism*. Durham, NC: Duke University Press.

Jansen, Sue Curry (1988) *Censorship: The Knot that Binds Power and Knowledge*. New York: Oxford University Press.

Jencks, Charles (1985) *The Language of Postmodern Architecture*. New York: Basic Books.

Joas, Hans (1987) 'Symbolic interactionism', in A. Giddens and J.H. Turner (eds) *Social Theory Today*. Stanford: Stanford University Press. pp. 82–115.

Johnson, Richard (1986–7) 'What is cultural studies anyway?', *Social Text*, Winter: 38–80.

Josephson, Matthew (1934) *The Robber Barons*. New York: Macmillan.

Journal of Aesthetics and Art Criticism (1989) 'Review of *America*', 47: 199.

Kael, Pauline (1986) 'Current cinema: out there and in here: review of *Blue Velvet*', *The New Yorker*, 52, 22 Sept.: 99–103.

Kakutani, Michiko (1987) 'John Huston's last legacy', *New York Times*, 13 Dec.: 1, 50.

Kaminer, Wendy (1990) 'Chances are you're codependent too', *New York Times Sunday Book Review*, 11 Feb: 1, 26–7.

Kaplan, Anne (1987) *Rocking around the Clock: Music Television, Postmodernism, and Consumer Culture*. New York: Methuen.

Kaplan, Anne (ed.) (1988) *Postmodernism and its Discontents*. London: Verso.

Kariel, Henry S. (1989) *The Desperate Politics of Postmodernism*. Amherst: University of Massachusetts Press.

Katovich, Michael A. (1990) 'Toward a postmodern theory of the past', in N.K. Denzin (ed.), *Studies in Symbolic Interaction*, Vol. 13. Greenwich, CT: JAI Press. pp. 130–47.

Kauffmann, Stanley (1984) 'Invasion of the culture snatcher; review of *Paris, Texas*', *New Republic*, 3 Dec: 26–7.

Kehr, Dave (1989a) 'Review of *sex, lies, and videotape*', *Chicago Tribune*, 11 Aug. (Sect. 7): A 37.

Kehr, Dave (1989b) 'When Rob met Woody: review of *When Harry Met Sally*', *Chicago Tribune*, 12 July (Sect. 5): 1, 3.

Kellner, Douglas (1988) 'Postmodernism as social theory: some challenges and problems', *Theory, Culture & Society*, 5: 239–69.

Kellner, Douglas (1989a) 'Jameson, Marxism, and postmodernism', in D. Kellner (ed.), *Postmodernism/Jameson/Critique*. Washington, DC: Maisonneuve Press. pp. 1–42.

Kellner, Douglas (1989b) *Jean Baudrillard: From Marxism to Postmodernism and Beyond*. Stanford, CA: Stanford University Press.

Kellner, Douglas, Leibowitz, Flo and Ryan, Michael (1984) 'Review of *Blade Runner*', *Jump Cut*, 29 (28 Feb.): 6–12.

Kempley, Rita (1989) 'Review of *When Harry Met Sally*', *Washington Post*, 12 July (Sect. B): 1, 11.

Kramer, Hilton (1982) 'Postmodern: art and culture in the 1980s', *The New Criterion*, 1: 36–42.

Kristeva, J. (1985) *Sexual/Textual Politics: Feminist Literary Theory*. London: Methuen.

Kroker, Arthur, and Cook, David (1986) *The Postmodern Scene: Excremental Culture and Hyper-Aesthetics*. New York: St Martin's Press.

Kroker, Arthur and Kroker, M. (1987) 'Body digest', *Canadian Journal of Political and Social Theory*, 11: 1–2.

Kroker, Arthur, Kroker, M. and Cook, David (1990) 'Panic USA: hypermodernism as America's postmodernism', *Social Problems*, 37: 443–59.

Krug, Gary (1989a) 'The eve of destruction: the nuclear war film', doctoral dissertation, Institute of Communications Research, University of Illinois, Urbana-Champaign.

Krug, Gary (1989b) 'Rumors of war: rhetoric and orientation in Reagan's "War on Drugs" speech', in N.K. Denzin (ed.), *Studies in Symbolic Interaction*, Vol. 10. Greenwich, CT: JAI Press. pp. 351–66.

Krug, Gary (1990a) 'Technology and the social: human interaction in four nuclear war films', paper presented to the 1990 Gregory Stone/Society for the Study of Symbolic Interaction Annual Symposium, St Petersburg Beach, Florida, 27 Jan.

Krug, Gary (1990b) 'Observations on the problems of film study as ethnography', paper presented to the 1990 Annual Meeting of the Midwest Sociological Society, Chicago, Illinois 13 April.

Krug, Gary J. and Graham, Laurel D. (1989) 'Symbolic interactionism: pragmatism for the postmodern age', in N.K. Denzin (ed.), *Studies in Symbolic Interaction*, Vol. 10. Greenwich, CT: JAI Press. pp. 61–71.

Krupat, Arnold (1989) *The Voice in the Margin: Native American Literature and the Canon.* Berkeley: University of California Press.

Lacan, Jacques (1982) *Feminine Sexuality.* New York: Pantheon.

Laclau, Ernesto and Mouffe, Chantal (1985) *Hegemony & Socialist Strategy.* London: Verso.

Lasch, Christopher (1990) 'The costs of our cold war victory', *New York Times*, 13 July: A13.

Lash, Scott (1988) 'Discourse or figure? Postmodernism as a "regime of signification"', *Theory, Culture & Society*, 5: 311–36.

Lash, Scott (1990) *Sociology of Postmodernism.* London: Routledge.

Lauro, Frank A. (1989) 'Lady sings the blues: a study of *Blue Velvet*'. Unpublished manuscript, English 273, November 23. University of Illinois at Urbana-Champaign.

Leavitt, Robin Lynn, and Power, Martha Bauman (1989) 'Emotional socialization in the postmodern era: children in day care', *Social Psychological Quarterly*, 52: 35–43.

Lefebvre, Henri (1984) *Everyday Life in the Modern World.* New Brunswick: Transaction Books. (Originally published in 1971).

Lemert, Charles (1979) *Sociology and the Twilight of Man: Homocentrism and Discourse in Sociological Theory.* Carbondale: Southern Illinois University Press.

Lemert, Charles (1989) 'Review of Jean Baudrillard, *Selected Writings*, edited with an introduction by Mark Poster', *Contemporary Sociology*, 18: 639–40.

Lennett, Richard (1985) 'Review of *Paris, Texas*', *Cinéaste*, 14: 60.

Lentricchia, Frank (1990) 'In place of an Afterword – someone reading', in F. Lentricchia and T. McLaughlin (eds), *Critical Terms for Literary Theory.* Chicago: University of Chicago Press. pp. 321–38.

Lévi-Strauss, Claude (1963) *Structural Anthropology.* New York: Basic Books.

Lohr, Steve (1987) 'Investors retreating from foreign markets', *New York Times*, 16 Dec.: 1, 32.

London Review of Books (1989) 'Review of *America*', 26 March: 13.

Lyman, Stanford M. (1987) 'From matrimony to malaise: men and women in the American film, 1930–1980', *International Journal of Politics, Culture and Society*, 1: 73–100.

Lyman, Stanford M. (1989) 'Sociology of the absurd and the micro–macro link', paper presented to the 1989 Annual Meeting of the Society for the Study of Symbolic Interaction.

Lyman, Stanford M. (1990) 'Anhedonia: gender and the decline of emotions in American film, 1930–1988', *Sociologial Inquiry*, 60: 1–19.

Lyman, Stanford M. and Vidich, Arthur J. (1988) *Social Order and the Public Philosophy: An Analysis and Interpretation of the Work of Herbert Blumer, Vol. 1.* Fayetteville: University of Arkansas Press.

Lyotard, Jean-François (1971) *Discours, figure.* Paris: Klincksieck.

Lyotard, Jean-François (1974) *Economie libidinale.* Paris: Minuit.

Lyotard, Jean-François (1984a) *Driftworks.* New York: Semiotext (e).

Lyotard, Jean-François (1984b) *The Postmodern Condition.* Minneapolis: University of Minnesota Press. (Originally published in 1979).

Lyotard, Jean-François (1985) *Just Gaming.* Manchester: Manchester University Press.

Lyotard, Jean-François (1986) *Le Postmoderne expliqué aux enfants: Correspondance, 1982-1985.* Paris: Editions Galilée.

Lyotard, Jean-François (1988a) *The DIFFEREND: Phrases in Dispute*. Minneapolis: University of Minnesota Press.

Lyotard, Jean-François (1988b) 'Interview with Jean-François Lyotard', by Willem van Reijen and Dick Veerman, *Theory, Culture & Society*, 5: 277–309.

Lyotard, Jean-François (1989) *The Lyotard Reader*, ed. Andrew Benjamin. Oxford: Basil Blackwell.

Macksey, Richard, and Donato, Eugenio (eds) (1972) *The Structuralist Controversy*. Baltimore, MD: Johns Hopkins University Press.

Maines, David R. (1982) 'In search of mesostructure: studies in the negotiated order', *Urban Life*, 11: 267–79.

Maines, David R. (1989a) 'On the liminality of post-positivism and the conceptualization of culture: an editorial introduction', *Cultural Dynamics* (special issue on 'Conceptions of Culture') 11: 1–10.

Maines, David R. (1989b) 'The alcoholic self and its social circles', *American Journal of Sociology*, 94: 864–73.

Maines, David R. (1989c) 'Myth, texts, and interactionist complicity in the assessment of Blumer's work', in Norman K. Denzin (ed.), *Studies in Symbolic Interaction*, Vol. 10. Greenwich, CT: JAI Press. pp. 383–413.

Maines, David R., Sugrue, Noreen and Katovich, Michael A. (1983) 'The sociological import of G.H. Mead's theory of the past', *American Sociological Review*, 48: 161–73.

Mandel, Ernest (1975) *Late Capitalism*. London: New Left Books.

Manning, Peter K. (1987) *Semiotics and Fieldwork*. Newbury Park, CA: Sage.

Manning, Peter K. (1988) *Symbolic Communication: Signifying Calls*. Cambridge, MA: MIT Press.

Manning, Peter K. (1990) 'Strands in the postmodern rope: ethnographic themes', in N.K. Denzin (ed.), *Studies in Symbolic Interaction* Vol. 12. Greenwich, CT: JAI Press. pp. 1–19.

Marcus, George E., and Fischer, M.J. (1986) *Anthropology as Cultural Critique*. Chicago: University of Chicago Press.

Marcuse, Herbert (1964) *One-Dimensional Man*. Boston: Beacon Press.

Marx, Karl (1983) 'From the Eighteenth Brumaire of Louis Bonaparte', in E. Kamenka (ed.), *The Portable Karl Marx*. New York: Penguin. pp. 219–92. (Originally published 1852).

Maslin, Janet (1989) 'Lately the lens frames moral issues: review of *Crimes and Misdemeanors, sex, lies and videotape*, and *Do the Right Thing*', *New York Times*, 22 Oct. (Sect. 2): 15, 25.

Mathews, Jack (1989) 'The Cannes file "c'est Magnifique" say the critics to US film maker, 26,' *Los Angeles Times*, 15 May (Part VI): 1, 4.

McCaffery, Larry (1990) 'White noise, white heat', *American Book Review*, 12: 4, 27.

McCall, Michael M., and Becker, Howard S. (1990) 'Performance science', *Social Problems*, 37: 117–32.

McGuigan, Cathleen and Huck, Janet (1986) 'Black and blue is beautiful? Review of *Blue Velvet*', *Newsweek*, 108 (27 Oct.): 65–7.

Mead, G.H. (1929) 'The nature of the past', in J. Cross (ed.), *Essays in Honor of John Dewey*. New York: Henry Holt. pp. 235–42.

Mellancamp, Patricia (1987) 'Images of language and indiscreet dialogue. *The Man Who Envied Women*', *Screen*, 28 (2): 87–102.

Merleau-Ponty, Maurice (1964) *Signs*. Evanston: Northwestern University Press.

Merleau-Ponty, Maurice (1973) *Adventures of the Dialectic*. Evanston: Northwestern University Press.

Meyer, Karl E. (ed.) (1990a) *Pundits, Poets and Wits: An Omnibus of American Newspaper Columns*. New York: Random House.

Meyer, Karl E. (1990b) 'Newspaper columnists: literature by the inch', *New York Times Book Review*, 18 March (Sect. 7): 1, 24–5.

Meyrowitz, Joshua (1985) *No Sense of Place*. New York: Oxford University Press.

Mills, C. Wright (1951) *The White Collar*. New York: Oxford University Press.

Mills, C. Wright (1956) *The Power Elite*. New York: Oxford University Press.

Mills, C. Wright (1959) *The Sociological Imagination*. New York: Oxford University Press.

Mills, C. Wright (1963) 'Women: the darling little slaves', review of S. de Beauvoir, *The Second Sex* (1952), in *Power, Politics and People: The Collected Essays of C. Wright Mills*, ed. and with an introduction by Irving Louis Horowitz. New York: Ballantine. pp. 339–46. Written (but unpublished) in 1953.

Mills, C. Wright, Senior, Clarence and Goldsen, Rose Kohn (1950) *The Puerto Rican Journey: New York's Newest Migrants*. New York: Russell & Russell

Mitchell, Juliet (1982) 'Introduction – I', in J. Mitchell and J. Rose (eds) *Feminine Sexuality: Jacques Lacan and the Ecole Freudienne*. New York: Pantheon. pp. 1–26.

Moore, Michael (1990) '"Roger" and I, to Hollywood and home to Flint', *New York Times*, 15 July (Sect. H) 11–12.

Morris, Meaghan (1987) 'Asleep at the wheel?: review of *America*', *New Statesman*, 113 (26 June): 28–9.

Morris, Meaghan (1988a) 'Introduction: feminism, reading, postmodernism', in M. Morris, *The Pirate's Fiancée: Feminism, Reading, Postmodernism*. London: Verso. pp. 1–16.

Morris, Meaghan (1988b) 'At Henry Parke's motel', *Cultural Studies*, 2: 1–47.

Mulvey, Laura (1989) *Visual and Other Pleasures*. Bloomington: Indiana University Press.

Nash, Nathaniel C. (1987) 'A new urgency for reforms in policing securities trades', *New York Times*, 17 Dec.: 1, 34.

Nelson, Carey (1987) 'Men, feminism: the materiality of discourse', in A. Jardine and P. Smith (eds), *Men in Feminism*. New York: Methuen. pp. 165–78.

Newman, Charles (1985) *The Postmodern Aura*. Evanston: Northwestern University Press.

Newman, Peter C. (1987) 'Wall Street's gutter ethics. Review of *Wall Street*', *Maclean's*, 28 Dec.: 61.

Newsweek (1987) 'A bull market in sin. Review of *Wall Street*', 14 Dec.: 78–9.

New York Magazine (1987) 'Review of *Wall Street*', 14 Dec.: 87–8.

New York Review of Books (1989) 'Review of *America*', 16 Dec.: 1391.

New York Times (1988a) 'The new traditionalist', ad for *Good Housekeeping*, 18 Aug.: 50.

New York Times (1988b) 'The new traditionalist', ad for *Good Housekeeping*, 17 Nov.: 46.

New York Times (1988c) 'The new traditionalist', ad for *Good Housekeeping*, 8 Oct.: 21, 32.

New York Times (1989a) 'The new traditionalist', ad for *Good Housekeeping*, 26 Jan.: 44.

New York Times (1989b) 'Text of President's Farewell Address to the American people', 12 Jan.: 8.

New York Times (1989c) 'The new traditionalist', ad for *Good Housekeeping*, 5 March.

New York Times (1989d) 'Symposium: Woody Allen counts the wages of sin', 15 Oct. (Sect. C): 15, 25–6.

New York Times (1989e) 'Symposium: *Do the Right Thing* issues and images', 9 July (Sect. 2): 1.

Norris, Floyd (1989) 'Time Inc. and Warner merge, creating largest media company', *The New York Times*, 5 March: 1, 15.

Oakes, Guy (1984) 'The problem of women in Simmel's Theory of Culture', in G. Oakes (ed. and transl.), *Georg Simmel: On Women, Sexuality, and Love*. New Haven, CT: Yale University Press. pp. 3–62.

O'Neill, John (1988) 'Religion and postmodernism: the Durkheimian bond in Bell and Jameson', *Theory, Culture & Society* 5 (2–3): 225–39.

Owens, Craig (1983) 'The discourse of others: feminists and postmodernism', in H. Foster (ed.), *The Anti-Aesthetic*. Port Townsend, WA: Bay Press. pp. 57–82.

Pfohl, Stephen and Gordon, Avery (1986) 'Criminological displacements: a sociological deconstruction', *Social Problems*, 33: S94–S113.

Plummer, Ken (1983) *Documents of Life*. London: Allen & Unwin.

Plummer, Ken (1990) 'Staying in the empirical world: symbolic interactionism and postmodernism', *Symbolic Interaction*, Vol. 13: 155–60.

Porter, J.N. (1990) 'Review of *Postmodernism*, edited by Mike Featherstone', *Contemporary Sociology*, 19: 322–4.

Prendergast, Christopher, and Knottnerus, J. David (1990) 'The astructural bias and presuppositional reform in symbolic interactionism. a non-interactionist evaluation of the new studies in social organization', in Larry T. Reynolds, *Interactionism: Exposition and Critique*, 2nd ed. Dix Hills, NY: General Hall. pp. 158–80.

Rabinow, Paul (1986) 'Representations are social facts', in James Clifford and George E. Marcus (eds) *Writing Culture: The Poetics and Politics of Ethnography*. Berkeley, CA: University of California Press. pp. 234–61.

Rabkin, William (1986) 'Deciphering *Blue Velvet*: interview with David Lynch', *Fangoria* 58 (Oct.): 52–6.

Ragland-Sullivan, Ellie (1986) *Jacques Lacan and the Philosophy of Psychoanalysis*. Urbana: University of Illinois Press.

Rattner, Steven (1987) 'A view from the trenches: an investment broker winces at *Wall Street*', *Newsweek*, 14 Dec.: 80.

Ray, Robert (1985) *A Certain Tendency in Hollywood Cinema: 1930–1980*. Princeton, NJ: Princeton University Press.

Reed, Rex (1984) 'Review of *Paris, Texas*', *New York Post*, 9 Nov.: 19.

Reed, Rex (1986) 'Review of *Blue Velvet*', *New York Post*, 19 Sept.: 9.

Richardson, Laurel (1988) 'The collective story: postmodernism and the writing of sociology', *Sociological Focus*, 21: 199–208.

Richardson, Laurel (1990a) 'Speakers whose voices matter: toward a feminist postmodernist sociological praxis', in N.K. Denzin (ed.), *Studies in Symbolic Interaction*, Vol. 12. Greenwich, CT: JAI Press. pp. 51–63.

Richardson, Laurel (1990b) *Writing Strategies*. Newbury Park, CA: Sage.

Ritzer, George (1988) 'Sociological metatheory', *Sociological Theory*, 6: 187–200.

Robertson, Nan (1986) 'The all-American guy behind *Blue Velvet*', *The New York Times*, 11 Oct.: 11.

Robertson, Robert and Turner, Bryan S. (1989) 'Talcott Parsons and modern social theory – an appreciation', *Theory, Culture & Society*, 6: 539–58.

Rorty, Richard (1982) *Consequences of Pragmatism: Essays 1972–1980*. Minneapolis: University of Minnesota Press.

Rorty, Richard (1985a) 'Habermas and Lyotard on postmodernity', in R. Bernstein (ed.), *Habermas and Modernity*. Cambridge, MA: MIT Press. pp. 161–76.

Rorty, Richard (1985b) 'Reply to Jean-François Lyotard', *Critique*, 41 (456): 570–1.

Rorty, Richard (1986) 'Freud and moral reflection', in J.H. Smith and W. Kerrigan (eds), *Pragmatism's Freud: The Moral Disposition of Psychoanalysis*. Baltimore MD: Johns Hopkins University Press. pp. 1–23.

Rorty, Richard (1989) *Contingency, Irony and Solidarity*. New York: Cambridge University Press.

Rose, Jacqueline (1982) 'Introduction – II', in J. Mitchell and J. Rose (eds) *Feminine Sexuality: Jacques Lacan and the Ecole Freudienne*. New York: Pantheon. pp. 27–58.

Rose, Jacqueline (1988) 'The man who mistook his wife for a hat or a wife is like an umbrella – fantasies of the modern and the postmodern', in A. Ross (ed.), *Universal Abandon*. Minneapolis: University of Minnesota Press. pp. 237–50.

Ross, Andrew (ed.) (1988) *Universal Abandon: The Politics of Postmodernism*. Minneapolis: University of Minnesota Press.

Ross, Andrew (1989) *No Respect: Intellectuals & Popular Culture*. New York: Routledge.

Ryan, Michael (1988) 'Postmodern politics', *Theory, Culture & Society*, 5: 559–76.

Ryan, Michael and Kellner, Douglas (1988) *Camera Politica: The Politics and Ideology of Contemporary Hollywood Film*. Bloomington, IN: Indiana University Press.

Said, Edward (1978) *Orientalism*. New York: Pantheon.

Salamon, Julie (1989a) 'Review of *Crimes and Misdemeanors*', *Wall Street Journal*, 12 Oct.: A14.

Salamon, Julie (1989b) 'Review of *sex, lies, and videotape*', *Wall Street Journal*, 3 Aug. (Sect. A): 9.

Sanger, David E. (1987) 'The computer's contribution to the rise and fall of stocks', *New York Times*, 15 Dec.: 1, 52.

Sartre, Jean-Paul (1948) *The Psychology of Imagination*. New York: Philosophical Library.

Sartre, Jean-Paul (1976) *The Critique of Dialectical Reason*. London: New Left Press.

Sartre, Jean-Paul (1981) *The Family Idiot: Gustave Flaubert, Vol. 1, 1821-1857*. Chicago: University of Chicago Press.

Saussure, F. de (1959) *Course in General Linguistics*. New York: Philosophical Library.

Schatz, Thomas (1981) *Hollywood Genres: Formulas, Filmmaking, and the Studio System*. New York: Random House.

Schatz, Thomas (1988) *The Genius of the System: Hollywood Filmmaking in the Studio Era*. New York: Pantheon.

Scheler, Max (1961) *Ressentiment*, New York: Free Press. (Originally published in 1912).

Schudson, Michael (1988) 'What is a reporter? The private face of public journalism', in James W. Carey (ed.), *Media, Myths, and Narratives: Television and the Press*. Newbury Park, CA: Sage. pp. 228-345.

Schutz, Alfred. (1967) *The Phenomenology of the Social World*. Evanston: Northwestern University Press. (Originally published in 1932).

Seidman, Steven (1990) 'Against theory as a foundationalist discourse', *Perspectives* (Theory Section newsletter, American Sociological Association), 13(2): 1-3.

Shils, Edward (1960) 'Imaginary sociology', *Encounter*, 14: 77-80.

Shumway, David (1989) 'Jameson/Hermeneutics/postmodernism', in D. Kellner (ed.), *Postmodernism/Jameson/Critique*. Washington, DC: Maisonneuve Press. pp. 172-201.

Simmel, Georg (1978) *The Philosophy of Money*. London: Routledge & Kegan Paul.

Simmel, Georg (1984) *Georg Simmel: On Women, Sexuality and Love*. Trans. and ed., with an Introduction by Guy Oakes. New Haven, CT: Yale University Press.

Simon, John (1986) 'Neat trick', *National Review*, 38 (7 Nov.): 54-6.

Siskel, Gene (1989) 'Review of *sex, lies, and videotape*', *Chicago Tribune*, 6 Aug. (Sect. 13): 6-7.

Siskel, Gene (1990) 'Review of *Wild at Heart*', *Chicago Tribune*, 17 Oct.: 13.

Sklar, Robert (1975) *Movie-Made America*. New York: Random House.

Smelser, Neil J. (1989) 'External influences on sociology', *International Sociology*, 4: 419-30.

Smith, Dorothy E. (1989) 'Sociological theory: methods of writing patriarchy', in R. Wallace (ed.), *Feminism and Sociological Theory*. Newbury Park, CA: Sage. pp. 34-64.

Sontag, Susan (1967) *Against Interpretation and Other Essays*. New York: Dell.

Sprinkler, Michael (1988) 'Review of *Wall Street*', in Frank N. Magill (ed.), *Magill's Cinema Annual: 1988*. Pasadena, CA: Salem Press. pp. 364-7.

Stahl, Sandra K.D. (1977) 'The personal narrative as folklore', *Journal of the Folklore Institute*, 14: 9-30.

Stauth, Georg and Turner, Bryan S. (1988) 'Nostalgia, postmodernism and the critique of mass culture', *Theory, Culture & Society*, 5: 509-26.

Sterngold, James (1987) 'Seeking a stronger safety net for the system', *New York Times*, 14 Dec. 1, 34.

Sterritt, David (1989a) 'Review of *Crimes and Misdemeanors*', *Christian Science Monitor*, 27 Oct.: 10.

Sterritt, David (1989b) 'Review of *When Harry Met Sally*', *Christian Science Monitor*, 2 Aug.: 11.

Sterritt, David (1989c) 'Review of *sex, lies, and videotape*', *Christian Science Monitor*, 28 Aug.: 11.

Strauss, Anselm (1978) *Negotiations*. San Francisco: Jossey-Bass.

Studlar, Gaylyn (1985) 'Review of *Paris, Texas*', in Frank N. Magill (ed.), *Magill's Cinema Annual, 1985: A Survey of 1984 Films*. Englewood Cliffs, NJ: Salem Press. pp. 359–64.

Suleiman, Susan Rubin (1986) 'Naming a difference: reflections on modernism versus postmodernism in literature', in D. Fokkema and H. Bertens (eds), *Approaching Postmodernism*. Philadelphia, PA: John Benjamins. pp. 255–70.

Tilman, Rick (1984) *C. Wright Mills: A Native Radical and His Intellectual Roots*. University Park, PA: Pennsylvania State University Press.

Time (1987a) 'In the trenches of Wall Street', 20 July: 76–7.

Time (1987b) 'A season of flash and greed. Review of *Wall Street*', 14 Dec.: 82–3.

Toulmin, Stephen (1983) 'The construal of reality: criticism in modern and postmodern science', in W.J. T. Mitchell (ed.), *The Politics of Interpretation*. Chicago: University of Chicago Press. pp. 99–117.

Treichler, Paula (1987) 'Aids, homophobia and biomedical discourse: an epidemic of signification', *Cultural Studies*, 1: 263–305.

Turner, Bryan S. (1984) *The Body and Society*. Oxford: Basil Blackwell.

Turner, Bryan S. (1987) 'A note on nostalgia', *Theory, Culture & Society*, 4: 147–56.

Turner, Bryan S. (ed.) (1990) *Theories of Modernism and Postmodernism*. London: Sage.

Turner, Jonathan H. (1987) 'Analytical theorizing', in A. Giddens and J. Turner (eds), *Social Theory Today*. Stanford, CA: Stanford University Press. pp. 156–94.

TV Guide (1990) 'The Best of Weekly Viewing', 6 October: 7.

Ulmer, Greg (1983) 'The object of post-criticism', in H. Foster (ed.), *The Anti-Aesthetic: Essays on Postmodern Culture*. Port Townsend, WA: Bay Press. pp. 111–25.

Ulmer, Greg (1985) *Applied Grammatology*. Baltimore, MD: Johns Hopkins University Press.

Ulmer, Greg (1989) *Teletheory: Grammatology in the Age of Video*. New York: Routledge.

Updike, John (1984) 'Modernist, postmodernist, what will they think of next?', *New Yorker*, 10 Sept.: 136–8, 140–2.

Urry, John (1990) *The Tourist Gaze*. London: Sage.

Utne Reader (1988) 'Are you addicted to addiction?: A skeptical look at AA and other 12-step programs', 30 (Nov.–Dec.): 2, 52–76.

Variety (1987) 'Review of *Wall Street*', 9 Dec.: 117.

Veblen, Thorstein (1899) *The Theory of the Leisure Class*. New York: Macmillan.

Veblen, Thorstein (1919) *The Vested Interests and The Common Man*. New York: Macmillan.

Veerman, Dick (1988) 'Introduction to Lyotard', *Theory, Culture & Society*, 5: 271–5.

Vidich, Arthur J. (1990) 'Baudrillard's *America*: Lost in the Ultimate Simulacrum', *Theory, Culture & Society* 8(2): 135–44.

Vogue (1987) 'Talking to Oliver Stone', Dec.: 166, 172.

Wall, John M. (1986) 'The best film of 1986: probing the depths of evil', *Christian Century*, 60 (Jan. 7–14): 7–9.

Wall Street Journal (1987) 'General News Index': 1124–5.

Wallace, Ruth A. (ed.) (1989) *Feminism and Sociological Theory*. Newbury Park, CA: Sage.

Warren, Robert Penn (1959) *All The King's Men*. New York: Bantam. (Originally published in 1946).

West, Cornell (1988a) 'Interview with Cornell West', by Anders Stephanson, in A. Ross (ed.), *Universal Abandon*. Minneapolis: University of Minnesota Press. pp. 269–86.

West, Cornell (1988b) 'Discussion', in C. Nelson and L. Grossberg (eds), *Marxism and the Interpretation of Culture*. Urbana: University of Illinois Press. p. 360.

West, Cornell (1989) *The American Evasion of Philosophy: A Genealogy of Pragmatism*. Cambridge, MA: Harvard University Press.

White, Hayden V. (1973) *Metahistory: The Historical Imagination in Nineteenth Century Europe*. Baltimore, MD: Johns Hopkins University Press.

Whitmore, George (1989) *Someone Was Here: Profiles in the AIDS Epidemic*. New York: North American Library.

Wiley, Norbert (1967) 'America's unique class politics: the interplay of the labor, credit, and commodity markets', *American Sociological Review*, 32: 531–41.

Wiley, Norbert (1986) 'Early American sociology and *The Polish Peasant*', *Sociological Theory*, 4: 20–40.

Wiley, Norbert (1988) 'The micro–macro problem in social theory', *Sociological Theory*, 6: 254–61.

Williams, Raymond (1977) *Marxism and Literature*. Oxford: Oxford University Press.

Williams, Raymond (1981) *Culture*. Glasgow: Fontana Books.

Williamson, Bruce (1986) 'Movies: review of *Blue Velvet*', *Playboy*, 37 (Dec.): 25.

Williamson, Judith (1987) 'Review of *The Morning After*', *New Statesman*, 12 June: 23.

Wilson, Charles Reagan, and Ferris, William (eds) (1989) *Encyclopedia of Southern Culture*. Chapel Hill: University of North Carolina Press.

Wolfe, Tom (1981) *From Bauhaus to Our House*. New York: Farrar Straus Giroux.

Wolfe, Tom (1988) *Bonfire of the Vanities*. New York: Knopf.

Wolfe, Tom and Johnson E.W. (eds) (1973) *The New Journalism*. New York: Harper.

Woolgar, Steve (1980) 'Discovery: logic and sequence in a scientific text', in K. Knorr, R. Krohn and R. Whitely (eds), *The Social Process of Scientific Investigation. Sociology of Sciences Yearbook, Vol. 4*. Boston: Reidel. pp. 239–68.

World Almanac and Book of Facts, 1990. New York: Pharos Books.

Yakir, Dan (1989) 'Rob Reiner's foray into "Maturity"', *Boston Globe*, 9 July (Sect. A): 6.

Index

About the Author

Norman K. Denzin is currently Professor of Sociology, Communications and Humanities at the University of Illinois, Urbana-Champaign. He is the author of several books, including *Sociological Methods* (1978), *Children and Their Caretakers* (1973), *The Values of Social Science* (1973), *The Mental Patient* [with S.P. Spitzer] (1968), *Childhood Socialization* (1977), *Social Psychology*, 7th edition [with A. Lindesmith and A. Strauss] (1991), *The Research Act*, 3rd edition (1989), *On Understanding Emotion* (1984), *The Alcoholic Self* (1987), *The Recovering Alcoholic* (1987), and *Interpretive Interactionism* (1989). *The Alcoholic Self* and *The Recovering Alcoholic* were nominated for the C. Wright Mills Award in 1988. *The Alcoholic Self* won the Cooley Award from the Society for the Study of Symbolic Interaction in 1988 and was nominated for the Sorokin Award, also known as the award for Distinguished Scholarly Publication, by the American Sociological Association in 1989. Denzin is the author of over seventy articles in various academic journals. He has been the editor of *Studies in Symbolic Interaction: A Research Journal* since 1978. He is past President of the Midwest Sociological Society and has served as Vice-President of the Society for the Study of Symbolic Interaction (1976–77), secretary of the Social Psychology Section of the American Sociological Association (1978–80) and editor-elect of the *Sociological Quarterly*.

Printed in the United Kingdom
by Lightning Source UK Ltd.
9725000001B/78-87